Nemanja Vidić

CAPTAIN FANTASTIC

THE BIOGRAPHY OF MANCHESTER
UNITED'S SUPERSTAR DEFENDER

Nemanja Vidić

CAPTAIN FANTASTIC

FRANK WORRALL

JOHN BLAKE

Published by John Blake Publishing Ltd,
3 Bramber Court, 2 Bramber Road,
London W14 9PB, England

www.johnblakepublishing.co.uk

First published in hardback in 2010
This edition published in paperback in 2011

ISBN: 978-1-84358-305-9

British Library Cataloguing-in-Publication Data:

A catalogue record for this book is available from the British Library.

Design by www.envydesign.co.uk

Printed in Great Britain by CPI Bookmarque, Croydon, CR0 4TD

1 3 5 7 9 10 8 6 4 2

Papers used by John Blake Publishing are natural, recyclable
products made from wood grown in sustainable forests. The manufacturing
processes conform to the environmental regulations
of the country of origin.

Every attempt has been made to contact the relevant
copyright-holders, but some were unobtainable. We would be
grateful if the appropriate people could contact us.

For Alan Feltham and the boys on *SunSport*

CONTENTS

ACKNOWLEDGEMENTS

SPECIAL THANKS: John Blake, Allie Collins and all at John Blake Publishing, and Andy Bucklow at *The Mail on Sunday*.

THANKS: Alex Butler, Tim Smith, Derek Whitfield, David Michael, Adrian Baker, Russell Forgham, Ian Rondeau, Pravina Patel, Martin Creasy, Colin Forshaw, John Fitzpatrick, Dave Morgan, Richard Orchard, Phil Chaplin, George Binyon, Phil Bryant, Howard Cooper, Lee Smith, Danny Bottono, Angela, Frankie, Jude, Nat, Barbara, Frank, Bob, Stephen, Duncan Williams, Meg Graham, Steven Gordon, Gary Edwards, David and Nicki Burgess.

Chapter 1
THE FIGHTER

HE ALWAYS wanted to be a professional footballer but his school pals and teachers would laugh at him, calling him a silly dreamer. 'Just how do you expect to even escape your troubled hometown, let alone make it as a footballer in Belgrade or further afield?' they would ask. But what they failed to realise was that this was a boy who thrived on adversity and one who would prove that miracles can happen, even in the most difficult environment and circumstances. Indeed, in the case of Nemanja Vidić, it would be this that would propel him towards his dream.

In 2009 he admitted as much when he said of his tough streak: 'I think you are born with that. My personality is like that – I don't like to give up, I like to fight for everything. Not to fight in a bad way but to go hard to chase something. That is how I am.'

Growing up in a harsh situation would make him tough – and far more determined than other boys to get just what he wanted. And in Europe, it didn't come much tougher than growing up in a war zone in western Serbia, in a grey industrial city, battling against the odds to make a name for yourself as a footballer – and then being forced to watch your best friend die of a heart attack at the age of 20, just as you were making that breakthrough.

This was no cosseted footballer enjoying the easy life, as many singled out for stardom in the English game now do. Here was a boy who had to do it the hard way – and one whose drive, durability and toughness would be reflected in his play when he finally made it.

This is the story of Nemanja Vidić – the hardman who won the hearts of thousands of football fanatics at Manchester United. Like Jaap Stam – one of his illustrious central defence predecessors at Old Trafford – he is a one-man defence, a man-mountain carved out of granite, who might as well hold up a sign to rival attackers bearing the proud, obstinate words: 'Thou shalt not pass'.

This is the story of a modern icon, one that made it against all odds: Vidić, the dreamer from Serbia, who would become a defensive rock at the Theatre of Dreams in Manchester.

It all began on October 21, 1981 – one year after the death of President Tito, the man who had directed the rebuilding of a Yugoslavia devastated by World War II – in the town of Užice (formerly Titovo Užice) when Nemanja Vidić was born to parents Dragoljub, a worker in a copper rolling mill, and Zora, a bank clerk. A medieval town with a population of around 50,000, Užice – which is 150 miles west of Belgrade – had been renamed in honour of President Tito in 1946 but reverted to its former name in 1992. At the time of Nemanja's birth it was – and remains even today – renowned for its non-ferrous metals, particularly copper and aluminum. It is also a livestock-breeding and fruit-growing region.

The Vidićs were not working-class people nor were they affluent, but they certainly weren't poor. They lived a frugal lifestyle, but they never went without. From the age of 3, Nemanja had kicked a ball about regularly, encouraged by his father, who was a fan of the Beautiful Game. By the time he was 7, he had become more serious in his kickabouts, but he was only small (later, he would shoot up in height during his teenage years) and would, according to family friends, 'zoom around the field like a bumble bee'.

It was at 7 that Nemanja was to make his first impression on the game, as he followed his older brother Dusana – who was then 9 – to play for the youth team of local outfit FK Jedinstvo Putevi. He did well at Jedinstvo and was then spotted by a scout at neighbourhood rivals Sloboda Užice at the age of 12. His parents were delighted – although Nemanja wasn't allowed to neglect his schoolwork and continued to attend classes while training with the club in his free time.

Sloboda had their own ground, with a capacity of 12,000, and had been Serbian champions 14 times over. They also boasted some major name former heroes – chief among them Radomir (Raddy) Antić, who starred for the club in the 1967–68 season, before going on to serve at Partizan, Fenerbahce, Real Zaragoza and, most famously in England at least, Luton Town, where he ended his playing career in 1984 after making 100 appearances and scoring 9 goals for the Hatters.

Antić would also go on to become a top-notch manager, taking command at Real Madrid, Barcelona and the Serbian national team.

This was the environment the young Vidić had always craved – one where the team and its history was well signposted, where he could make a name for himself and get noticed, thanks to the size of the club. Despite his size, he settled in well and quickly at the club – he was still 'tiny' according to family friends. When he reached 13, he had a growing spurt and this, in turn, brought a newfound confidence. He moved from 'buzzing around everywhere' to occupying the centre of defence, a position he liked because he could see what was going on and direct operations.

Two years later the biggest club in the country came knocking at his door and he was signed as a junior by Red Star Belgrade, where he would eventually begin his professional career. He would need that tough streak of his when he moved to Belgrade in 1996.

He was 15 and living in alone in a hotel. His mother made the journey with him, but she soon had to return home to work, leaving the teenager to fend for himself. Zora shed many tears and would later admit that 'it had been the hardest day of my life', but her son consoled her, telling her that he was going to be a star footballer and one day she would be able to give up her job and follow his career, whenever or wherever she wanted. He would certainly be proved right on that count.

Dragoljub was also distraught that his son had to leave home, but somehow managed to hide his emotions well. He told the boy that he needed to be well organised if he was to make the big-time with Red Star and apparently tried to cover up his sense of loss by giving Nemanja a series of instructions to live by concerning his training, social life and relaxation. Dragoljub stressed the importance of the latter: if his son was to progress he needed to ensure that he was fit, healthy and ready for training. He must take it easy when he was away from football and had to make sure he got enough sleep.

Nemanja later recalled: 'I left Užice when I was 15 and moved to Belgrade to live and play football for the club. That was the generation of '91 [when they won the European Cup]. [Dejan] Savicević, [Robert] Prosinecki, [Darko] Pancev, [Vladimir] Jugović... they had a great team at that time – they were my idols. At Red Star it was like here [Manchester United]. Every game we played we had to win. You never think about drawing.'

Heeding his father's advice to look after himself, his career moved forward at a rapid pace. He worked hard and dedicated himself to his dream. Physically and emotionally, he grew bigger and stronger, and enjoyed his first three years in Belgrade.

Then, in 1999, he experienced the other side of life: the gloom, hopelessness and darkness as the bombs fell on Serbia during Operation Allied Force. Both his hometown, Užice, and his new home, Belgrade, were bombed by NATO planes in the offensive against Serbian forces in Kosovo. Užice suffered its worst damage on 6 May 1999, when NATO forces bombed a number of roads, the airport and government buildings. Ironically, just 20 days later and about 1,000 miles away, the club that he would eventually join in England were finally breaking a 31-year jinx. On 26 May 1999, his future employers Manchester United would win the European Cup for the first time since 1968 and the glory days of George Best and Sir Matt Busby.

In western Serbia, however, the locals had much weightier issues on their minds than football matches – such as staying alive.

Homes were also destroyed that dark grey day in Užice – leading to thousands of civilians gathering to protest in the main square against the random bombings and killings and the ruin of their town. It was hard for Nemanja to take as he heard from his parents by telephone what was happening back home – he was fraught with concern and also had to contend with the regular bombing incursions on Belgrade, where he was still living.

He said: 'It was a very bad time for our country and for us people as well. Everything stopped in the country, you could not do anything. People stopped working. As a boy [in Belgrade] I couldn't play football for three or four months.

Belgrade was a dangerous place to be; you just couldn't train because of the planes. It was a bad time, many people died. I don't really know what to say. It shouldn't happen to anyone.'

But he had to set the darkness in his soul aside and get on with his life – and his career. Now 19, he was ready to become a professional footballer and Red Star were glad to grant his wish. Years of hard work, determination and self-sacrifice had paid off.

The club's management team decided the youngster was not quite ready for action in a Red Star shirt, but felt that he would benefit from first-team workouts, so he was loaned out for his first season (in 2000) to a smaller Serbian club side, FK Spartak Zlatibor Voda. The team played in the Serbian Second Division and Vidić found his stay worthwhile, as he battled against rough-and-ready forwards. In this part of his career he learned to give as good as he got – there were no frills or fancy play in the Second League; your reputation lived (or died) on the strength and courage of your game.

That season Nemanja Vidić the hardman was constructed and developed and when he returned to Red Star in the summer of 2001, he was ready and raring to go. Now he wanted to test himself against the best players in the country – and, he hoped, in Europe and beyond.

Sure enough, he was parachuted straight into the Red Star first team the next season and quickly gained a reputation for his hard-tackling, no-nonsense approach. The fans loved him and so did his team-mates. Vidić and Red Star embarked on a fine run of performances that would ultimately lead to them claiming the Yugoslavia Cup in the summer of 2002.

But, just as everything was going so well, more darkness descended upon Nemanja's life – swiftly and agonisingly in the autumn of 2001. His best friend and team-mate Vladimir Dimitrijević, who also came from Užice, died during training following a heart attack on 1 October. The striker was just 20. The previous June, he had signed a five-year deal with Red Star and had won plaudits on his debut for the club against Mladost in August of that year.

Nemanja's official website sums up the heartbreak he must have felt: 'First October 2001 will be written in black letters. Red Star and Serbian football have lost one of the biggest talents.'

Inconsolable, he found the tragedy hard to come to terms with, saying, 'It will stay with me forever. There was no warning; he just went over. I could not tell what was happening, but it was clear something was seriously wrong. That is as much as I want to say about that day. It is too painful to keep going over.

'Vladimir is with me every day, but the memory is not of what happened during that training session. We had so many great times together. Growing up and going to school, kicking a ball about on the streets and being taken on by Red Star. Those are the thoughts I keep with me.

'We were inseparable. We shared the same dreams and wanted to be successful together. We both came from Užice and we both moved to Red Star. We wanted to touch the sky with Red Star, but unfortunately Vlada is not with us any more,' he said, after captaining Red Star to a domestic double in 2004. 'When I play, I think about my friend and I will do everything I can to save his memory. Every goal I score is for him.

'He would have been very proud of what I have achieved since, and I would have been just as proud of him if he had achieved the same. And he would have done. Vladimir was so talented; he would have been a great player. But now he is gone and I want to preserve his memory for ever.'

In the close season of 2009, Nemanja returned to Užice to pay a personal tribute to the friend he still misses so deeply. He travelled to the Vladimir Dimitrijević football school that exists there in Vladimir's memory, where he spoke to his friend's father and took time out to encourage the youngsters who attend the academy.

Indeed, Vidić was also at the school when it first opened in 2002 and Vladimir's father, Nedeljko, explained just how much Nemanja's support had meant to him over the years. In a letter to *SunSport* in March 2007 he outlined his gratitude: 'Vlada and Nemanja shared the same dream – to reach the highest level in football and, after Red Star, to play together for Manchester United. But fate was harsh on them and, on October 1, 2001, Vlada died.

'They were training and Vlada, who was just 20, had his problem and his heart failed. Nemanja went with him in the ambulance to the hospital but it was too late. They went to Red Star at the same age and at the same time. They were always together, best friends. They respected and cared for each other.

'Vlada told me that Nemanja was the most honest and revered of all his friends. After they finished their time in the youth team they were separated when they went on loan to different teams. They were far away from each other but used to talk on the phone for hours and dream of going back to Red Star.

'They played well and were recalled to Red Star in 2001 and signed contracts with the club they loved. They were very happy and from that time they were like brothers. Nemanja never forgot about Vlada and a year after he died, he came to open a memorial centre. He played all his games in a T-shirt with Vlada's picture under his shirt and showed it whenever he scored.

'He has never forgotten Vlada's family and often comes to visit us when he can, to go to the cemetery where Vlada rests. We are very happy for Nemanja because he is playing for the biggest club in the world. We are always grateful when Nemanja mentions Vlada in his interviews and the many things he does to keep his memory alive.'

In 2002, six months after his friend's death, there would be some light in the darkness when Vidić played a key part in helping Red Star to the final of the 2001–02 Yugoslav Cup. And on 29 May 2002, he was part of the victorious Red Star team that lifted the Cup, after they overcame FC Sartid 1923 Smederevo 1-0 in the final. It was a sweet moment for Red Star as, a year earlier (and without Nemanja), they had lost the final by the same scoreline to their biggest rivals, Partizan.

Now, Nemanja was lifting the Cup as a part of the team that had returned to the final in fine form, a team that had banished the misery of that defeat some 12 months earlier. Vidić was still only 20, but as he paraded the trophy with his jubilant team-mates he knew that finally, he had arrived on the world footballing stage. The Red Star line-up that day – with Nemanja in his favoured centre-back role – read: Randelović, Marković, Vidić, Vitakić, Lalatović, Bratić, Gvozdenović, Milovanović, Bocković, Pjanović and Bogavac.

After just 20 minutes, Mihajlo Pjanović would score the winning goal and, perhaps somewhat surprisingly given his reputation, Vidić was not among the six players booked. It was his first major honour in football, but this was just the start.

A year later, at the tender age of 22, Nemanja was appointed Red Star's captain by then boss Zoran Filipović and went on to lead his team to a remarkable League and Cup double in 2004. Afterwards, he would admit that the only downside to the prestigious appointment was that his friend Vlada was not there to share his joy.

Vidić was under no illusions about the weight of his new role: being captain of Red Star Belgrade would mean pop star-style scrutiny from the club's fanatical supporters and the sports press. 'When you play for Red Star, there is nowhere you can go in Serbia where people are not talking about you and Red Star,' he told Ian Stafford of the *Mail on Sunday* in 2008. 'Winning the double with Red Star was, for me, as big as winning the Champions League with United, but when it comes to pressure, playing for United is not as big as being made captain of Red Star at 22.'

Being skipper of Red Star certainly meant that he was constantly in demand. The club's supporters are some of the most fanatical in Europe and they expect their captain to be just as committed and tough. For the most part, they loved Vidić and the zeal and courage he brought to the job and his role as a no-nonsense centre-half. However, they fell out big-time on one occasion, when Vidić rather foolishly agreed to do a fashion photoshoot with Saša Ilić, captain of Partizan.

Dave Fowler, writing in the *Observer* in 2004, best summed up the bitterness between Red Star and Partizan when he said: 'Whenever Red Star Belgrade meet their local city rivals Partizan, the atmosphere is rancid with hatred and aggression. Their rivalry is as fierce and embedded as any in world football.

'I have been to games in Belgrade where the violence between supporters was worse than anything I have witnessed in England, or indeed anywhere outside the former Eastern bloc. The violence is not restricted to football: Partizan and Red Star have affiliated clubs in other sports, such as basketball and handball, which are infected by hooliganism… The ultras of Red Star – the *Delije* or heroes – are the most feared, organised and uncompromising of the Serbian hooligan gangs.'

Given the hatred and bitterness between the two sets of fans in Belgrade, it was probably no surprise that some Red Star fans considered themselves betrayed by Nemanja – they felt that he was conspiring with the enemy. As Dave Fowler explained, the reaction of one of the leaders was to teach their emerging man a lesson – it was a hard one too, as he wrecked his car with a baseball bat.

'Padja, another young *Delije* leader, explains how he is responsible for smashing up the Red Star players' cars whenever they perform badly. He carries a handgun under his jacket and boasts of how he recently destroyed the car of Red Star's captain, Nemanja Vidić, after he appeared in a fashion shoot with the captain of Partizan.'

Vidić, who was also part of a group attacked by a gang of masked fans armed with clubs and knives, somehow forgave them but came to understand the nature of some of the footballing fans. Certainly, he trod a little more carefully in his choice of sponsored activities after that little incident.

One of his best matches for Red Star was in December 2002. By then he was coming to terms with life in the first team and what was an emerging side by scoring for them in the 2-0 win at Radnicki Obrenovac.

Vidić struck a fifth-minute penalty to set Red Star on their way and Branko Bošković added the second, seven minutes from time. The win moved them up to third in the table – they were improving all the time, as was Vidić, and it would not be long before he would lead his team to that historic double as skipper.

He told friends that the win at Radnicki – and his fine performance capped by the goal – was a turning point. It gave him much more confidence and spurred him on to believe that, yes, he could captain Red Star one day and even play at an even higher level, in a bigger club league in Europe.

Vidić had always been a player who looked for the next opportunity, the next step up as his career developed. He was, and remains to this day, a man driven by intense ambition and determination to win everything, to reach the absolute top of his trade.

He would go on to grab another vital goal when he fired Red Star ahead on the hour in their crunch match at Zemun as the season drew to a climax in April 2003. The hosts would draw level on 85 minutes with an equaliser from Sasa Stojanović, but Vidić and Red Star were by now making their mark. They had moved up to the runners-up spot from third and were confident of making a fight of it in the following season with their rivals and neighbours Partizan, who were a massive 19 points ahead of them.

Nemanja and Red Star might have been viewed as also-rans that April, but their time was nigh. They were becoming a more coherent, powerful unit over the season, with Vidić chipping in with key goals as well as impressive displays at the back. All this provided invaluable clues as to what was about to happen next.

The following season, there would be a seismic shift in power, with Vidić being the man at the helm, the man who would wrest the power from Partisan for Red Star.

On May 9 2004, Red Star finally won the League title they believed should be theirs from birthright, from their biggest rivals. That was the day skipper Nemanja Vidić proudly held the trophy aloft in front of adoring fans in Belgrade.

It was Red Star's 23rd League title and they had achieved it by beating Vojvodina of Novi Sad 3-0. The result was a real turnaround on the previous season, when, as we saw, they finished a massive 19 points adrift of Partizan, who were managed by German legend Lothar Matthaus.

The breakthrough – which meant Red Star had qualified for the second preliminary round of the Champions League – was thanks principally to two men: Vidić, who had rallied the team and inspired them, and their manager, Slavoljub Muslin, who took over from Zoran Filipović (the man who had appointed Nemanja to the captaincy), who had told the big defender that he trusted him wholeheartedly as his on-field commander.

Muslin played for Red Star from 1975 to 1981. Like Vidić, he was a defensive stalwart and his performances at the back were important in helping the club win three League titles. He also played in the 1979 UEFA Cup final for Red Star, but this ended in disappointment as Red Star lost the final 2-1 on aggregate to Borussia Monchengladbach.

In 1988, Muslin turned to coaching. Eleven years later, he arrived back at Red Star as their manager. It had been a long journey home, via clubs in France and Morocco, but he would only stay two years – from 1999 to 2001 – before resigning over an apparent dispute over a key player.

Muslin spent a season at Levski Sofia in Bulgaria, taking them to the title and Cup double, and then returned to Red Star after he was sacked by Levski in 2003. By the following spring, he had brought his third title to the club as a coach, thanks to his link-up with star man Vidić.

After lifting the League trophy in 2004, Muslin commented: 'At the start of the season, I said we had the best players and they have now proven me right. This is my dearest trophy to date, especially because we were very much underrated earlier this season.'

Vidić was delighted with winning the trophy, saying that it was as if a weight of anticipation had now been lifted. He also made it clear that he wanted to beat rivals Buducnost a few days later to add the cup to his League winner's medal: 'It's been like unloading a heavy burden from my back. It has been said that if you play for Red Star and do not win a title, it's as if you hadn't played at all. But now we want the double – we will be very cautious against Buducnost and will do everything to double the celebrations.'

And he and his team did just that, emerging triumphant in the Serbia and Montenegro Cup Final, with a 1-0 win over Buducnost. For Vidić and Muslin, the dream was complete: in their first season together as skipper and boss, they had lifted the coveted double. It was some feat and now their fans dreamed that the duo might conspire to aim for success in Europe.

But Muslin added a note of caution to the celebratory atmosphere, saying: 'We'll do our best to qualify for the forthcoming Champions League, but first we have to keep the squad intact and maybe even acquire a reinforcement or two.'

Serbian football analyst Ozren Podnar also urged caution at the time, saying: 'The word is already out that Atletico Madrid have an eye on full-back Marjan Marković and the captain Vidić. Inter Milan and Manchester United want Vidić as well, while Hamburger, Ajax and Besiktas are after the centre forward Nikola Zigić.'

Already the vultures were circling for Vidić. He was becoming a big name, thanks to his achievements for Red Star.

Journalist Podnar also made this point in April 2004:

Red Star may never win another European crown again, but they want at least to emulate their arch rivals who played in the Champions League group phase this season, after knocking out hot favourites Newcastle in the third preliminary round – and preferably not finish bottom of the group, as Partizan subsequently did against Real Madrid, Porto and Olympique Marseille.

A fair point, it summed up just why Nemanja did not stick around for long after such a remarkable achievement. Always a boy with stars in his eyes, he wanted to test himself against the best, to win the biggest and most prestigious trophies, and he could not see himself doing that in Belgrade. As Podnar pointed out, the yardstick by which Red Star then judged their success in the Champions League was to make the group stages – and not be embarrassed when they got there.

But Vidić wanted much more than that, so a parting of the ways was inevitable. It wouldn't be long coming – just two months after lifting the Cup with Red Star, he was on his way to Moscow in a move that left his fans in Belgrade and his admirers at bigger clubs in Italy and England stunned. Why move to Moscow? Was this really a step up from Belgrade? Nemanja's friends simply stated that he had 'fancied a change' and 'had always liked the idea of living and playing football in Moscow'. The feeling was that it would be only for a year or maybe two and then he would move on to one of the bigger outfits in world football in either England, Italy or Spain.

Vidić was quick to praise the Red Star fans when it was formally announced that he would be leaving after securing that historic double. He told the press how they had made him 'feel like a king' and he had wanted to win trophies to thank them for supporting him as he came up through the ranks.

As a result, in the eyes of Red Star fans he would always be seen as a legend – even when he walked away, leaving them heartbroken. He had won one League winner's medal and two Serbo-Montenegran Cup winner's medals.

Nemanja signed for Spartak Moscow on Monday, 5 July 2004, putting pen to paper on a four-year deal. By then he had won six caps for his country and was renowned for his hardline defending and wonderful leadership skills. The details of the transfer fee were not revealed, though the rumour was that Vidić had become the most expensive defender in the history of the Russian Premier-Liga. Sources close to the Moscow outfit claimed the fee was actually £4.5 million.

Vidić would play a season and a half for Spartak. It was not a period that would bring him further honours, but he was chosen in the Russian Football Federation's list of the country's top 33 players in 2005 – one of three left centre-backs, along with Dmitri Sennikov of Lokomotiv Moscow and Erik Hagen of Zenit St Petersburg.

Sure, he was loved by the Russian fans for his tough tackling and no-nonsense physical approach, but it is difficult to see what his time in Russia brought him – apart from maybe a hatful of roubles. Friends of his claimed the experience of playing in the snow and cold had 'toughened him up even more' and that Nemanja himself 'in no way felt it was a wasted experience.' In his first and only full season in Moscow, Spartak finished runners-up in the Russian Premier League, eventually losing out to Moscovite rivals CSKA.

In total, Vidić made 39 appearances for Spartak and grabbed four goals. He told friends that he had a 'fantastic time in Moscow' and was glad that he had experienced life and football in the Russian capital. Of course, in May 2008 he would make an emotional return to the Luzhniki Stadium, where he had spent 18 months with Spartak prior to his move to Old Trafford, when Manchester United played Chelsea in the Champions League final.

Just over 12 months after he joined Spartak, Nemanja Vidić's life was moving upwards yet again. Not only was he becoming known as a defender of true class – who was again starting to draw admiring glances from Italy, Spain and England – but he was ready to settle down not only as a footballer, but as a man.

The Serb was settling down with his sweetheart, Ana – and the couple would eventually marry on July 17, 2006. Typically for Nemanja, and the way he prefers to live the quiet life, their wedding was hardly the stuff of *Hello!* magazine. Instead, he and Ana, a refugee from Kosovo who met him when she was studying economics at Belgrade University, were married at a little restaurant in the Zlatibor mountains close to his hometown, Užice. Ana now brings up their two children, Luka (born in December 2006) and baby Stefan, born on May 27, 2009 – the day of Manchester United's appearance in the Champions League final.

The guest list was not one that would have attracted the paparazzi – it was made up of close family and friends. 'That's the way he is,' said a friend. 'He doesn't like being in the limelight or showing off. He is a man who likes peace and quiet and stability – he is the opposite of what he becomes when he steps onto a football field. Off it, he is a gentle giant – on it, he is a warrior, a true footballing hard man.'

Indeed he is: at 6ft 4in and weighing 14 stone, Vidić cuts an imposing figure. But by the end of 2005, he would no longer be able to stay out of the limelight. Sir Alex Ferguson had already decided that Vidić was the man to steady his rocking defensive ship; he would also help to steady Rio Ferdinand, thus benefiting the England man's game, too. And he would also be the man around whom Ferguson could build a Champions League-winning team.

Then Portsmouth captain Dejan Stefanović, who played alongside Vidić in the Serbian national team, said that United were buying the genuine article: 'He is not scared and that is a very important thing. He will go in every challenge for the long balls and he can play football as well. He is a young lad and he is a good character. He is the sort of player who can score goals as well and he will be a big success for Man United.'

Some pundits from Serbia suggested that Ferguson, once he had secured Vidić's signature, should follow the advice given to Serbia's coach at the time, Javier Clemente, by one of his backroom staff: 'Clemente should go to church and light a candle every morning praying for the health of Nemanja Vidić.'

Yes, the hero from Serbia was on his way to Old Trafford, but the initial passage would not go to script as Vidić struggled to settle and find his feet. Let's now examine the details of his transfer from Russia to Old Trafford – and assess just why he found it tough going in his early days at the biggest club in the world.

Chapter 2

TAKE IT AS RED

'If I have to walk to Manchester to play there, I'll walk'
— *Nemanja Vidić , December 2005*

ON 5 JANUARY 2006 Vidić finally signed on the dotted line for Manchester United. The fee was not officially revealed, but a reliable United source said that Spartak Moscow received in the region of £7.2 million. The Russians had initially asked for £11 million, with United offering closer to £5 million, but agreed a compromise when it became clear that Nemanja was desperate to complete the move. He had set his heart on becoming a Red and would earn a basic starting salary of £50,000 a week.

The deal had taken a couple of months from start to finish. United were not the only club in the frame: Liverpool and Aston Villa in England, and Fiorentina in Italy, had also made concrete inquiries at the start of November 2005. But it was United that Vidić wanted to join, despite claims in the British press that Italy was his preferred destination.

United are a club who like to conclude their transfer negotiations in private and they were happy to go along with Vidić and his agent, Paolo Fabbri, when it was suggested in November 2005 that a suitable smokescreen would be to hint that he really wanted to go to Italy. There was even talk that the Serbian had signed an agreement to join Fiorentina that month, although this would be rigorously denied.

But the idea that Vidić might be off to Italy at least kept the British press at bay, while United and Spartak conducted preliminary negotiations without the added pressure of journalists camped outside their respective doors. Of course, another major fear within United was that big-spending Chelsea might also try to muscle in and hijack the deal – Sir Alex Ferguson had already privately voiced his concerns that he was afraid of 'bigging any player up' in case it alerted Chelsea owner Roman Abramovich. With Vidić playing for a Russian outfit and Abramovich one of the most important and influential men in both Russian society and football, there was a real risk that he could nip in and take the man who was acclaimed as the best defender in the Russian League.

Despite the efforts of United, Spartak and Vidić himself to keep the possible transfer low-key, the cat was out of the bag by the middle of December 2005. On 16 December 2005, the *Guardian* reported that the Red Devils had made their move, saying, 'Manchester United have opened formal talks with Spartak Moscow for their Serbia & Montenegro international defender Nemanja Vidić with a view to bringing him to Old

Trafford either in the next month's transfer window or at the end of the season. The approach was confirmed last night by the Spartak president Sergey Sharlo, who said that he had quoted a fee of around £11 million. United value him at much less and a deal could hinge on whether the two clubs can reach a compromise.'

Sharlo also told the press that he would certainly regret losing the Serbian hardman; that he had become the man around whom the Spartak team revolved, their most important player. But the president of the club also understood that he could not stand in his player's way if he wanted to move to United. Sharlo commented, 'Vidić is a player in our team and we wouldn't like to let him go. We'll try to do our best to keep him at the club. But if any club can offer us the proper price which we can use for signing another player of the same level, we can accept that.'

Yet even as United's move was becoming public knowledge, the extent of the success of their 'keep it secret' agreement with Spartak and Vidić could be gauged by comments coming from Italy. Stories appeared in the Italian press that Nemanja was indeed on his way to Fiorentina – and Vidić's Italian representative, Silvano Martina, was happy to follow the party line and say that his man would prefer to sign for an Italian club than United. Martina, who would have been the man who would have negotiated the transfer in Italy, had Vidić opted to move there, told *PA Sport*, 'There is no interest from Manchester United so far or from Arsenal either. Liverpool showed an interest one month ago, but they never made an official offer.

'Vidić has a contract from Spartak Moscow until 2008 but has a release clause he can exercise at any time, provided a payment of €7 million is made. The player has been happy at Spartak, but would like to move on. He will leave in January and his intention is to move to Italy, but if Manchester showed an interest then he may consider it. Vidić's dream is to play in Serie A and he came very close to signing for Parma, but the deal fell through following the scandal of Parmalat.'

The quotes highlight the success of United's clandestine methods when dealing with transfers. Sir Alex Ferguson likes to keep things undercover and low-key to avoid getting caught out by a counter-offer if someone thinks United are interested. If news of any negotiations breaks and he is drawn into an auction, these days the United boss's inclination is always to pull out of any possible deal. His approach is the result of a harsh slap in the face that he and United had suffered back in July 2003. That summer, David Beckham left United for Real Madrid and Ferguson believed he had snared just the man to stop the fans getting on his back for allowing their hero to depart to Spain.

Fergie was convinced a deal was in the bag for the Brazilian superstar Ronaldinho. The then United chief executive Peter Kenyon had lined up a deal with the French club Paris St Germain and he shook hands on a fee of £17 million. Indeed, Sir Alex was so confident of the deal going through that he even revealed, 'We are just about there but we don't know for sure. We are very close; we are pursuing it very intensely. I don't want to be counting chickens – that never works. Disappointment can come very quickly in football and people can change their minds in an instant.

'The signs are OK, but we just want to get that seal on it before we can talk about it more openly.'

But the Brazilian eventually signed for Spanish giants Barcelona – after they agreed to pay PSG £4 million more than Manchester United had offered. United were left smarting at being gazumped and with a stinging assessment of their transfer policy from PSG president Francis Graille ringing in their ears. He said, 'Manchester United have been too sure of themselves, believing that they'd done the hard work by negotiating directly with the player and going behind PSG's backs. Manchester started their negotiations at a very low level on the financial front... their offers were always inferior to Barcelona's.'

Ferguson is said to have decided there and then that he would never again negotiate his transfers in public – and never again would he or Manchester United be left a laughing stock.

But the Italians were not the only ones to fall foul of United's softly-softly success in securing the Vidić transfer. A week before their interest became public, Liverpool skipper Sami Hyypia made it clear that he would not be the fall guy if, as he expected, Vidić arrived at Anfield in the January transfer window. The *Sun* reported that Kop boss Rafa Benítez had bid £4.5 million for Vidić – and Hyypia told the newspaper that he wouldn't be losing any sleep over Vidić's likely arrival at Anfield!

Meanwhile, Vidić himself remarked, 'All the talk about new

signings doesn't affect me at all. I will just continue to do my best. Last season I was sitting on the bench for a while after the club signed Mauricio Pellegrino on loan from Valencia. I believe I am playing well at the moment and that's not because I feel threatened that someone might come in and take my place. Anybody can try to take it; I am up for the fight.'

It was obvious why Benítez would have loved to add Vidić to his squad – he was light on numbers. Already the Spaniard had established his credentials at Liverpool by leading them to that extraordinary European Cup final win over AC Milan in 2005, but as he weighed up his options before his 50th game in charge of the club at the end of November 2005, he knew that his squad was not good enough to win the Premiership; that was why he put in a bid for £4.5 million for Vidić although the offer was laughed off by Spartak. Benítez admitted at the time, 'It was hard last season to cope with Europe and the Premier League. I hope to improve the squad so we can cope better.'

There had also been much interest from then Aston Villa boss David O'Leary, who, like Benítez, was keen to improve a team that had potential but at the time was struggling near the foot of the Premier League. O'Leary, to give him his due, was the only Premier League manager to actually fly out to Moscow to see Vidić in action for himself. He attended the Russian Primera Liga game between Shinnik Yaroslavl and Spartak Moscow in October 2005 and admitted he was very interested in signing one of the Spartak players.

Later he would admit that it was Vidić that he had travelled to see, although at the time he was understandably reluctant to show his hand, saying: 'I've visited Yaroslavl to watch some Spartak players we're interested in. There is one player in Spartak I'd sign now but the final decision, as you understand, will be made by our board, not me. Moreover, according to the regulations we can register new players only from January 1, so my trip is of a reconnaissance kind.'

Clearly he needed Vidić more than the powerhouse centre-back needed him, for at the start of November 2005 Villa had won only two Premiership games and were just two places and two points above third-bottom Everton. They had conceded 19 goals in 11 games and O'Leary admitted, 'I am aware of our problems and the need to do something about them but if we don't stop conceding the sort of goals we have been, life is going to be hard.'

Vidić would have been a lifesaver for the big bluff Irishman and his demoralised Villa troops and O'Leary was deflated when it became clear the Serb only had eyes for United. Sir Alex too needed Vidić to prop up a faint-hearted United defence as much as O'Leary could have done with him for the same purpose at Villa Park.

At the time, much was made of the fact that Vidić had become the first signing of the Glazer era at Old Trafford. The previous June the Americans had bought the club for almost £800 million after a bitter campaign that had seen fans burning an effigy of new owner Malcolm Glazer and cancelling their season tickets.

United supporters were unhappy that Glazer was burdening the previously well-run, cash-rich club with a massive debt. It had been revealed that Glazer would be investing only £272 million of his own money to fund the deal. He would borrow £265m, set against the club's assets, and would raise a further £275m by issuing securities.

Fans were worried that the level of debt would mean there would be no available cash for transfers. As Christmas 2005 came and went, they appeared to have been proved right: United had spent precisely nothing while the team struggled and so Vidić's signing from Spartak Moscow for £7 million on that cold January morning was heralded by the club as a sign that the Glazers did have money for transfers and that they would splash out, if the price and the player were right.

Sam Wallace, writing in the *Independent*, summed up the situation on Boxing Day 2005, when it was announced that Vidić would put pen to paper as soon as the transfer window opened on 5 January 2006: 'The Glazer family may have a reputation for being the Premiership's Scrooges but the new owners of Manchester United sanctioned a £7m Christmas Day spending spree yesterday that allowed Sir Alex Ferguson to sign the highly sought-after Serbian defender Nemanja Vidić from Spartak Moscow.

'In the biggest single pay-out for a player since the Glazers assumed control of United in May, the club paid close to Spartak's asking price of £8m to secure the services of the 24-year-old…'

And how United needed him – they struggled to keep up with Chelsea in the League, and disappointingly exited the Champions League at the group stages on December 7.

Taking a closer look at the team's showings back then, it is clear that the defence was simply not good enough. United needed a hardman like Vidić to complement the more refined touches of fellow centre-back Rio Ferdinand. An example of the failings at the back can be seen in the sobering trip to Middlesbrough on 29 October 2005. The perennial strugglers walloped United 4-1 and the make-up of the defence that day gives a fair inkling of just why United were on the wrong side of a hiding. Apart from the evergreen Edwin van der Sar, United's backline read: Phil Bardsley, Rio Ferdinand, John O'Shea and Mikael Silvestre. Bardsley was never going to be a top-notch fullback, while Silvestre was reaching the end stage of his United career and mistakes were all too often creeping in. And O'Shea? He was a competent journeyman whose key claim to fame was his versatility. Silvestre partnered Ferdinand in the heart of the defence, but he was hardly the rock that Ferdinand needed to steady his own game – which, at the time, was certainly up and down.

Within half an hour at Boro, United were two down and Ferguson responded by trying to stabilise his troubled backline. He took Bardsley off and replaced him with Kieran Richardson. The latter moved to left-back, with O'Shea shifting over to right-back.

So how did it work out? Well, United shipped another two

goals and it did not solve the problem of the rocky Ferdinand-Silvestre partnership. Rio needed a new, full-time steady man to link with and he was to tell Ferguson that in private.

United were dreaming of catching Chelsea, the new top dogs in the Premier League, but after the Middlesbrough débâcle they were 13 points adrift of the leaders. Ferguson was honest enough to admit that his defence needed urgent remedial work and that the dream of overhauling Chelsea was rapidly turning into a nightmare. He said: 'It was a shocking performance. We conceded some terrible goals and we cannot afford do that with what we are trying to achieve. We conceded in the second minute to a free shot from 25 yards and we never recovered from that. A lot of people look at us as a team who can stop Chelsea – but not on this showing.'

One indirect result of the Middlesbrough loss would be the imminent departure of United legend Roy Keane. In an interview he gave to United's in-house TV channel, MUTV, the skipper lashed out at the quality of the performance. At the last minute, the programme was pulled, although details of Keane's attacks on certain players would filter through to the press.

His harshest words were said to be aimed at the club's then record signing, Rio Ferdinand: 'Just because you are paid £120,000 a week and play well for 20 minutes against Tottenham, you think you are a superstar.' The interview left Ferguson incensed – he had always maintained a policy of keeping any disputes or disagreements out of reach of the press – and two weeks later Keane was gone. Sources said that the final straw for Ferguson was that the Irishman had criticised his then number two, Carlos Queiroz. The manager felt duty-bound to back his assistant against Keane, who he considered had, on this occasion, strayed too far out of line.

Four days after the Middlesbrough loss Ferguson switched the backline around again, with Silvestre moved out to left-back and Wes Brown brought in to partner Ferdinand, who had suffered heavy criticism over his display at the Riverside. But the changes failed: United lost 1-0 against Lille in the Champions League, with ex-Spurs striker Milenko Acimović scoring from close range after 37 minutes.

The result left United in real danger of exiting the competition at the group stages – a prospect that had the board of directors shuddering as they thought of the massive loss of cash that would accompany such a devastating scenario. United were booed off the field by their 4,500 travelling supporters, while the boss himself admitted that he could understand their grievances.

Ferguson said: 'Without question, those fans want to see us win. They have followed us through thick and thin. They were like that when we had not won the title for 20 years and I am sure they will be like that again. We are going to have to regroup and win our next two matches against Villarreal and Benfica because they are vital now. We were not in our best form – that has to be said – we are going to have to fight our way through this.

'No one's going to help us with that. We are going to have

to do it ourselves and we don't want to feel sorry for ourselves.'

But star striker Ruud van Nistelrooy didn't help matters by admitting that he thought the United side of November 2005 was the worst Old Trafford team he had played in since joining the club in April 2001. The Dutchman said: 'When I came to Manchester United four-and-a-half years ago, we were unbeatable. I remember games when I had four or five opportunities, constant service and we attacked. It was great and I enjoyed it. We all want those days to come back. The question is, how do we do it?

'We need to look at the squad, look at everything. Each of us knows within themselves what is going to happen. Without doubt, this is the most difficult time I have had since I came to United.'

Hardly the glowing endorsement that Ferguson would have wanted from one of his players, but the United chief was realistic enough to know himself that the wheels were threatening to come off the great institution that he had breathed fresh life into over two decades. He was well aware that fresh blood was needed throughout the team, particularly in the defence. He knew that he would eventually get Vidić, but he didn't know if he could keep United on track until January 2006 – and he was also unable to hazard a guess as to how long it would take the Serb to settle down and find his form.

By the middle of December Ferguson would breathe a sigh of relief when he could finally officially announce that he had secured Vidić's services. But by then it was too late to save the club's season as far as the Champions League was concerned.

On 7 December, United crashed out of the competition with a 2-1 defeat at Benfica. Silvestre again partnered Rio at the heart of the defence – and again that partnership was not up to scratch. The result meant United finished bottom of Champions League Group D, an indignity that left them without even the consolation prize of a place in that season's UEFA Cup competition.

Paul Scholes had put United ahead after just 6 minutes with a close-range effort, but almost inevitably, their porous defence had leaked once again as Geovanni headed the Lisbon club level just 10 minutes later after he lost Ferdinand and Silvestre, and Beto secured the win with a speculative effort that beat van der Sar from 25 yards out just after the half-hour mark.

This was a disastrous outcome – the first time United had failed to qualify from the competition's group stages for 11 years. It would cost them money (up to £15 million, had they gone all the way) and prestige. Inevitably, there would be calls for the manager's head from some quarters.

After the match Ferguson called for calmness and level-headedness, saying that he was in the midst of a rebuilding programme and that he needed time and patience: 'We have a job to do and the rebuilding will carry on. We are disappointed, there's no doubt about that. It's a blow and you have to regroup. This club has always risen from difficult situations and we will again. We gave away possession far too easily so we only have ourselves to blame in that sense. We were desperate to win the match and with that came a sense of anxiety.

'I give my team 10 out of 10 for determination and effort, but in the end it was not to be. You couldn't argue it was an unfair result, but I don't think it would have been unfair if we had got an equaliser either.'

But he refused to answer questions about his own position at Old Trafford, saying, 'I am not going to answer that; the press will have plenty to say. I've got a job to do, it's a great job and I've confidence in my players.'

Yet the day after the Lisbon débâcle there were widespread calls for Ferguson to resign. As the *Independent* newspaper pointed out, these were not just from those so-called fans who went to Old Trafford once or twice a season, but diehards too: 'Even United's official website, in its Fanzone section, reflected the dissent – much of it directed against the man whose 19 years at Old Trafford have been strewn with silverware.

'"It's time Fergie retired," one writer said. "I know we're in transition but the last consistent run we had was at the end of 2002–03." Another weighed in: "Big changes have to be made because we're not good enough." A third argued: "It's the lowest point in 10 years – they couldn't even get through a group with three very average teams."'

The back pages of the newspapers were, of course, chock-a-block with pieces speculating that the end of the Ferguson reign was near. *The Times*'s Oliver Kay wrote: 'A new defender is also on Ferguson's wish-list, with Spartak Moscow claiming that United will rival Liverpool for the signature of Nemanja Vidić, the Serbia and Montenegro centre-half. The Glazers have indicated that they are prepared to back Ferguson's judgement during the January transfer window and that there will be no restriction on his budget if he is able to agree deals to sign the players he wants, but doubts persist about the amounts of funds that will be made available, particularly now that it seems a new man may be in charge of the team by the summer.'

But Ferguson would have none of it. In his mind there would be no 'new man in charge', just himself, reconfirmed in charge.

The manager responded as expected: he came out fighting. He said that he would spend in the January transfer window to improve his team in defence and that the club's controlling Glazer family had offered him a public vote of support, saying they were not unduly concerned at the loss of Champions League football. A spokesman for the Glazers commented: 'There's enough slack in their investment, corroborated by the experience of running another large franchise in the [Tampa Bay] Buccaneers, to take this loss in their stride.'

In other words, it was business as usual and would remain that way – as long as Ferguson spent well in the transfer window, and as long as he bought a player (or players) who not only had talent, but who also were winners.

In that sense, Nemanja Vidić was not only a top-class buy by Ferguson, he was a saviour of sorts when he eventually established himself , helping to settle down an underperforming Ferdinand and forming a formidable, often unbreachable backline. He was the rock on whom Ferguson could rely to repel all invaders, who could perform so consistently well that the boss no longer had to worry about saving his own skin. No, with Vidić on board, Ferguson could work on developing a team that would eventually bring him his second Champions League trophy. Within 30 months of Vidić joining what appeared to be a sinking ship, United were once again champions of Europe.

A Coincidence? Hardly.

The importance of Vidić to Ferguson's own planned revival could be seen by the fact that the very day when the Serbian finally put pen to paper with United, the manager had him straight outside at Carrington, training with his new team-mates, just hours after he had received his work permit. No gentle settling in period – Ferguson knew that he needed this giant of a man to fit in quickly if he was to maintain control indefinitely.

Vidić was, after all, a member of the renowned backline of the Serbian national side – the so-called 'famous four' defence – that would concede just one goal while qualifying for the 2006 World Cup finals. He was a rock indeed to build on.

Ferguson was like the man who had won the lottery as he showed off his new signing to the press and public. He almost purred as he said, 'Good defenders win you things. Nemanja is a quick, aggressive centre-half and will be a terrific addition to the squad. This lad is a natural athlete.'

Vidić also expressed delight at moving from Moscow to Manchester. He remarked, 'To be playing for United, the biggest club in England and probably the world, is an absolute honour. Manchester United have a huge amount of great supporters and the club represents something absolutely fantastic to me. I really hope my time in Manchester will be one of the best periods in my life.

'I received an offer from Liverpool but when I heard United were interested, I wanted to sign immediately.'

These were the sort of words which would endear any player to United fans, particularly the news that he had snubbed their most bitter rivals for a move to M16. He was given the No. 15 shirt and said that he was looking forward to making his debut and that he felt that he would easily fit into English football: 'The players have accepted me already, been very friendly and made me feel very welcome. I cannot see anything else presenting a problem now. I am sure English football would suit me and I will adapt very quickly.'

After all, he had already proved himself to be hard as nails and a tough competitor. In the event, his settling-in period would take rather longer than expected, but more of that in the next chapter.

Vidić's first match involvement with United would come on 22 January 2006, when he was named as a sub for the home match with Liverpool. He would not be called upon, but had some interesting observations to make prior to kick-off when it was suggested to him that he might become the next Steve Bruce at the club. He said: 'When I was a child there were some fabulous players but really I don't try to imitate or copy anyone and I don't have any role models. I am trying to be myself, make my own style and produce my own image.'

Sir Alex certainly felt that centre-back Vidić and fullback

Patrice Evra – his other transfer window signing that January, a £5.5 million buy from Monaco – would reinforce his stumbling back four and his own reign. A month before he signed for United, Vidić himself had admitted that they had problems at the back, leaking holes that he felt confident he could fix: 'Defence is United's weakest link. After I was told that they are interested in signing me, I watched several tapes of their games.

'They do have problems in defence, to say the least. And the most problematic is their centre-back zone from where their opponents score much too often.'

Evra would also take time to settle in. Ferguson was to say: 'In football, there is never the last piece of the jigsaw. You are always chasing the rainbow, no matter how successful you are. You always look to improve, which is what we are trying to do here. We may do things differently to some other clubs but the one great thing I have always had at my time at United is the backing to take a long-term view of things.

'We have the opportunity of looking a little bit further ahead to see how players will be in two or three years' time. Obviously, we also have to try to maintain success at the same time. It is not easy, but we are not far away. We think the present squad, staying together, can achieve that.'

Certainly Belgrade journalist Zoran Panjković, who had watched Vidić's career with interest since he broke into the Red Star Belgrade team as a teenager, was convinced that Sir Alex had spent his money well.

'He's a really great defender and it is a very good move for Sir

Alex Ferguson,' Panjković told BBC Sport. 'He is similar to Rio Ferdinand but maybe with a bit of John Terry's qualities as well. He is a very aggressive player and very physical. I think he will be a really special player in English football – and I think he will form a formidable partnership with Ferdinand.'

Panjković said that Vidić had told him that he had always wanted to join United and play in the Premier League. He added: 'He has become a player that almost makes no mistakes. He's a very strong player and a leader.'

Indeed he was – although it would take a little while for United fans to realise the gem Ferguson had unearthed from Eastern Europe.

Ferguson knew from the start that he had struck gold with Vidić. That was why the United boss was much more relaxed and confident as he surveyed his squad at the end of January 2006. The dark mist of depression and dismay surrounding himself and the club after the stunning blow of that defeat by Benfica had all but evaporated. Ferguson felt that United were now back on track and that in Vidić he had finally located the leader who would end the defensive nightmares that had pushed him close to the edge.

It was a new start and Vidić would live up to all his expectations. Let's now take a look at those first few months of Nemanja's induction into English football – January to May 2006, five months that would begin with a tricky settling-in period but would also include him picking up silverware in his first season at Manchester United.

Chapter 3

STARTER'S ORDERS

THE FIRST WEEKS of the Vidić era at Old Trafford were uncomfortable and unconvincing – and that is being kind to the man who would go on to establish himself as a new hero at United. He struggled to find his feet and his form, and it appeared to the outside world that Sir Alex had dropped an almighty clanger in signing the big Serb.

Even some fans in United's massive Red Army were questioning the wisdom of spending £7.2 million on a player who was obviously struggling at the Theatre of Dreams. There were also questions posed as to whether the money splashed out on Vidić, and fellow newbie Patrice Evra, might not have been better invested in a top-class, top-quality midfielder. After all, wasn't that the area in which United most needed a new recruit after the sudden exit of Roy Keane?

There was some validity in the questions – particularly the

idea that United were short of quality in midfield. Many criticised Ferguson at the time for spending the first readies he had seen from the Glazers on a pair of defenders that no one knew anything about. Since when did defenders win titles?

The truth was that Evra and Vidić did help United win titles once they had settled in – which just goes to show that Sir Alex, with a network of spies all over the world, knows a great deal more than many of his critics about which players to buy and when.

There was also the little matter of Evra and Vidić needing time to settle in, both at United and into the rigours of the Premier League. The British game is much more demanding and physical than either the Russian or the French game and the duo found their fitness was not at the required level.

In Vidić's case there was also the fact that he had not played competitive football for a couple of months by the time he made his debut for United. The Russian season finished in November 2005 and when United's medical staff assessed his fitness, they told Sir Alex that his new signing was nowhere near ready for the demands of a full second half of the season in England. Instead they suggested that he was put through a tough pre-season schedule – the sort the players are normally given in July prior to the new campaign – and that only when his fitness levels improved dramatically, should he be trusted in the first team.

They had decided Evra was the fitter of the two (he had, after all, come from a French League that was still in progress) but the chasm in the fitness levels required was clear when Patrice made his debut at Manchester City on 14 January 2006. He had a torrid time of it at the City of Manchester Stadium, so much so that he was withdrawn at the interval and replaced by Alan Smith. United had lost just three of their last 28 matches against City and as they were struggling to keep pace with leaders Chelsea (who were 13 points clear of the Red Devils before the Manchester derby), the defeat was a double body blow. It was probably just as well that Ferguson had listened to his medical staff and resisted the temptation to blood Vidić – the experience of a derby defeat might have blunted his confidence, as it certainly did with Evra.

Vidić made the bench when United entertained Liverpool at Old Trafford on 22 January, but was not called into action for a match that they would win 1-0, thanks to a last-gasp Rio Ferdinand goal. But three days later – on 25 January 2006 – Nemanja would finally touch the ball as a first teamer at United, albeit for three minutes of normal time. Sir Alex decided that it wouldn't be too much of a gamble to bring on Vidić in the 87th minute of the League Cup semi-final first-leg clash against Blackburn at Old Trafford. United ran out 2-1 winners – and Vidić's confidence was boosted by knowing that he had played a part, albeit admittedly a small one, in helping to take the Reds to the final of the competition.

The night after the win over Blackburn, he was in action again, this time for the reserves as United's staff stepped up his training in preparation for his full debut. Vidić played well for the second XI, putting in a 45-minute shift before being rested, and he helped them to a 3-2 win in his first competitive outing since finishing the Russian season with Spartak Moscow on 22 November.

His solid display contributed to United's reserves returning to the top of the table and encouraged club officials told Sir Alex that it might be worth taking a gamble with him in the FA Cup tie at Wolverhampton three days hence.

Fergie listened and gave the idea the thumbs-up for the fourth round match, believing, correctly as it transpired, that the Championship team would not prove too daunting a mission.

So it was on 29 January 2006 that Nemanja made his full debut for Manchester United at Wolves. United, in cruise control, dismissed the challenge of their former midfield general Paul Ince and his team-mates with ease. Vidić was hardly tested – and that was without the man he had expected to partner. Yes, on that cold January day at Molineux, Sir Alex sent Rio Ferdinand out in an unaccustomed central midfield role... with Wayne Rooney! Instead, Vidić would line up with Wes Brown in the heart of the defence.

The *Independent* summed up Vidić's full debut in this way: 'The Serb produced a decent first start for his new club, though he will have to encounter more potent opposition than this to prove himself a worthy acquisition. Vidić, who was booked for a cynical body-check on Kenny Miller in the second half and occasionally required the insurance policy of Ferdinand to cover his hasty runs out of position, helped seal the victory in first-half stoppage time with a long clearance that exposed a static home defence. Saha was played onside by Gabor Gyepes as the ball dropped over the top and he dispatched an emphatic finish beyond Postma before the old gold rearguard had finished looking for an offside flag to rescue their indecision.'

United keeper Edwin van der Sar begged to disagree, arguing that Vidić had done well at Molineux. He said: 'Nemanja is an old-fashioned defender who makes a lot of challenges. Everyone is pleased with his performance at Wolves. I think the manager looked to see what we already had and what we needed to add. He has been here a month now and has had to catch up a little bit on fitness because he had a break after the Russian season finished. But he has done a lot of training separately. We have all seen him running quite often after we have finished our own sessions but it was important for him to get 90 minutes.'

But Nemanja's morale would be shattered in a series of tough matches after that encounter at Molineux, until he finally found his full fitness and adjusted to the tough physical demands of the English game. The first lesson did not take long in coming, either – just three days, in fact.

On 1 February, United played away at Blackburn in the Premier League, losing 4-3, and Vidić suffered a chastening evening. Once again he was partnered with Wes Brown in central defence, with Rio Ferdinand in the 'Roy Keane' central midfield role. But this time Vidić's lack of fitness and Premier

League nous, and Ferdinand's square-peg-in-a-round-hole status were horribly exposed.

All evening Vidić struggled against the pace and wizardry of David Bentley and the battering ram power of Shefki Kuqi. The Serbian and his partner Brown were booked for reckless challenges as they tried in vain to stop the onslaught – and Ferdinand was sent off for two bookable offences.

At the end of a demoralising night Bentley left Ewood Park with the match ball after grabbing a well-earned hat-trick while Vidić left with his reputation in tatters. The result also meant that United had fallen 15 points behind leaders Chelsea at the top of the Premiership.

Sir Alex, as stubborn as ever, refused to accept United had been in disarray – although he did concede his defence had been in trouble at times: 'I think our performance was terrific but mistakes at the back cost us. We dominated the first half, but we were down 3-1 at the break. In fairness to the players they kept going and going. They were fouled and fouled, and the referee has to be strong. Blackburn are very difficult to play against because the game is stopped all the time.'

He was asked if he would be changing the backline for the next match – Fulham were due at Old Trafford three days later. However, he refused to comment on that and also when asked whether he believed Vidić and Evra needed more time to settle into English football.

In the event, Ferguson would drop Vidić for the Londoners' visit but keep faith with Evra, who was looking a little lightweight compared to Gabriel Heinze, who was still absent through injury.

Mikael Silvestre was drafted in to replace Vidić as United emerged 4-2 winners. Two and a half years later, in August 2008, Vidić would be able to laugh about being dropped – and how he and Evra used to feel homesick, saying: 'Neither of us started well and we used to say we wanted to leave. We can laugh about it now because we have both reached 100 games for the club. I am really pleased. I have worked hard to achieve that and I'd like to play many more games for United.'

But it was no laughing matter at the time, although Vidić did not argue with Ferguson's decision to give him a break from the firing line. In fact, he was more than a little surprised when the United manager told him a week later that he was back in the team. Vidić had expected to be given a couple of weeks out of the limelight to improve his fitness and confidence but that is not how Ferguson works: he makes decisions whenever he believes they are needed. In this instance he believed Vidić's confidence would benefit from what would surely be a gentle stroll in the park against a struggling Pompey – especially as he would be playing for the first time alongside Rio Ferdinand, who had served a one-match ban and was eager to return to the fray.

He was proved right as Ferdinand encouraged and cajoled his new partner. United won 3-1 and Vidić's only real setback of the day came when he and substitute keeper Tim Howard got in each other's way late in the second half and were almost punished by Pedro Mendes. Howard, to his credit, recovered in time to save Mendes's shot on goal.

But Vidić would have nightmares after he struggled in the next match, particularly as his lapse of concentration was directly responsible for the fifth-round FA Cup loss at Liverpool. Ferdinand, who had been a calming influence on Nemanja at Portsmouth, was out with a hamstring injury, which meant Vidić was paired with Brown – unfortunately. He really could have done with the reliable Rio at his side all the time as he settled precariously into English football.

United had held their own at Anfield for just 19 minutes – that was when Vidić and Brown both lost Peter Crouch at a corner, leaving the 6ft 7in frontman with a free header which he gratefully powered past Edwin van der Sar. Sir Alex agreed that Ferdinand's absence had been a hammer blow for his troops, saying: 'We lost Rio Ferdinand after training on Friday then Mikael Silvestre got a knock. It has been 85 years since Liverpool beat us in the FA Cup and I was hoping it would be another 85 years, then I wouldn't be around to see it. We found it hard to get our momentum going, but we stuck at it and I felt we dominated the second half.

'We started the game badly. We didn't have enough height at the back when Liverpool pumped it forward. Liverpool can play for only five minutes and win the game, that is the way they are. They pump the ball into the box and with good set-piece delivery, they keep you under pressure.'

It meant the Red Devils realistically had only one chance of avoiding a second season without a trophy – in the following week's Carling Cup final against Wigan.

As if Ferguson did not have enough problems, Alan Smith was ruled out for months after suffering a broken leg and a dislocated ankle towards the end of the game. Poor Smith – known as Eminem in the United dressing room at the time because of his likeness to the American rap star – had only come on as substitute for Darren Fletcher on 76 minutes.

A week later Fergie showed the ruthless side of his nature by dropping Vidić from the Carling Cup final team. Ruthless, yes, but undoubtedly the correct decision: Nemanja was still struggling to tune into the pace of the Premier League and it wouldn't have done him much good, had he put in an indifferent shift against the Latics, who liked to employ the bruising pair of Jason Roberts and Henri Camara up front.

There was also no place in the starting line-up for Evra, who had similarly struggled since his move from Monaco. The Frenchman was so out of touch that he had not even been on the bench in the previous match at Anfield and Ferguson's has not forgotten that the only time he had paired Vidić and Evra together, United had conceded four goals at Blackburn.

Yet now the United manager would name them both among his substitutes for the Carling Cup final and, in an astute piece of man-management, would send them on to lap up the atmosphere and claim their first medals at the club. Together, they jogged onto the Millennium Stadium pitch in Cardiff after 73 minutes, Vidić replacing Brown at centre-back and Evra taking over from Silvestre at left-back.

By then the Cup was already on its way back to Manchester – it was 4-0 – and so there was little danger in giving them a workout and a morale booster despite their floundering form. On a sidenote, while Vidić was delighted to have picked up some silverware within two months of joining the club, his joy would prove to be Ruud van Nistelrooy's misery. The big Dutch striker had expected to play, but was left out after a training bust-up with Cristiano Ronaldo. Boss Ferguson was so annoyed by van Nistelrooy's refusal to apologise to Ronaldo that he did not even give him a cameo role in Cardiff, much to the player's consternation. He had already started to rise from the bench when Ferguson signalled that he would be making two substitutions, only to sit back down again angrily when Vidić and Evra were called on.

It was said to be the final straw in the rapidly deteriorating relationship between the United boss and the man who had been his star striker for the previous five years. Four months later, van Nistelrooy would be sold off to Real Madrid.

Vidić had already been given an inkling from the boss that he was to play some part in the Cardiff showdown when Ferguson said that he was not too worried about the form shown by Nemanja and Evra in the first couple of months after they signed: 'Parts of their game are very good. All we need to do now is improve their understanding of the game in this country.'

That boosted the duo's previously flagging spirits and, a

couple of days before the Final, Vidić remarked: 'I'm very much looking forward to the match. The team has given 100 per cent in every match and winning a final would be the crowning glory at the end of it. Winning a trophy is always a special memory in every player's life.

'I want to be at Manchester United for a long time and I hope I can win many trophies with the team.'

He accepted that his form had not been good since the move from Spartak Moscow – and that his lack of fitness had contributed to that and the three yellow cards he had picked up in the past five matches – but promised the fans that he would eventually prove a real asset to Manchester United.

Vidić said: 'I think this is the right league for me. I hadn't played since November 22 – my last match in Russia – so I have been training but I don't think I have reached my peak because it takes time to reach full fitness. My future, as far as I'm concerned, is in front of me and I will fulfill my potential.

'I am hoping to have a good career [at United] but that depends on my game. But the way I am playing, I hope in my period of time in Manchester it will be one of the best of my life.

'It is an absolute honour to be playing for United. There were offers from other teams and the United offer came last-minute but it is an absolute honour. United presented me with something which was absolutely fantastic.'

Nemanja also paid tribute to his manager and team-mates for helping him settle in: 'I can only say thank you because they have all been very helpful, the players and the manager.

Obviously it takes time to settle down. All along, everyone has been most helpful. I would now like to prove myself to show what I can do.'

He would not get that chance immediately, though. In one of those footballing quirks of fate, United would play Wigan again in their first match after the Carling Cup triumph, in the Premiership at the JJB Stadium. Vidić would find himself once more on the bench, but would not feature this time, as United won 2-1. He was also on the sidelines, but not used in the next match – the 2-0 win over Newcastle at Old Trafford.

But then his fortune would change for the better – and for good. Again, his promotion would be at the expense of another United stalwart: this time Wes Brown would be the man to suffer after he was sidelined with a hamstring injury: an injury that allowed Vidić to stake a claim in the first team in the game against West Brom at the Hawthorns and against Birmingham at Old Trafford. Ever since that point, Vidić has maintained his position as the No. 1 partner to Ferdinand at the centre of the United back four.

Brown, who had considered the position his own best natural role, would now be left to pick up the pieces of his career as an initial stand-in to Gary Neville at right-back and eventual successor to the club skipper in that spot.

On the day that Vidić became a fixture in the team, United ran out 2-1 winners at West Brom. He kept his place in the next match – the 3-0 home-win over Birmingham – and cemented it in the 1-0 home triumph over West Ham and the 2-1 victory at

Bolton. By now, he had played in four consecutive matches for United and was beginning to strike up a powerful partnership with Rio Ferdinand.

For the first time in years United had a central defensive pairing that looked the business. It was the beginning of a new era that would propel them to an eventual Champions League and World Club championship win. However at the time, and after four wins out of four, the real test of the blossoming Vidić-Ferdinand partnership was now upon them as Arsenal arrived at Old Trafford for a Premier League showdown.

There would be no hiding place for Vidić with Robin van Persie, Emmanuel Adebayor and Thierry Henry in town. He had performed well in those four previous wins, dispelling the doubts from his first two months at the club, but this would now be the moment of truth. It was a huge challenge to keep three of the Premiership's most prolific strikers quiet, but it was one that the Serb proved more than capable of. The legend of Vidić was about to take shape on the Stretford End: a new hero was born as he bravely placed himself in the line of battle against the aggressive Londoners to emerge triumphant.

United ran out 2-0 winners in a match that was watched at Old Trafford by 70,908 fans – back then a record attendance for the Premier League. Wayne Rooney and Ji-Sung Park stole the goalscoring honours, but Vidić and Ferdinand also deserved the plaudits that came their way as they shackled the powerful Arsenal attack. 'Rio and Vida were awesome,' said Rooney after the match, summing up the contribution of the rock-solid pair.

Wayne had reason to be grateful: Nemanja had won possession of the ball for United in the 55th minute, passed it to Silvestre and, from the Frenchman's cross, the Liverpudlian smashed the ball past Jens Lehmann for his goal.

It was United's ninth successive Premier League win and a strong signal of intent to Chelsea that they would be going all out to regain their title the following season. The win moved the Reds to within 7 points of the Blues, but they had just five games remaining to catch the reigning champions. Ultimately, it would prove too great a task, but their form was a warning to Chelsea that they meant business. Their new-found defensive strength – with Vidić and Ferdinand at the heart – and a wonderful strike combination of Rooney and Ronaldo was heralding in a new era of domination for the Old Trafford giants.

Before the crunch encounter with the Gunners, Vidić said he felt confident that he was up to the challenge, that he was now fit enough to deal with any physical contest. He told the *Manchester Evening News*, 'The Russian League is a tough competition and so is the Serbian League but physically, the Premiership is even harder. Every game is a big battle here in England. I have discovered it is like a boxing match for me; I just have to make sure I am not the one on the floor in future.'

And at a press conference before the game, he had told how his confidence had been boosted by words of encouragement from his Serbian international team-mates Savo Milošević and Mateja Kežman. Both had failed to make an impact in England, with Aston Villa and Chelsea respectively, but both were convinced Vidić would prove a success.

Vidić explained: 'Before I joined United, I had a very long discussion with Mateja Kežman and Savo Milošević about their experiences in England. I believe my biggest strengths are my physical toughness and my speed, and both Mateja and Savo felt those qualities would be much better suited to the English game than theirs.'

Another indication of Nemanja's improving form came after the win when Wes Brown paid tribute to him, saying he knew he faced a struggle to get back into the side at centre-half. Brown was back in the squad for the match against the Gunners after recovering from his groin strain, but ended up as an unused sub.

Brown said: 'Vida has been excellent for the team and played some great games, and when you're playing well, you stay in. It's frustrating because I was having a good run before I got injured, but that's how it goes.

'There's no point looking back and saying "if only" – I've just got to get on with it and try to get back into form and fight for my place.'

If the win over Arsenal represented a first-season high for Vidić, the 3-0 thumping United suffered at Chelsea three matches later, at the end of April, was one of the lows. Before the clash Sir Alex had said that his squad was getting better all the time, that it was 'as good a squad as we have ever had.' He was talking about potential for the season to come, but some critics joyfully shoved those words of praise back down his throat as Chelsea crushed United at Stamford Bridge to show why, at least for now, they deserved to retain their crown.

The Blues had needed just a single point to clinch a second successive title, but ended up with all three after overpowering United.

Vidić was culpable for the first Chelsea goal, allowing Didier Drogba to outjump him on 5 minutes, with William Gallas then heading the ball home. Nemanja was also one of three defenders to blame for the second goal on the hour. Joe Cole scored after first beating Rio Ferdinand, then waltzing past Vidić and leaving Silvestre for dead, before finally slamming the ball home past a hapless van der Sar. Ricardo Carvalho completed the rout, grabbing the third goal on 73 minutes.

Sir Alex claimed his team were hard done by, but was honest enough to also concede Vidić and Co. had not had their best day at the office. He said: 'It was harsh and I don't think 3-0 was a fair reflection of our performance. We had a lot of the play and made some good chances, but we didn't make it count. If you lose goals as softly as we did today, you have to take your medicine for that.'

United now had just two matches left of the 2005–06 season to reach the target of 4 points set by their manager – 4 points that would take them to 83, the number they had accumulated when they last won the title back in 2003. They did just that: drawing 0-0 with Middlesbrough at home and then beating Charlton 4-0 in the final match of the campaign at Old Trafford.

The results meant they finished runners-up to Chelsea, and importantly, automatically qualified for the following season's Champions League.

Vidić ended his first season at the club by coming on as a substitute for Gary Neville on the hour. After the defeat at Chelsea the manager once again opted for caution and protection: taking Nemanja out of the firing line so he could regroup following the bruising battle with Drogba, the big Serb was a sub for the Boro match.

So what was the final verdict on Nemanja's first season in England? Well, the stats say that he started just 9 League games (out of a possible 17) after joining United in January 2006. But there certainly were mitigating circumstances: he was struggling for fitness, struggling to adjust to a new country and it was no fun living in a hotel.

As he would admit: 'It was very hard for me. When I arrived in Manchester I had not trained for 40 days because the Russian season was finished. The players were asking me every day if there was anything I needed, but it was difficult for me to communicate.

'I was living in a hotel and trying to acclimatise to a different style of football and culture. Everything was thrown at me at once. And on top of that I was very aware that the fans were asking, "Who is this player?" I was unknown and people wanted to see what they were getting for £7 million. I was very aware I was under the spotlight. I had a few injuries and the first few months were very difficult.

'When I moved from Belgrade to Moscow it wasn't such a big move in terms of the cultural differences – the way of life and the weather in those cities is not so different. But when I arrived in England, it was a very big difference. Things like driving on the other side of the road were very difficult for me to get used to. I started driving on my second day in Manchester and it was very confusing at first; I hit the kerb a few times.

'The food is also very different to the food in Serbia and Russia. People putting milk in tea was so strange although now I have tried it, I have to say that I don't mind it.'

Yet, when Nemanja finally began to make his presence felt as a central defensive partner for Rio Ferdinand during that tough debut season, he would show glimpses of the form that was to lead to him becoming a first-team regular and a colossus at the back.

Certainly, the best was yet to come. The following season, with a full pre-season behind him and settled, we would see the real Vidić and the forging of an unbreakable bond between him and the fans who loved him for his wholeheartedness.

Chapter 4

THE JOY OF SIX

A T THE END of his first full season at Old Trafford – the 2006–07 campaign – Nemanja would be honest enough to admit that he had entertained thoughts that he was not going to make the grade in England. He revealed: 'My first couple of months were difficult. It's true – I didn't think I had a future in England; I did worry that I wasn't going to make it at United – the football is different. It wasn't that I was scared but I had lost my confidence because of what happened in those first couple of months. I missed passes I had never missed before; it was like I had forgotten how to play, but players need to be strong in the head to play at a big club here.'

He went on to explain that the start of the campaign had been vital to his success, how he had been worried about how the knee injury he had suffered the previous June in Serbia's World Cup build-up might affect his season, but he had worked hard in the gym and eventually in training to get fully fit. Also, he had enjoyed several morale-boosting talks with Sir Alex, and by August 2006 he was on the way back. He would not return to the first team squad until 13 September, but by then he was convinced that he could become a key man for United.

Now he felt fit and refreshed and confident that in the coming season he would prove to the fans that he was worth the £7.2 million he had cost.

He would be proved right.

After a two-year spell in the title wilderness, United would finally wrench the Barclays Premier League crown back off Chelsea, ending the Stamford Bridge club's dreams of winning it for a third consecutive year.

True, the manager's personal holy grail of lifting the European Cup again would not come to pass, but the team was developing and even that dream was on the horizon. Meanwhile, Vidić's rating in the eyes of the supporters who had initially barracked him would shoot through the roof as he went about his business like a marine on operational duty: full-on, with no thought of his own safety and determined to win at all costs. In turn, they adored him for his bravery and his commitment to the cause. Very soon that acclaim would be backed by a series of terrace chants and T-shirts proclaiming their love for the man.

Once they realised that he would do just about anything for Manchester United, it did not take long for the Stretford End to pay homage to a man who looked uncannily like the villain from the movie *Rocky IV*. Ivan Drago, like Vidić, was also of Eastern European stock. The Russian boxer, played by Dolph Lundgren in the Sylvester Stallone drama, was billed as a red superman. He knocks out Rocky's best friend, former heavyweight champion Apollo Creed, and when asked at the post-fight press conference to send a message of hope to the critically-ill boxer in hospital, he callously shrugs his shoulders and says, 'If he dies, he dies.'

The parallels with United's big Serbian lookalike warrior were obvious and it was not long into the 2006–07 season before T-shirts started to appear adorned with Vidić's face and Drago's motto: 'If he dies, he dies.'

Later that season Nemanja would laugh when asked about his likeness to Drago and admit: 'Every game is like a boxing match for me.' He would go on to explain: 'English football is so demanding and I don't think you can play unless you are 100 per cent fit. The game here is so quick and when you are playing every Saturday and Wednesday, it can be very tough. It's one of the best leagues in the world, but it's also very physical. That's why I say it's like a boxing match – nowhere else can you be as physical with opponents. I prepare for every match telling myself that I will be up against the best striker in the world because you always have to be ready for a battle.'

Another terrace T-shirt appeared that season, again with Vidić's face on the front, accompanied by the words: 'Veni, Vidi, Vidić... He came, he saw, he kicked their f***** heads in.'

There were also a few terrace chants about Vidić emerging –

the first, to the tune of 'Volare', which had the player himself cringing: 'Nemanja ohhh, Nemanja ohhh. He comes from Serbia, he'll f***in' murder ya!'

Initially, Vidić would smile and wave when he heard the song booming down from the stands at Old Trafford but as time went by, he found it difficult to do so for it was hard to reconcile the image the fans loved to foster of him with the real man, the man he was off the pitch. For all his reputation as a hardman, Nemanja Vidić was a gentle giant in his private life and nothing like the man demonising centre forwards.

He was a family man, one who liked to spend his time with his wife and son and socialising with friends. In short, he was nothing like Ivan Drago and the terrace song about him murdering someone came to trouble him, especially as he was still sensitive about the destruction that had so devastated his homeland during the Kosovan War.

In 2008 Vidić would admit that he found the song rather distasteful. He said: 'If the fans sing your name then you should be happy, but the song they sing about me at the moment has some very strong words. It mentions killing people and maybe that is because of the country I am from and what happened there in the past. Perhaps it is a little bit too much to sing, because I don't see myself as a hard player. I am a defender so it is my job to be aggressive on the pitch, but off it I am like everyone else.

'I like spending time with my family, listening to Serbian music and going out to eat good food in Manchester. Nobody has ever died on the pitch because of a challenge.'

At the same time, in an interview with the *Independent*, he also conceded that he was a different character when he pulled on a football shirt – that he changed personality, that he wanted to win and that he allowed his competitive nature free reign on a football pitch. He said: 'I don't act tough because I want to be tough. It just depends on the situation. The last few years I have had a number of injuries. I have put my head where maybe I don't need to put it – it's just me trying to stop a goal. Sometimes you can't go strong because the guy you are playing against is stronger than you. Sometimes you have to be more clever to take the ball – you cannot win 100 balls out of 100; it is about finding a way to win it.'

He said that he believed he had always been a courageous person and that translated onto the football field: 'I don't like to give up – I like to fight for everything. Not to fight in a bad way, but to go hard to chase something. That is how I am in training and in games.'

In 2008 he also explained his philosophy on life and football to *Sport* magazine, saying: 'The man you see on the pitch is very different to the man you see off it, the man you speak to today. When I play football, I become more aggressive – I have to give everything to the team. Maybe I don't always have great form, but I always give everything I have and I think the fans like to see that. I play strong, yes, but I am not a dirty player or a killer, as the fans sing. I don't want to hurt or injure anyone, I just want to win. I have to win – I am a bad loser.'

But Vidić had no problem with the ditty that the fans had

come up with in 2006 to celebrate their bond with him. It was nowhere near as heavy or controversial, sung to the tune of The Automatic's 'Monster': 'What's that coming over the hill? Is it Nemanja? Is it Neman-jaaa?'

The season would end with United finishing on 89 points, 6 clear of Chelsea and a remarkable 21 clear of third-placed Liverpool. United ended the season as Premiership champions for the ninth time in 15 years – their glory being confirmed after Chelsea failed to win against Arsenal at the Emirates on 6 May 2007. The 1-1 draw left them 7 points behind United, with two games to go. United were out of reach – home and dry.

But that was not the end of the season's story. Two weeks later, the Blues would get their revenge in the FA Cup Final, beating United 1-0 at Wembley. Vidić was to be honoured by making it into the PFA Team of the Year award – along with the other members members of United's brilliant backline.

The PFA team lined up like this: Goalkeeper: Edwin van der Sar (Manchester United); defence: Gary Neville, Patrice Evra, Rio Ferdinand, Nemanja Vidić (all Manchester United); midfield: Steven Gerrard (Liverpool), Paul Scholes, Ryan Giggs, Cristiano Ronaldo (all Manchester United); attack: Didier Drogba (Chelsea), Dimitar Berbatov (Tottenham Hotspur).

United had begun the campaign in blistering form, notching up four straight Premier League wins in the first month. They opened with a 5-1 thrashing of Fulham at Old Trafford and followed that up with a 3-0 win at Charlton, a 2-1 victory at Watford and a 1-0 home win over Spurs.

That was the good news... the bad news was that Vidić (who had now become known as 'Vida' to his team-mates) was involved in none of those games. He was still getting back to full fitness after suffering the devastating knee injury that had ruled him out of Serbia's World Cup campaign in June 2006.

Finally, he would reappear in United's squad for the Champions League Group F match against Celtic at Old Trafford on 13 September 2006. Unlucky for some on the 13th, his role in the 3-2 win was to be that of an unused substitute. He was also an unused sub in the next match: the 1-0 home loss to Arsenal in the Premier League.

That defeat ended United's unbeaten start to the season, but the result signalled the beginning of the Vidić era proper at Old Trafford. After the defeat by the Gunners, Wes Brown was dropped and Nemanja recalled for his first full start since the 3-0 loss at Chelsea on 29 April 2006. One man's misfortune was certainly another's big break. In the next match – a Champions League clash in Lisbon on 26 September – Vidić would replace Brown at the heart of United's defence and never look back. It was the start of a partnership with Rio Ferdinand that would provide the rock-steady base from which United would go on to dominate England and Europe.

United won 1-0 against Benfica to banish the demons of the traumatic defeat by the Lisbon giants the previous December – the defeat that had brought demands for boss Ferguson's dismissal from some disgruntled fans, and a defeat that had ushered in the signing of Vidić and Patrice Evra to bolster a sometimes flimsy backline.

Now Vidić and Ferdinand started to settle down as a partnership and prosper. United benefited enormously, notching up some terrific results over the next month, including a 2-0 home win over Liverpool and a 4-0 drubbing of Bolton at the Reebok. Snuggled in between the sequence of heady results, Nemanja also reached another personal landmark: on 14 October 2006 he scored his first goal for Manchester United in the 3-1 win at Wigan.

On 5 minutes, United had fallen behind to a Leighton Baines goal, but Vidić headed United level on the hour, hammering home a Ryan Giggs cross. Ferguson was quick to praise his man, saying: 'Nemanja is such a brave lad, he's not afraid to stick his head in – he's like Steve Bruce in that sense. If you do that, you're going to get goals and hopefully the one at Wigan is the first of many for us.'

The result sent United 3 points clear at the top of the Premiership.

It didn't take long for Vidić to follow up with his second goal for the club and this time it was in front of the masses at Old Trafford. On 4 November, he grabbed the final goal in the 3-0 demolition of Portsmouth. The goal was extra-special for his boss – it came on Ferguson's 20th anniversary as manager at Old Trafford.

Once again Giggs was involved in providing the ammunition for Vidić, passing the ball to Gary Neville from a short corner, with the club skipper floating over an inch-perfect cross from which Vidić (again) nodded home. United's then assistant manager Carlos Queiroz was quick to praise Vidić. He said: 'Nemanja is showing the form that persuaded us to bring him in last year. He is brave, determined, speedy and not afraid to put his head in where it hurts – as you saw with the great goal he scored today.

'It was a big moment for him to score at Old Trafford and I'm sure there are many goals from him to come – he is that sort of attacking centre-half.'

Queiroz was bang-on with that assessment: Nemanja would prove a regular headache for defences up and down the country as he prospered at corners and set-pieces.

Vidić was also pleased to have got off the mark at Old Trafford. He said: 'It was a great feeling to score in front of my own supporters. My first goal for the club at home – I'll never forget it. The fans have been great and so have the players and the manager. I really feel part of the club now and I'm learning what it means to be a Manchester United player.'

Ferguson was glowing after the win and said that he thought Vidić had done a great job and was making his presence felt at the heart of the defence. He added: 'We have had a fantastic start to the season. Historically, we don't always have good starts. We have made one this year and we need to take advantage of it. I have to be honest and say there is a confidence about the place that suggests we are now in a position to pull out all the stops and go for it.'

And United did just that – by Christmas they were battling with Chelsea for the Premier League title and had also successfully made it through to the next phase of the Champions League, much to the relief of their manager, the players and the fans after the disastrous showing a year earlier when they were eliminated at the group stage.

Progress to the knockout stage was all the sweeter as they would beat Benfica 3-1 to secure it – almost a year to the day after they had lost to the same outfit in Lisbon, a defeat that had confirmed their ignominious exit from the competition.

Once more, Vidić was prominent in the victory. He stood firm with Ferdinand to repel the Lisbon side's attacks and set United on their way to victory with their first goal on the night. The Reds had gone behind to a piledriver from Marcos Nelson, but Nemanja pulled them level with a bullet header.

Again, Ryan Giggs played a part in the Vidić goal. On the stroke of half-time Ronaldo was fouled by Simao and Giggs floated in the free kick. Vidić rose higher than anyone to head the ball home, much to the delight of the 75,000 strong-crowd.

Goals from Giggs himself and Louis Saha put the result beyond doubt.

With rivals Celtic losing in Denmark, United leapfrogged them to take top spot in their group. It was a remarkable turnaround from 12 months before.

Ferguson praised Vidić for his towering header, saying he was grateful as it had taken away some of the stress that engulfed United's games. He added: 'We always torture ourselves in these games. We started very slowly. The players struggled quite badly early on and the crowd took a while to get into the ground because of all the traffic. It needed Benfica to score for us all to get started. Suddenly the crowd got going and we found our rhythm and looked decent.

'We have a young, inexperienced side and I am not sure we can play a patient game. We can only really play one way and that's to bomb forward and to play the game in an exciting way – the Manchester United way, if you like.

'Before the game I would have taken a 1-0 win with a scabby goal off someone's kneecap but I'm always happy when we play well, like we did in the second half tonight. Now we have a lot of big League games before the next stage starts in February.'

And FA Cup games...Vidić and Giggs were up the field combining yet again in United's FA Cup fourth round 2-1 win over Portsmouth at Old Trafford on 27 January 2007.

Vidić looked as if he had headed United ahead from a Giggs corner. Replays showed the ball had crossed the line before it was hacked away by Pedro Mendes. Ironically, the same player had himself had a legitimate goal beaten away at Old Trafford in January 2005. Mendes, then in the white shirt of Spurs, had a shot from the halfway line cleared by United's keeper Roy Carroll when the ball also crossed the line.

'It was disappointing not to be credited with another goal,' Vidić would say after the match. 'I knew at the time it had crossed the line – it was a clear goal. But at least we went on to win the tie.'

United moved up a gear when Wayne Rooney came on just after the hour, the Scouser marking his arrival with a fine brace that destroyed Pompey's resistance.

A week later, Nemanja's disappointment turned to joy when he claimed the second goal in United's 4-0 thumping of Spurs at White Hart Lane.

Vidić crashed home a fine header from Michael Carrick's corner as the Red Devils made light work of their hosts. Goals from Ronaldo, Paul Scholes and Giggs completed the rout and Vidić commented: 'That was one of our best performances of the season and it was great to score the second goal. It sets us up nicely for the run-in.'

Boss Ferguson agreed: 'The scoreline is very good. To come to Tottenham and win 4-0 is exceptional. It looked as if once we got in front, we started to get a bit careless and casual. You can't do that. Zeros against your name is the name of the game.'

The *Independent*'s Sam Wallace argued that Vidić had proved to be United's spiritual leader as they romped home, saying they were 'a team reaching the height of their powers driven on by Nemanja Vidić, who added the second before goals from Paul Scholes and Ryan Giggs sealed the contest.'

It was an interesting point. Since Roy Keane had left the club 14 months earlier, United had been without a clear leader. Others stepped up to the role he had bequeathed – particularly Rooney and Ferdinand – but none caused fear and panic in the ranks of the opposition, unlike Vidić, the battering ram hardman. He had proved he was a leader – already he had the

T-shirt from his days as captain of Red Star Belgrade and Spartak Moscow – and now he was coming out of his shell at Old Trafford and taking up a role that came to him naturally.

There was also something of the Bryan Robson about the big Serb – the way he would throw himself fearlessly into any tackle and not pull out of a physical confrontation. United's original Captain Marvel had suffered the impact of several crunching tackles – his career glories interspersed with a string of serious injuries – and so it would prove with Vidić.

Some commentators in Robson's era had described his unrelenting bravery and no-holds barred style as reckless and irresponsible, but the majority preferred to talk about his honour to the club he would clearly die for. So it would prove with Vidić as he put himself in the line of unrelenting pressure from opposition forwards and defenders. And yes, the man should be praised, not criticised, for his bravery – but it would cost him and United dear in his first full season at the club.

The win at Spurs meant that United were 6 points clear of Chelsea at the top of the League and on their way to retaining the crown after two barren Premier League campaigns. It seemed to inspire Vidić and United: they now believed they were destined for greatness after a couple of years of relative obscurity with Nemanja in the outpost that was the Russian League, and United struggling to stay afloat in Chelsea's slipstream.

The Reds went on a 10-match unbeaten run – a sequence that included some terrific results, including a 1-0 win at Liverpool in the League and a similar scoreline in the Champions League over French side Lille at Old Trafford. The win over Lille – with Henrik Larsson heading home – meant United progressed to the quarter-finals, 2-0 on aggregate.

Vidić was now ever-present in the first eleven and his link-up with Rio drew ever-bigger plaudits. It seemed nothing could spoil what was turning into a fine first full season for the Serb at United.

Then disaster struck – and United would pay dearly.

On the last day of March, the Reds were hosting Blackburn in what looked, on paper, to be a nice easy afternoon's stroll in the park. And so it proved as they ran out comfortable 4-1 winners – a victory that meant they needed just five more wins to wrap up the title.

But the afternoon proved a nightmare for Nemanja. His day would end 28 minutes into the match when he was forced off with a broken collarbone after he fell awkwardly while challenging for a header from a corner. Vidić said: 'I knew something was badly wrong the moment I felt the pain. It was terrible, I was in absolute agony. I didn't even think of playing on – I knew I was out of the match and that I would probably be sidelined for a few weeks. I knew it was something very serious.'

Ferguson was understandably buoyed by the result, but sickened by the injury to his star defender. He said: 'It's a real blow to lose Nemanja at this time of the season. The great thing we showed was the composure to not lose our heads, keep our nerve and keep on playing and by doing that, we kept on making chances.'

The loss of Vidić would have a serious impact on United's quest for glory, and effectively end their European campaign. Though clearly unfit, he would be rushed back for the semi-final match against AC Milan and United would exit the competition.

When the injury struck, it was believed that Vidić would be absent for up to two months, with some pundits even suggesting he might not be fit until the following season.

One United fan on the club's official fans' forum summed up the panic in the ranks when he posted: 'United have no chance in Europe now Vidić is out for a couple of months!'

In the event, the tough nut would be out for just five weeks, but that was down to his bravery and his commitment – he was not ready for top-class action.

Immediately after Vida suffered the injury Sir Alex was faced with a nightmare shuffling of his pack for the Champions League quarter-final away tie at AS Roma.

Mikael Silvestre was also missing with a dislocated shoulder and captain Gary Neville was out with ankle ligament damage suffered a fortnight before in the 4-1 home win over Bolton. This meant United had to field a makeshift central defensive pairing, with John O'Shea partnering Rio Ferdinand.

Given the last-minute disruption, it was little wonder the Reds lost 2-1 in the first leg of the tie.

To their credit, even without the imposing figure of Vida at the back, United turned the tables on the Italians in the return leg. Wes Brown proved a capable stand-in as the Reds swamped Roma 7-1 to progress to the semi-finals.

Two weeks to the day after United suffered the blow of Vidić's injury at Blackburn, they would be dealt another setback when his defensive partner Rio Ferdinand was struck down by the injury jinx that had afflicted the backline of late.

Playing in the FA Cup semi-final against Watford on 14 April, Rio limped off with a groin injury. Ferguson replaced him with Darren Fletcher, a move which saw a shuffle in the entire back line. Midfielder Fletcher had to fill in at right-back, with Wes Brown and Gabriel Heinze as centre-backs, and Patrice Evra completing the back line.

United went on to win 4-1 with two goals from Rooney, one from Ronaldo and the other from Kieran Richardson, but the victory had been bought at a heavy cost. The last thing they needed was the loss of their other defensive lynchpin as the season reached the business end.

Their Premiership campaign was still rolling along nicely – even without the combined skills of Vidić and Ferdinand, they won two out of their next three League matches – but it was the Champions League that had become Ferguson's personal holy grail as the years rolled by.

It had been almost 8 years since he had achieved his first European Cup win in that thrilling finale against Bayern Munich in the Nou Camp. That win, after 13 years at the helm, had calmed Fergie. Finally, he had matched Sir Matt Busby's achievement of winning the European Cup, but he still hankered after at least one more victory.

Quite rightly, he believed that a club of Manchester United's stature should have won more than two European Cups. Plus there was also the small matter of United having been British trailblazers in the competition – they were the first British team to take part and the first English team to win it.

United – and English involvement – had been down to the vision of the late great Matt Busby who, in 1955, had realised this was the future of football. Testing his brilliant Busby Babes against the best Europe had to offer could only be good for the game and for their development. So it had been that Manchester United began England's European Cup participation in the Preliminary Round in Brussels on 12 September 1956 against the Belgium outfit, Anderlecht.

Fifty-one years later, in 2007, Sir Alex needed no reminding of this history – nor the fact that United had not delivered consistently enough in Europe given their role in the competition to date. In his eyes, their two wins in those 51 years compared miserably with the haul of Real Madrid, AC Milan and, more painfully, the five wins that his eternal enemy, Liverpool, had to their name.

No, just winning the League was not enough for the tough Scot by 2007. He had told friends that he wanted the European Cup again more than anything else and that he would feel he had underachieved if he was pegged back to just the one win by the time he finally put away his chewing gum and stopwatch. Yet the injuries to his key defenders – first Nemanja, then Rio – would undermine and ultimately thwart his major ambition for at least one more season.

Both men would be declared fit for the semi-final second-leg clash in Milan on 2 May 2007 – but neither was fit in terms of match sharpness. Nemanja had not played since 31 March, Rio since 14 April. Both struggled to overcome their injuries and Nemanja had suffered most with his collarbone injury.

Ferguson decided his two players would travel to Milan and that he would assess their relative strengths in training there. Looking back on the match, it still seems illogical that the manager decided to go for Vidić rather than Ferdinand. The Serb had been out longer, was even less sharp than Rio and there was an understandable feeling that he had probably not been given long enough to recuperate. Of course, part of that was down to his toughness and desire to get back in the side more quickly than expected, but Ferguson may well have picked the wrong man that night.

Ultimately, it would show in Vidić's performance – he had a stinker, definitely one of his worst showings in a United shirt as he struggled for speed, sharpness and to come to terms with the game. United lost 3-0 in the San Siro, 5-3 on aggregate, as a Kaka-inspired Milan left them for dead.

The magical Brazilian forward scored the first goal as he slammed the ball home in the eleventh minute.

Vidić was directly at fault for the second goal, scored by Clarence Seedorf. First, he failed to clear an Andrea Pirlo cross into the box, then he allowed Seedorf to get the better of him and hit the ball past Edwin van der Sar. The Serb's horror show was complete towards the end of the 90 minutes when substitute Alberto Gilardino raced past him to score and end the contest.

United were out of the European Cup.

Afterwards Ferguson admitted: 'It is very disappointing, given how well we have done to get here but I'd have to say we never came out the blocks. Milan were better prepared physically than us but we never coped with our start to the match. We lost two goals cheaply and you cannot do that at this level. Milan were fresher, but you have to say they put in a fantastic performance.

'If there was a difference in us tonight it was because we have been using the same players for the last two weeks without any respite. Milan have been resting players at the appropriate times, but that is not taking anything away from their performance. We had a gruelling test at Everton on Saturday, where we had to go the extra mile, but I still expected more from my team. We just have to take it on the chin and see where we go from here.'

Pressed on whether he had rushed Vidić back too early, Ferguson waved the question aside angrily, dismissing the idea and instead pinning the blame on the inexperience of his two potential matchwinners, Rooney and Ronaldo. He added: 'Wayne did OK, but it was a disappointing night for Cristiano and he knows it. They are young and on nights like this, the professionalism and experience of Milan gives a good indication of where we've got to go. That doesn't just apply to Rooney and Ronaldo, it applies to all the players.'

Yet the criticism that he had erred in picking a rusty Vidić would not go away so easily. Former United manager Tommy Docherty was one of his biggest critics, labelling the decision 'a disaster'. Docherty told Radio Five Live: 'When you're out for four or five weeks and the surgeon says you're fit to play, you're fit – but not fit to play. Playing Vidić was a disaster.'

Yet to his credit, Nemanja would show just what a star he was three days later, mounting a brilliant rearguard action with his partner-in-crime Ferdinand, as United withstood all Manchester City could throw at them at the City of Manchester stadium. It was an excellent riposte to those who had questioned his quality after the nightmare in Milan.

United won 1-0, thanks to a penalty converted by Ronaldo and the disappointment of going out of the Champions League would now be lifted as Vidić and Co. moved within a whisker of lifting the Premier League title that had been Chelsea's for the previous two seasons.

They secured it just a day later when Chelsea could manage only a 1-1 draw in their match against Arsenal at the Emirates. It was a remarkable achievement given United had looked so far away from Chelsea after Roman Abramovich had moved in and started spending all his millions.

In reality, Ferguson's team had been in transition for three seasons, with young players replacing older ones and new stars such as Vidić being brought in to bolster the spine. However, Nemanja would not be used by the manager in the final two League games of the season – the 0-0 draw at Chelsea and the 1-0 home loss to West Ham. Ferguson wanted to keep him fresh and fit for one final throw of the dice in what had proved to be a massive first full campaign at Old Trafford for the Serbian hero. He was keen for him to help inspire United to the double, by beating arch rivals Chelsea at Wembley in the FA Cup final.

But like the Champions League, winning the FA Cup would prove an obstacle too far for Ferguson's now-weary troops. Vidić would link up with Ferdinand once again and on this occasion the partnership came up against a man with whom Nemanja would have plenty of fiery run-ins as his United career progressed. Yes, Didier Drogba. While the Ivory Coast striker has a reputation for being somewhat petulant, he can also be one of the best players in the world when he is in the mood.

On 19 May 2007, in the first FA Cup final to be played at the new Wembley Stadium, it was fair to say Drogba was in the mood – most specifically during extra time. Chelsea were also hunting their own double glory at Wembley – a domestic cup double after securing the Carling Cup in February. And it would be they who would emerge triumphant at the 126th final, thanks to Drogba's winner.

The goal, in the 116th minute, broke the monotony of what had been a disappointing finale to an otherwise exciting season. Frank Lampard set Drogba up with a fine pass, leaving the big hitman the relatively simple job of slamming the ball past van der Sar.

This was only the second time in the game that Drogba had escaped the clutches of Vidić and Ferdinand – he also managed an effort that curled out off the post during normal time – but it was to prove the difference between the teams. The 1-0 scoreline, which could have gone either way as Ryan Giggs missed an equally fine chance to kill off the Blues when he had just Petr Cech to beat in normal time, was a fair reflection of the dour, dull game.

Boss Ferguson conceded that fatigue had been to blame for United's disappointing showing. He said: 'There was a bit of tiredness. The number of games they played eventually gets to them. It was the same for both teams, but I think in two or three positions we were tired.

'The pitch was slow, maybe that didn't help, but from our point of view we were tired. There was nothing between the two sides. Neither deserved to win or lose and we are disappointed we have lost. It has been exceptional what my players have been through – we just couldn't cross the line.'

There would be no third successive FA Cup final being decided on penalties, but more's the pity was the general feeling after the fodder served up over 120 minutes. Many agreed that a shootout would at least have made up for the defensive shut-out that ensued.

Not that Nemanja Vidić was concerned about shut-outs – it was part and parcel of his job description, after all – but he was gutted by the loss. Vidić, who was booked in the match for a foul on Frank Lampard 10 minutes from time, said: 'My first FA Cup final and I am very down that we lost. The match is shown all over the world, including back home in Serbia. I had hoped to be running round with the Cup, but it was not to be. We did our best and we will be back again, I am sure of that. And at least I have ended my first full season in England with a Premier League winner's medal. That is the big one as far as I am concerned.'

It was a fair appraisal of his first full campaign. The high of winning the title tempered by the disappointing Champions League exit to AC Milan and the FA Cup loss at Wembley to old rivals, Chelsea. But Vidić had certainly made his mark on the English game – he was a hero with the fans at United and viewed as a man it was wise not to mess with by his rivals.

The next season would be the one when he really upped the ante as he and United together stormed to a remarkable level of glory, at home and in Europe.

Chapter 5

MAGNIFICENT SEVEN

I F VIDIC'S FIRST full season in the red and white of United had been memorable for his first Premier League winner's medal, the second would be off the radar as he notched up a dazzling run of successes. He and United would finally bring the coveted Champions League back to Old Trafford and he would be rightly acclaimed as having become one of the world's best central defenders.

Yes, he had come a mighty long way in the two years since United had signed him as a promising, but raw, player from the Russian League. Few would have predicted the plaudits and medals he was to accumulate that season as he and United got off to a stuttering start in the campaign of 2007–08.

It would begin as it had ended with Chelsea as their opponents in the traditional FA Community Shield season setter at Wembley on 5 August 2007. This time, United would emerge triumphant, winning 3-0 on penalties after the match ended 1-1. Ryan Giggs had put the Reds ahead on 35 minutes, only for Florent Malouda to level, 10 minutes later.

In 30°C heat the teams once again struggled to put on a show, just as they had in the FA Cup final the previous May.

Vidić and Ferdinand anchored the centre of the defence with Wes Brown at right-back, Patrice Evra to their left, and van der Sar in goal. The five of them were now established as United's number one defence and Chelsea found it difficult to break them down. Vidić was in fine form and his afternoon was made all the easier as Drogba missed out through injury. The Serb even had a hand in the United goal, floating an excellent pass over to Evra who, in tandem with Ronaldo, then set up Giggs.

Despite the win there was a certain lethargy to United's play and they would still be suffering from it a week later when they opened their Premier League campaign with a home clash against Reading. They were out of sorts and the loss of Wayne Rooney in the first half, with what turned out to be a fractured foot, did not help their cause.

The Reds couldn't even muster a breakthrough when the visitors were reduced to 10 men after substitute Dave Kitson was sent off for a disgraceful tackle on Evra. United boss Ferguson refused to press the panic button despite seeing his team struggle in two consecutive matches. Instead he blamed the loss of two points on the absence of Wayne Rooney due to injury, saying: 'If he'd been on the pitch, I think we'd have won the

Above: Vidić (in the background) playing in an Under-21 match against England in 2002. He made his full international debut in November of the same year.

Below: In action for Red Star Belgrade in a 2002 Champions League match against Lazio.

Nemanja quickly established himself in the Serbian national team. As these pictures from 2003 show, he has never been afraid to put in a strong tackle – which can sometimes get him in trouble with referees.

Nemanja celebrates with the Serbia and Montenegro National Cup, which he won with Red Star in 2004. He joined Russian side Spartak Moscow a month later.

Serbia and Montenegro in World Cup qualifying action in 2005, with Vidić, *below*, holding off Raul of Spain.

Above left: Vidić takes defensive action for Spartak in the 2005 Russian season finale against Lokomotiv. The game finished 1-1, which was enough to guarantee Spartak Champions League football.

Above right: Nemanja makes his debut for Manchester United on 25 January 2006, coming on as a substitute during United's 2-1 win over Blackburn Rovers in the Carling Cup.

Below: New boy Nemanja jokes with Patrice Evra on the bench.

Above left: Nemanja in training with Serbia team-mate Mladen Krstajic in May 2006. Sadly Nemanja damaged his knee ligaments before the World Cup and played no part in the tournament.

Above right: Nemanja looks dejected after United's 1-0 defeat to Celtic in the Champions League group stage in November 2006.

Below left: Vidić celebrates scoring his first Champions League goal for United, against Benfica on 6 December 2006.

Below right: Nemanja intervenes to calm then team-mate Cristiano Ronaldo during Serbia's Euro 2008 qualifier against Portugal.

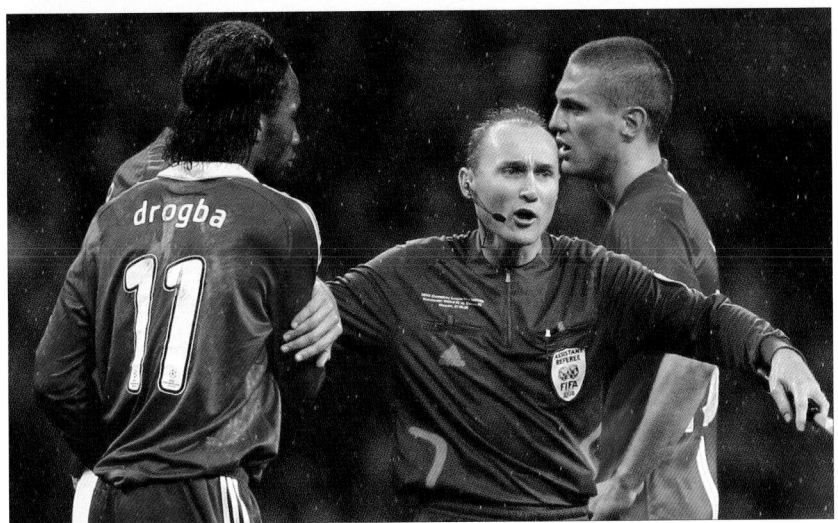

Above: Manchester United's 2007/8 Champions League team line up before their game against Olympique Lyonnais. Vidić is in the back row, second from the right.

Below: The assistant referee steps in to break up an argument between Nemanja and Chelsea's Didier Drogba during the 2008 Champions League final, which ended with Drogba being sent off after lashing out at Vidić.

Nemanja with the Champions League trophy. United clinched the trophy on penalties to seal a historic victory over bitter Premier League rivals Chelsea.

match. In the second half chances started to come. We had some good chances and we just didn't take them.'

Three days later United travelled to Portsmouth and before the match Vidić told the press that he was confident United would soon turn the corner – and that the Reading result would hopefully prove to be merely a blip. He said: 'We have dropped two points already and we are disappointed with that, but we cannot afford to think about it too much. It is a long season, so all we can do is assess where we made the mistakes and try to improve. Portsmouth are always a difficult team to play against anyway, so we cannot afford to go into the match still thinking about what happened against Reading.'

He admitted that the United boys were mourning the loss of Rooney and had accepted it would be all the more difficult to kick-start their season without the injured Scouser. Vidić said: 'Wayne is a big loss because he has been in such good form during pre-season. Hopefully, he will be back quickly but we have a big squad, with lots of competition for places, and there are plenty of others who have the ability to score.'

Manager Ferguson agreed with Vidić that the trip to Portsmouth would be no walkover. He said: 'Fratton Park is not an easy place to go to. It means Portsmouth have a big advantage overall in terms of their likely home record.

'Harry [Redknapp] has made a few interesting additions too, especially David Nugent, John Utaka and Sulley Muntari, who we have watched quite a bit, and I would expect improvement from them this season.'

Both Vidić and Sir Alex were right to be wary of Pompey. United had to settle for another point, coming away with a 1-1 draw, after Paul Scholes put them ahead with a blistering drive on 15 minutes, only for Benjani to equalise just after the interval. Carlos Tevez marked his Manchester United debut by setting up Scholes for the goal, but the Reds stumbled after Ronaldo was sent off for violent conduct.

He followed Portsmouth's Sulley Muntari in being red-carded 5 minutes from time for what looked like an attempted headbutt on Richard Hughes. Two minutes before him, Muntari had traipsed down the tunnel for an early bath after a second booking.

Boss Ferguson felt Ronaldo had been harshly dealt with. He told Sky Sports: 'I've looked at the replays and there's nothing conclusive. My take was that he was provoked. He's fallen into the trap and he's paid the penalty... it's his own fault, really.

'It was a disappointing result, but not a disappointing performance. There was a great contribution from Carlos Tevez, even though he had to endure a lot of tackles from behind, a lot of abuse [because he is an Argentine], and he came through that.'

And assistant boss Carlos Quieroz added: 'We played much better than we did against Reading and created lots of opportunities. We controlled the game in the first half, but Portsmouth put more pressure on us in the second half and we lacked a bit of composure.'

Queiroz praised Vidić and Ferdinand and absolved them of any blame for the Pompey equaliser. He said: 'Nemanja and Rio did well to keep Nugent and Benjani quiet for most of the match. No one was to blame for the headed goal, it was unstoppable.'

But United's slow start to the campaign would continue into the next match – the derby against Manchester City at Eastlands – and Vidić was to suffer as the ball deflected off him for the host side's winning goal in a 1-0 sickener. Vidić did his best to make amends, however, hitting the bar with a header from a Giggs cross and keeping City's frontmen at bay.

Afterwards he admitted the goal was a killer, but no one was blaming him for it. It came about on the half-hour when City's Brazilian midfielder Geovanni let rip with a shot from 30 yards out, the effort cannoning in past van der Sar after hitting Vidić on the calf. It was a freak goal – and City's only shot on target in the first half – but it meant they had chalked up three consecutive wins at the start of their Premier League campaign and were sitting pretty at the top of the table while United had just two points from their three games.

While Tevez had made his League debut at Pompey, Owen Hargreaves followed suit at City, lining up alongside Michael Carrick and Paul Scholes in midfield. It would take time for the new faces to settle in comfortably and without the injured Rooney and the suspended Ronaldo, United lacked a little in terms of their normal flair and invention.

Ferguson told everyone who would listen to calm down, that United would be back in business – and soon. He was proved right when just a week later the Reds finally got their 2007–08 title bid on the road with a 1-0 win over Spurs at Old Trafford, with the Portuguese winger Nani scoring his first goal for the club. United had begun the match second bottom in the League, but rarely looked in real danger once they had settled down after an early scare when Robbie Keane hit the bar in the first minute.

Afterwards Sir Alex made the valid point that his team were finding it hard to fire on all cylinders because anxiety had crept in: an anxiety borne out of expectations after they had reclaimed their League title the previous campaign. He said: 'That was narrow, touch-and-go, nothing to choose between the two sides. They dug in and got forward a bit and there was really nothing in it in the second half.

'I thought we lacked a little bit of confidence. Players are anxious, there is a lot of expectation here, and what was required was to dig in, show great commitment and we did that.'

Certainly there was a feeling among the fans that this could be a very big year for United. Lifelong fan Dave Moore explained: 'Right from the start of that season there was a tinge of excitement and anticipation in the air. We had finally brushed away the cobwebs of the transition years by winning back the title from Chelsea – and had proved we were number one again, despite Abramovich's millions.

'We expected to retain the title but also felt we could go on and win the Champions League for the third time. There was all that stuff about the final coming on the 50th anniversary of the Munich Air Disaster. It seemed as if we were pre-destined.

That's why there was a little unrest and anxiety among the fans at the start of the season when we got off to such a stinker. It hadn't been expected: we had thought we would open up with all guns blazing, but we should have known better really, shouldn't we?

'United had always been renowned as poor starters and so why should it have been any different that year? The team started off like a car that was stuttering, but gradually picked up speed and ended the season like a Rolls-Royce. But it was still a blow to our pride to lose at Man City back in August!'

Asked if he felt Vidić had started the campaign well, he replied, 'Yes, he was one of the most consistent performers. I know the goal went in off him against City, but it wasn't his fault. Him and Rio were solid at the back and a threat up front. I thought Vidić was getting better with every game, becoming more polished – although he was still a bit of a nutter! He had no fear when he went in for the ball and you could hear the shudder among the fans when he collided with an opponent and hit the deck.

'No, Vidić was a top man, even when we were struggling for form – the main reason it was such a bad start was down to Rooney getting injured. He was really badly missed.'

United followed up the 1-0 win over Spurs with another 1-0 win, this time over Sunderland, again at Old Trafford. Their football was far from pretty but still they were grinding out results and that, when things are not going quite as expected, is recognised as being the sign of true champions.

On 15 September, they battled to a third consecutive 1-0 Premier League win, getting the better of Everton at Goodison Park. Vidić was the hero of the hour, his headed goal 7 minutes from time helping United to continue their steady, if dour, progress up the Premiership table. It was a winner that would typify the Vidić trademark goal: he would meet a corner (in this instance, from Nani) after escaping the clutches of a couple of desperate last-line defenders to ram the ball home with unstoppable power. The legend was growing: not only was Vidić the defensive hardman, now he was becoming the Steve Bruce-like kingpin, who would get you that vital goal when you most needed it.

The match at Goodison had draw written all over it until Nemanja popped up with the winner, escaping the attention of Yobo and Tony Hibbert, much to Everton's dismay. It was a brilliant goal and afterwards he would be honest enough to admit United had come to Goodison with such a finish in mind; that they had determined that if they could keep things tight at the back – which he, as Man of the Match, and his partner-in-crime Rio most certainly did – then the door might open for one of them to sneak in a late winner at a corner or some other set piece.

And so it transpired.

Vidić admitted: 'We knew we could get a goal like we did. We came for that and we got it.'

Or to put it another way, he came, he saw, he conquered – and he also made a point of blowing his and Rio's trumpets in holding the backline together when he added, 'Sometimes it's more important not to lose a goal.' It was a valid point, especially given that he and Rio were undoubtedly United's star performers of the season thus far.

Vidić and United were beginning to pick up momentum and they would chalk up yet another 1-0 triumph just four days after the Everton win. Playing in the Champions League group stage, they overcame old European foes Sporting in Lisbon. Cristiano Ronaldo, returning to his native Portugal, grabbed the winner just after the hour mark, but it was Vidić who caught the eye with his brilliant, no-nonsense 'thou shalt not pass' brand of defending.

In particular, he caught the eye of his boss, who would now mention for the first time in public how he saw something of Steve Bruce in his Serbian rock. He praised Vidić and gave a succinct summary of the qualities that made him such an outstanding centre-back. Ferguson said: 'Nemanja reminds me of Steve Bruce in the sense he always asks a question of defenders. He wants to know whether they have the courage to put their head in front of his.

'There is no question he can play, there is not a doubt about it. But he doesn't mess about in terms of clearing the ball. He acts like a defender.'

Ferguson also told how delighted he was with Vidić's threat at the opposite end of the field. He said: 'He got me 5 goals last season and has already got one this year. I think he can easily get between 5 and 10 because he has got just the right qualities.'

It was probably at this point, as he extolled his man's virtues, that the United boss started to give serious thought to the idea of tying him down to a longer-term contract. Certainly, he was aware how envious eyes around Europe – particularly from Italy – were being cast towards the centre-back. Two months after Vidić's wonder shows at Everton and Lisbon, Ferguson would reward him with that new deal, which we'll examine shortly.

After the Champions League Group F win, it was back to the bread and butter of the Premiership and the first acid test of the new season for Vidić and Co.

Yes, the Chelsea boys were heading for Old Trafford, determined to show who were the real top dogs after suffering the ignominy of having the title crown they had begun to believe was theirs snatched by United the previous May.

That was the plan at least: in reality the Reds would prove too strong for the visitors, overpowering them with goals from Tevez and Saha in a 2-0 victory. Chelsea's cause was not helped by the dismissal of Jon Obi Mikel on the half-hour for a clumsy challenge on Evra.

It was hardly the start that Avram Grant, installed as a willing puppet by owner Roman Abramovich after the sacking of José Mourinho, had dreamed of, but it could have been much worse. After Mikel's red card, Chelsea lost their shape and discipline. Vidić and Ferdinand had little trouble in mopping up sporadic breaks by Andriy Shevchenko, Florent Malouda and Salomon Kalou in the absence of the injured Drogba. Indeed, Vidić almost netted from a free kick in the first half, only the alert Czech in goal thwarting his shuddering effort.

United had moved up to second in the table and their run of League wins continued with a 1-0 victory at Birmingham on 29 September, their fifth on the trot. A few days later, they notched yet another 1-0 triumph courtesy of the fit-again Wayne Rooney against Roma in a Champions League Group F clash at Old Trafford, but then Vidić suffered an injury setback in the Premier League encounter at home to Wigan. After just 21 minutes, he had to leave the field after suffering a facial injury and concussion. It was a blow for United, taking some of the gloss off a 4-0 win courtesy of a brace from Ronaldo and one apiece for Tevez and Rooney.

John O'Shea was also injured and in his post-match press briefing Sir Alex admitted that he was upset that both the Irishman and Vidić could be sidelined: 'Considering all the things that happened, I think we've done fantastically well. I was very pleased with the football in the second half. We had 10 players missing, but great credit to the players who played today. We speeded the game up in the second half, the flow of the game was much better; it's coming together.'

Fortunately for Vidić, he would miss only one match – the 4-1 away romp at Aston Villa – before he was declared fit and ready to go again. His return would be in the tough-looking Champions League match in Kiev as he replaced Gerard Pique. Before the game, he admitted the prospect of facing Kiev's forwards did not scare him in the least, but the flights to and from the Ukraine were something else altogether. He told *Inside United* magazine: 'Both me and my wife Ana do not like flying. It frightens us. I'm starting to get more worried each time I fly. My wife isn't very good on planes and the more travelling I do with her, the more she makes me nervous.'

He admitted that he was in awe of United legend Bobby Charlton, who survived the 1958 Munich air disaster: 'He was involved in a terrible air crash, yet he still flies. He is a very, very courageous man. I cannot imagine doing that, definitely not.'

United ran out 4-2 winners in the Ukraine, although Sir Alex expressed his disappointment at some of the defending, in particular the performance of goalkeeper Edwin van der Sar. The big Dutchman was beaten from 25 yards out by Guinea forward Ismael Bangoura and the boss reacted by substituting his goalkeeper 10 minutes from time.

Vidić also did not look his usual assertive self and later admitted he had taken a little time to settle down after his absence due to injury. He did look rusty and on the hour, when he pulled down substitute Artem Milevskiy in the box, he was lucky not to be punished with a penalty and a sending-off.

Yet United were all the better for his presence – and Rio Ferdinand was certainly glad of his return to action. Ferdinand admitted that he felt confident enough to go up for United free kicks with the big Serb back in the team: 'I knew we were safe at the back with Nemanja back in the side, so I left him alone at the back and ambled up for a free kick Ryan [Giggs] was taking after 10 minutes. Luckily enough, I got my head to it!'

That headed goal put United one-up and on their way to a memorable win.

Vidić joked: 'If Rio keeps going like this, he is going to finish up top scorer. He did brilliantly for his goal and he had another chance apart from that.

'We have always felt there were a lot of goals in this team and now it seems to have clicked for us at last. Obviously, the strikers are the ones we tend to rely on, but if defenders can chip in as well, that can only be good news for everyone.'

Nemanja admitted he had had to work his way into the game after returning from injury. That in itself had meant he was a little more cautious than usual in joining Rio upfront at corners. He said: 'I had two knocks against Wigan, not one. I did try to carry on for another 10 minutes or so, but I didn't feel well at all, so I had to come off. Now, I feel much better. I did stay back at corners against Kiev, but only because it was my first game back and I wanted to see how I felt. I am sure I will go up for corners against Middlesbrough on Saturday.'

United were on a roll now. They would go on to beat Middlesbrough 4-1, draw 2-2 at Arsenal (in a match they were just 8 minutes away from winning) and then thrash Kiev 4-0 at Old Trafford in the return Champions League Group F fixture.

In the win over Kiev, Vidić also had the honour of skippering United for the first time – even though it was just for 45 minutes. He took the armband when stand-in skipper van der Sar was withdrawn at the interval and admitted he felt 'so proud' at leading his team-mates out for the second half.

Vidić said the decision to make him captain was typical of his boss's 'brilliant' man-management and was just the latest in a string of gestures Ferguson had made to help him settle in and to feel as if he were a vital cog in the United machine. Nemanja revealed, 'I knew all about his reputation for sometimes losing his temper and I couldn't have blamed him for having a go at me [in the early days when Vidić struggled to acclimatise]. But instead, he walked over and went out of his way to calm me down. It seems funny now, when you think what he can be like, but he was telling me not to get angry.

'I realised then that he is a master at psychology. He knows what makes every one of his players tick, whether it's in training, out on the pitch or even at home. He knows how we breathe. I think he realised that bawling me out might have made it worse. He just said: "Come on, calm down. Players always need time to settle into a new environment and you're no different. It's normal, so stop worrying. I bought you because I knew you were right for this club. Your time will come."

'Hearing all that from him made an incredible difference – it put me completely at ease. Once I had stopped being anxious, I began to adapt to the English game. Wearing the armband, even for 45 minutes, made me so proud.'

Before the Arsenal match, Vidić and Ferdinand had been looking to notch a tenth clean sheet of the season as a central defensive partnership and Vidić declared himself confident this could be achieved, while expressing his hope that at the other end of the field Rooney and Tevez could link up to destroy the Gunners.

He said: 'Why shouldn't they score? They are playing so well at the moment – and not just them, but Ronaldo, Nani, every one of the attackers. At the back, though, we will take just as much pride from a clean sheet as they will do with a goal. Arsenal will be a big test, but I believe we can stop them and have another clean sheet to our names.'

Then he told of his delight when Ferguson had mentioned the partnership between himself and Rio in the same breath as the legendary one between Bruce and Gary Pallister. He said: 'I have heard of the comparisons with Bruce and Pallister. They are part of the Manchester United legend. To be compared with them is great, it makes you want to try even harder.'

Nemanja also told how he respected Arsenal and how he had watched keenly from Serbia and Russia (in the days when he played for Red Star Belgrade and Spartak Moscow respectively) when United and the Gunners had met in the past. He said: 'Arsenal have been playing very well this season. They are not just winning, but playing good football too. I watched their match against Liverpool and thought they were especially good in the first half.

'I always used to watch those games and they were always great. It didn't matter what position either team was in or their form going into the game. Players live for this sort of game and as both teams are playing really well right now, everyone will want to watch.'

Vidić said that he believed United were stronger now and that they could do better than the previous season when they had fallen at the final hurdle, in the FA Cup final loss to Chelsea at Wembley, in their double bid. He observed: 'We have a big squad this season. Last season we got a lot of injuries towards the end and did not have the power to go that one step further. Now we are much stronger and, with the competition for places, everyone is pushing that much harder.'

But he suffered more bad luck after starring in United's next match – the perfunctory victory (2-0) over Blackburn at Old Trafford on 11 November. Away on international duty with Serbia, he suffered a back injury that kept him out of the Premier League encounter at the Reebok against Bolton. It would be United who would suffer most as the 1-0 loss to the Wanderers vividly highlighted the massive impact Vidić had made at the club.

United were left short at the back as his replacement for the day, the young Spaniard Gerard Pique, struggled to contain Nicolas Anelka. Pique was to blame for the winner on 11 minutes as he missed a fairly easy header, with the ball dropping nicely for the man known universally as 'Le Sulk' to say 'thank you very much for the gift'. Anelka fired home his seventh goal of the season.

It was a sickener for United and for Ferguson, who was sent off by ref Mark Clattenberg for arguing with him in the tunnel at half-time. The defeat was United's first at the hands of Bolton since December 1978 and their first of the 2007–08 season since the loss at Manchester City in August.

Fortunately, Nemanja's absence was limited: he was back for

the next match and it was a case of business as usual as United beat Sporting Lisbon 2-1 at home in the Champions League. They would now embark on a seven-match unbeaten run up to Christmas, which included two particularly impressive results: a Mersey double over Liverpool and Everton.

Nemanja had already commented on his love of the matches against Liverpool. He said he was hypnotised by the atmosphere, the intense rivalry and the desire to win at any cost. This was another area in which he would rub shoulders with United's fans – they too looked forward to the Liverpool duels more than any other and, like Vidić, enjoyed nothing better than getting one over on their bitterest rivals. As the years went by, the big Serb's legend would grow alongside his antics in the matches against Liverpool – he would score against them, be sent off against them twice in one season, and declare again and again how he so loved to beat them!

Nemanja put in a towering performance as United won 1-0 at Anfield on 16 December, with a goal from Carlos Tevez. Later, he would rub Liverpool's noses in it by admitting the victory by a similar scoreline the previous season had been the most satisfying moment of his career so far. Then, United had somehow held on after Paul Scholes was sent off for a scuffle with Xabi Alonso, with John O'Shea grabbing the winner in injury-time.

Vidić said: 'My best memory has to be winning at Anfield last season, when O'Shea scored. Even though we played much better at Liverpool when we won again this season, that one was at such an important part of the season. Sure, this season's win at Anfield was important too, but it's easier to fix something when it happens at the beginning of the season. Those three points gave us the chance to win the Premier League – it was one step closer to the title.'

This was an attitude that would endear him to United's army of fans, as would his wholehearted showings when the matches against Liverpool came around each year. It was as if he was one of them: he wanted to beat the Scousers as much as they did. He also explained why it meant so much to win every match – why he went into battle buoyed by that single-minded ambition – and how it had been part of United's heritage and was now his own philosophy: 'Everybody knows United's name throughout the world. Everybody knows about the history of the club. The winning mentality is famous and I came to Manchester to win the most trophies possible and to be part of that history.

'I used to watch games on TV in Serbia and that meant I know all about the players who have been at United for the past 15 years. I am proud to follow those players.'

The win at Anfield in December 2007 was a huge one in that it kept United battling at the top for supremacy, but also left Liverpool 9 points behind them. It was the beginning of the end of their title challenge, and had a demoralising effect on the Kop outfit.

For Vidić, it meant the happiest Christmas of his life. Not only was he an integral part of a United team who were on their way into the history books in a fabulous season of achievement, but he had also cemented his own reputation as one of the best central defenders in the world. Proof of that had come a month earlier, when he was rewarded for his consistently fine displays with a new contract deal from Sir Alex Ferguson. The United boss had noted the regular stories on the back pages of the tabloids about the likes of AC Milan coveting his player and decided to take pre-emptive action to show them they were wasting their time.

Fergie sensibly tied Vidić down to United by offering a two-year extension to his contract, which meant that he would be with them until at least 2012. It showed just how highly the boss rated the man who had settled in so well at the heart of the defence with Rio Ferdinand – and who had also already scored five goals in what at the time had been 69 appearances for the club.

The new deal was announced after the win in Kiev and both Ferguson and Vidić expressed their delight. Nemanja would also get a much-improved salary package as part of its terms – his wage rising £23,000 a week, from £50,000 to £73,000. That gave him parity with the wages earned by most of the stars at the club, but of course, it still left him way behind Rio Ferdinand's deal.

Ferguson was confident that Vidić was well worth the investment and remarked: 'Nemanja has made a terrific impact at the club and has formed a partnership with Rio that was a major part in us winning the title last year. He is an extremely popular member of the squad and it's great news that he wants to be part of this exciting side.'

In turn, Vidić said he was 'privileged' to extend his stay – and made it clear his top priority was now bringing the European Cup back to Old Trafford after a 9-year absence. He commented: 'Playing in this team is a great privilege. I'm delighted to be able to extend my stay and I hope I can now do my bit to help us win more trophies. I certainly believe that can happen because the way we are playing at the moment, we are a danger to everyone.

'We may need a bit of luck along the way, but we must believe we can win the European Cup. We have top-quality players in attack and the feeling in defence is that we can always keep a clean sheet. We don't lose too many goals and this is the way we need to play in the future, if we want to win the trophy.'

He pointed out that United had qualified from Group F with four wins and that it was well within their grasp to go one better than their semi-final exit of the previous season: 'We have a bigger squad than last season and more good players, and because of that you have to say we are stronger than last season. Sometimes you need a bit of luck as well. Milan didn't play particularly well last season, but won the Champions League and there is a pattern of teams winning the competition when they are not going for their domestic league. But we're feeling confident about every match.'

Little did he know how prescient his comments back in November would be when the final of the Champions League came around the following May and United would finally emerge once again as the kings of Europe. However, he and the Reds would receive a setback just after Christmas 2007 when their unbeaten run would come to a shuddering halt with a 2-1 loss at West Ham on 29 December. It was a setback, but hardly unexpected – United had often come unstuck at Upton Park over the years and the Hammers had become a bogey team. Ronaldo had put United ahead, but goals from Rio's brother Anton and Matt Upson killed them off.

It was a wake-up call: 'don't expect to canter to the League title and Champions League glory', but it would prove a stutter, not a pivotal setback when viewed in the light of the season as a whole. Indeed, after the loss United would go on another unbeaten run – this time 7 matches – that would only end when they lost once again to neighbours Manchester City, who wrapped up an unlikely double at Old Trafford with a 2-1 win on 10 February 2008.

Again, it would prove to be a stutter rather than a setback: it would not bring about a run of bad results. On the contrary, similar to the defeat at City earlier in the season and the one against West Ham after Christmas, the February loss would prove to be a single blemish followed by a run of 16 matches unbeaten out of 17, with that single loss coming at home against Portsmouth in the FA Cup, a competition Sir Alex had already stressed was way down his list of priorities after the Champions League and the Premiership.

It was a run that would put United in a strong position

towards retaining their League title and set them up for that elusive Champions League crown.

There were some mighty results in the run and some fabulous contributions from Vidić, which also showed just how resilient the United team was. They would lose only occasionally and then, unlike most of their domestic rivals, would not allow it to weigh them down. On the contrary, they would dismiss any occasional defeat as one of those things, and press on determinedly to colouring in the bigger picture. They would not allow themselves to be distracted from their central ambitions. It was an excellent attribute and one that characterised the nature of both the team and Vidić, the rock at the back, who inspired his team-mates by going in where others feared to tread (or head).

Two results particularly stand out in the run – against Liverpool and Roma. On 23 March 2008, United disposed of Liverpool 3-0 at Old Trafford in the League. Vidić was a tower of strength, nullifying the threat of the boy from Spain, Fernando Torres, who was rapidly shaping up as the best centre forward in Europe.

Javier Mascherano hardly helped the visitors' cause by earning himself a red card for arguing with ref Steve Bennett over a booking for Torres just before half-time. Torres was lucky not to follow the Argentine down the tunnel after a disgraceful challenge on Vidić in the second half – clearly an indication of his frustration at the Serb's domination.

A year later Torres was to turn the tables – by turning Vidić inside out in the corresponding fixture – but that afternoon in March 2008 would belong to Nemanja. The result left United 6 points clear of second-placed Chelsea, who had won 2-1 against Arsenal.

Ferguson was full of praise for the way Vidić and Ferdinand combined so effectively to keep Torres and Steven Gerrard at bay – and made the point that this United team had now developed into one that was a real force in world football. He said: 'It was a really good performance – a performance of maturity. The team has matured over the last six months and today they hit their peak.'

There were more peaks to come as the season's end games unfolded.

On 1 April, United proved they were no fools by winning 2-0 at the Olympic Stadium against Roma in the quarter-final of the Champions League. It was a win that was all the more remarkable given that Vidić would only survive the first 34 minutes. He twisted his left knee and was replaced by Wes Brown, but goals from Ronaldo and Rooney saw the Reds home. There were fears that Nemanja might miss the run-in and that their Champions League dream would suffer, as had the previous campaign away in the San Siro. It was almost a year to the day that he had broken his collarbone against Blackburn and had subsequently been rushed back for the semi-final against AC Milan when he was clearly neither fit nor ready for top-grade action.

After the Roma setback Vidić left the Olympic Stadium on

crutches and his importance to United's season was highlighted by Sir Alex Ferguson's comment before they jetted home: 'I pray it is not serious, because he is such an integral part of our team. We think it might be a nerve injury, but we can't be sure at this moment.'

At least Ronaldo was upbeat – he voiced the belief that if Vidić could recover for the semi-final, then United could go all the way. He said: 'I think we have a great chance to win it. The team really played fantastically well in this game and has matured. Everybody knew what a tough game this was going to be for us and what a hard place Rome is to come to.'

Vidić was to miss the return leg against Roma but a 1-0 win, courtesy of a Tevez goal, was enough to ease United through, 3-0 on aggregate, and set up a potentially mouthwatering, if nerve-racking semi-final clash against the attacking aristocrats of Barcelona. As the Premier League fight hotted up, he also missed the 2-2 draw at Middlesbrough and the vital 2-1 win over Arsenal. But, just 18 days after he was injured in Rome – and much to the relief of United's players, manager and fans – he was back in business at Ewood Park on 19 April, helping United to a 1-1 draw that kept their title ambitions on target.

Nemanja was delighted with his comeback and spoke after the Blackburn match about how determined he was to face Barca to banish the memory of the 5-3 aggregate semi-final loss to AC Milan the previous season: 'We want to play much better at this stage and go on and win the trophy. Near the end of last season we had to play with some injured players.

Maybe that was the reason we did not do so well in the final stages.'

Vidić stressed that he and Rio would not simply be focusing their attentions on the great Lionel Messi over the two legs: 'Of course he is one of the best players in the world, everyone knows that, but the game is not all about Messi. Like many good teams, Barcelona have many good players.'

Clearly, the big Serb was relishing the imminent battle with the Spanish giants, but then disaster struck as illness and injury forced him to miss *both* legs of the semi. He was forced to pull out of the first leg after suffering a stomach complaint and would miss the return in Manchester after suffering a facial injury in the 2-1 defeat at Chelsea. The injury happened after a clash with Didier Drogba and was the latest spat in a growing vendetta between the pair that would eventually explode out of control in the final of the Champions League in Moscow.

To their credit, a patched-up United backline held out 0-0 in the Nou Camp and went through, thanks to Paul Scholes's winner at Old Trafford. It was the one goal of a tie that had threatened, on paper at least, to be a goal festival. Scholes's strike at once helped to erase his own personal nightmare and offered him the chance of redemption in Moscow – he had missed the final of the Champions League in 1999 because of suspension, but boss Ferguson promised him that, fitness permitting, he would be involved this time.

The defeat at Chelsea, sandwiched in between the two ties

against Barca, was a bitter blow for United and Nemanja. It meant the Blues were right back in the frame for the title – they were now joint top with United – and Vidić was despondent after being carried off on a stretcher just 11 minutes into the game, as he knew his hopes of playing against Barca in the return leg, four days later, had now also disappeared.

The Champions League was proving something of a jinx for him, but there would be a wonderful silver lining when it really mattered in Moscow at the end of May. And even though Chelsea had drawn level on points in the Premier League, their goal difference was inferior. Ferguson had decided to move Wes Brown into Vidić's position and bring in Owen Hargreaves at right-back. But two goals from the powerful Michael Ballack, one a penalty, won the points despite Rooney's equaliser.

Assistant manager Carlos Queiroz admitted the loss of Vidić had been 'a terrible blow', but expressed the hope that United would cope against Barca without him: 'Of course, he is a great player, a wonderful defender and a leader and we will miss him. But we have a job to do at this club and we have to win our next few games. It is important to support the players because after 90 minutes of effort and commitment, we want them to feel it is a fair game for them. The defeat by Chelsea has not caused any damage for us. We will concentrate and do our job and stay committed.'

He was proved correct: United were without Vidić against Barca at home – and won; also against West Ham at home – and won. Privately, Sir Alex admitted that if Vidić did not play again before the Champions League final, it would be difficult for him to be selected in Moscow.

Nemanja now faced a race against time to be fit. As already suggested, he was much like United's Captain Marvel of the 1980s, Bryan Robson, who would throw himself into every tackle and loose ball as if his life depended upon it and miss out on some of the glory games. But Vidić would prove tougher than even Robson, returning from injury much earlier than expected.

On 3 May 2008, he sat in the stands as United beat West Ham 4-1 in the Premier League, thanks to a brace from Ronaldo and one apiece for Tevez and Michael Carrick. But he could be seen smiling and joking: clearly he was on the mend and on the way back as United moved to within one win of another title as they ended their home campaign for the season.

United won comfortably even with 10 men – Nani was shown a red card on 37 minutes for headbutting Lucas Neill – and Ferguson now expected his men to finish off the job of winning the League at Wigan the following week, saying: 'We have not won anything yet, but we hope we can win the League next week. There was a bit of nervousness in our play at times, but we killed the game in the second half to continue what has been a fantastic season so far.'

Ferguson said he was confident that Vidić would be back for the final League game at the JJB Stadium and confirmed that he was doing well. He also praised Cristiano Ronaldo for grabbing his 39th and 40th goals of the season. He observed: 'How many players could score that many? He is improving all the time. Plus he has spent 90 per cent of the season on the wing. It's been a great day for us and we've got a big chance.

'Our players have been absolutely fantastic this season. We were down to 10 men and I said to try to run the clock down, keep possession and be patient in the second half, and I'm very pleased because there was a bit of tiredness.' He also criticised Nani for his indiscipline: 'There is no excuse for Nani. He showed a measure of immaturity and we will deal with it.'

United headed for Wigan on 11 May – and all the more buoyant because Vidić's comeback was confirmed a couple of days before the big match. He himself said that he was 'delighted' to be back and hoped he would now have a clear run to the Champions League final, 10 days later. His timing was perfect – all he had to do now was to show that he was fit and well, put in a composed showing and he was on his way to the biggest date of his life. Indeed, it was as if he had never been away as United strolled to a comfortable 2-0 win over Wigan, securing their 17th League title in style. Ronaldo put United ahead just after the half-hour and Ryan Giggs scored the goal that secured his 10th title winners' medal with 10 minutes remaining.

Yet again, Vidić and Ferdinand were commanding at the back, both directing and mopping up operations on what turned into a terrible playing surface as the heavens opened. At the end, both were dancing in the rain, along with manager

Ferguson and their team-mates, as they celebrated the win. It was Nemanja's second League title winner's medal in two seasons, but he – and United – weren't finished yet.

There was the little matter of the Champions League final to come and the possibility of winning the biggest medal in club football, but if they were to achieve this, then they would have to overcome biggest rivals, Chelsea. Vidić would have to get the better of his nemesis, the abrasive Didier Drogba.

With all the makings of a classic battle for Nemanja and his team-mates, it would prove to be just that.

Chapter 6

FROM RUSSIA WITH LOVE

NEMANJA ADMITTED he had pinched himself when he arrived in Moscow for the Champions League final with the rest of the United squad a couple of days before the match. There he was, back in the city where he had made his name with Spartak and attracted the attention of United – a Serb who had dared dream that he might escape his ravaged homeland to make it big in world football, playing in club football's biggest global competition.

Now he would be performing for the world's biggest and most popular football club in front of a live TV audience of almost one billion. He had come a long way and he was determined that he would not leave Moscow without a winner's medal.

Of course, he was also going to play again in the stadium where he had been a colossus of a defender – to the Luzhniki

Stadium, home of Spartak Moscow, the club he had left to join United. Nemanja said: 'I always dreamed of playing at the highest level and the final in Moscow was the highlight of my career. I was very proud to be there representing Manchester United – and to be representing my country. I will never forget the night, it was a dream come true, and a dream come true in a stadium that meant so much to me – the stadium where I enjoyed my time in Russian football as a Spartak player.'

Sir Alex Ferguson had picked a strong squad and the boys from Old Trafford flew out of Manchester airport on a private charter at lunchtime on Monday, 19 May 2008, two days before the crunch match. Vidić was delighted as some Spartak fans greeted him warmly when he walked through the airport in Moscow. They hadn't forgotten the man who had performed so heroically for their club and Nemanja was all smiles.

Twenty-four players travelled to Moscow as part of the United squad. Of them, only three had been part of the match-day squad that had touched down in Barcelona for the 1999 final against Bayern Munich in the Camp Nou. Ryan Giggs and Gary Neville had been in the starting line-up while Wes Brown was on the bench. Paul Scholes, who had been promised a start in the final in Moscow, had been with the squad in Barca, but of course, missed out on the game itself – he and Roy Keane were both suspended.

Chelsea arrived in town the same day – with an entourage of 44. It was their first European Cup final, but they were brimming with confidence, convinced that their time had come.

But United's destiny was linked to the event that had devastated the club, yet at the same time had also made it the best known in the world, some 50 years earlier. The Munich air disaster of 1958 was in the minds of many United staff and fans as they prepared to do battle: 8 of the team's players had been killed that black day as they returned from a European Cup game. United boss Ferguson was more aware than most of the significance of the 50-year anniversary and said: 'We won't let the memory of the Busby Babes down.'

And the boss was right. Certainly, with Munich survivors, including Sir Bobby Charlton, in attendance, the 2008 United side would not let them down. Vidić and his team-mates grafted and earned the right to have their names mentioned alongside those European Cup heroes of 1968 – Best, Charlton and Kidd – and of 1999 – Sheringham, Schmeichel and Solskjaer.

'It was only fitting,' Ferguson would tell the press ranks after the match. 'It was such an emotional occasion. I said the day before the game that we would not let the memory of the Busby Babes down. We had a cause and people with causes are difficult to play against. I think fate was playing its hand today.'

The day before, Sir Alex had added to the growing build-up by claiming that the final was now the biggest event in world football. He said: 'I think it is better than the World Cup now and has been for some time. The Champions League gets better each year, whereas World Cups are not what they used to be. You have to go back to 1986 in Mexico to get a real sense of what World Cups used to be like. Or the one before that: in

Spain. France and Brazil were both knocked out by the semi-finals that year; that shows how high the standard was. They were two of the best teams ever.'

Ferguson was convinced he now had a strong enough squad to lift the trophy, but added that the winning team would also need a bit of luck. He said: 'You need a little bit in terms of who you've got on the Saturday before your Tuesday night game, or in domestic terms who you play on the Saturday after a Wednesday. The Premier League is so competitive you can't ease up for a minute and it can be difficult picking your teams, if you are going for the League as well as Europe. You need a strong squad and we didn't have that last year, or at least not when we needed it.'

He also admitted he took a certain pride in the fact that the final would be between two English clubs – that it was a brilliant advertisement for the strength of the Premier League, commenting: 'There has been an English team in the last three finals. We are getting some consistency from English clubs in Europe now. The recent record suggests English clubs will get to the later stages, and once you do that there is always the chance of reaching the final or even winning it.

'Two European Cups over the history of the Premiership is not a lot, but there are reasons for that and the balance has been between Milan and Madrid, anyway. But the Premier League has improved, the quality of players in England has improved, and although English clubs have no divine right to succeed, we have a better chance of consistency in Europe now.'

The Moscow extravaganza was the third Champions League final between clubs from the same country in less than a decade. Spain's Real Madrid had defeated Valencia in 2000, while AC Milan beat Juventus in an all-Italian final in 2003.

The build-up was colourful and noisy as 25,000 fans from each club converged on the city the day before the big game, massing in Red Square, where special tents and entertainment had been lined up to keep them occupied. They mixed amicably for what one newspaper dubbed 'the biggest invasion since Napoleon'. Of course, there were problems getting into the country and finding somewhere to stay. Queues at immigration were long, tiring and testing, and the hotels in Moscow – all of which had cashed in by putting up their tariffs – were full. Even Wayne Rooney's then-fiancée Coleen suffered at Moscow airport, after spending 90 minutes filling in forms. She remarked: 'I am looking forward to the game, but I could have done without having to spend all that time filling in a load of forms about a lost suitcase.'

The missing Louis Vuitton suitcase that was lost on the way to Moscow belonged to a relative of Coleen's and the delay was irritating for the other United WAGs, who had to wait on a hot, stuffy coach until she was finally able to join them.

Yet the queues and delays would have been far greater for United's contingent of fans and staff, had the club's chief executive David Gill had his way! He reckoned they could have quadrupled their support for the match: 'We have actually allocated the tickets broadly in accordance with UEFA instructions prior to knowing whether we would be there. Our allocation is just over 21,000 tickets and with season-ticket holders, box-holders and other internal usage, it is a difficult process. We could sell well over 100,000 tickets for this final, so there will be a lot of disappointed people.'

By the day of the game itself, the atmosphere had become more serious, not because of the fans, but because of the Russian authorities' *fear* of the fans. Shops were banned from selling alcohol and some closed completely. On the journey from the city centre to the Luzhniki Stadium, which hosted the Moscow Olympics in 1980, police and militia had been employed by the Russians, who were wary and (as it turned out) over-sensitive to the threat posed by their visitors. They had heard all the stories about the infamous English hooligans and were determined to stamp hard on the merest suggestion of trouble.

Sports Minister Gerry Sutcliffe did not help assuage the Russians' fears when he felt it necessary to appeal to both sets of fans not to cause trouble. He said the eyes of the world would be on their final and that bad behaviour could wreck England's bid for the World Cup finals of 2018.

Sutcliffe remarked: 'I was really impressed and pleased that the European Champions final will be an all-English final, but that brings some responsibilities for the teams involved and their supporters. They have to make sure that we have a showcase final, which may help us in terms of our World Cup bid. When you think what the global audience will be for the Champions League final, their every move will be watched.

'It should be a great advert for the Premier League and for English football, but it will also be the place everyone will be looking at, if anything goes wrong. If that happened, it would not only be damaging for the two teams participating but could also have a big impact on the reputation of our game at a time when we are trying to encourage football nations to support our World Cup bid.'

However, apart from a few minor scuffles among fans that might have downed just little too much Russian vodka, the police needn't have bothered with such a massive intimidatory presence. In the end, it proved unnecessary and the sight of the massed fans made Vidić smile as the United team bus drove past them on its way to the stadium. The Serb had enjoyed some nights out in Moscow when he played for Spartak, and had shown his family around the sights of St Basil's Cathedral and the Kremlin when they visited him, but he had never seen anything like this. 'It's unbelievable,' he told Rio Ferdinand, who was sitting next to him on the coach. 'It shows how big football has become worldwide.'

And he wasn't wrong about that – the match would be watched by millions of people and millions of pounds would exchange hands in a cash bonanza that would help United continue to build and fund the team that following season.

Professor Simon Chadwick of the Centre of International Business of Sport summed up the sheer scale of the financial spin-off that the Old Trafford giants could expect when he told the *Sun*: 'The 2008 Champions League final will be the biggest prize yet in economic terms. The cumulative impact of this match could amount to upwards of £210 million – with more than half of that going to the two finalists.'

Which meant the final even eclipsed America's famed SuperBowl in terms of financial impact – a truly remarkable feat.

The proof of how big a cash cow the final had become was clear when a newspaper halfway around the world explained just what the match meant to people in India and how its successful model could even be used as a base for India's own sporting events.

After the match, the *Hindustan Times* commented: 'Soccer finals don't get any bigger than this: Manchester United playing against Chelsea in the Champion's [sic] League final in Moscow… but what struck beady-eyed us sitting here in 'indoostan, glued to our tallies [sic]… was the sheer mixture of quality and high-octane entertainment provided.

'Television cameras beaming the match live to millions worldwide lingered lovingly on the fouls and the battered bodies, as well as on the goals and the subsequent faces. This was Jacobean theatre performed by the two English clubs full of a non-English dramatis personae.

'For us sitting here in Delhi, Mumbai, Kolkata or Bhatinda, cheering on either Man U or Chelsea might seem a tad strange to the guys at the bar in the Old Mancunian or Stag's Head. It may seem odd to even the supporters from non-Manchester and non-London, who follow the tricks of the trade of their non-English heroes playing in either club to find Indians roaring in cheer or collapsing despair to the proceedings of a "European" tie. But, as the gladiatorial spectacle evident from Moscow's Luzhniki Stadium in the wee hours of Wednesday night here showed, Lalit Modi and gang could pick up a tip or two about truly globalising a spectator sport.'

Yes, it was that sort of final – a defining moment for the world of sport and business and English football. And it would be the cavaliers from Manchester who would emerge triumphant against the power players from London. OK, United had their own men of power in the rock-hard Vidić and his partner-in-crime, Rio, and Rooney could also hand it out when the mood took him, but Chelsea were a team built from granite: rock-steady and rock-hard; big men, who would not be pushed around and who could hold their own in any physical battle. John Terry, Michael Ballack and Didier Drogba – a rock-hard spine to a more than intimidating frame.

Yet United, to their credit, stood firm and refused to buckle as Chelsea's hard men confronted them. And at the end of the match it would be two of those men, Drogba and Terry, who would take it on the chin for their side's defeat.

After extra time, match was at 1-1, but 4 minutes from the end, Didier Drogba was sent off for an assault on Vidić and England skipper Terry missed the vital penalty that would have won it for the Blues.

Drogba's early bath might be considered karmic retribution for the run-ins he had had with Vidić since the Serb came to England. The Ivory Coast striker had frequently squared up to

Nemanja in previous encounters, often leaving him bruised and battered. This time, Drogba would go a little bit too far – he would be forced off the field and his team would pay a terrible price for his petulance. Certainly, he would have been one of the key penalty-takers in the shootout.

In being sent off, Drogba achieved the notorious distinction of becoming only the second player to see red in a Champions League final. Jens Lehmann had the notoriety of being the first, when he was dismissed for Arsenal against Barcelona back in 2006. The German goalkeeper brought down Samuel Eto'o in the box after the striker rounded him and was set to shoot on goal.

Lehmann had been dismayed at his sending-off, but Drogba was outraged and at first, refused to go. When he eventually left the field many commentators believed this would be his last action in a Chelsea shirt, although he would in fact live to fight another day and to court yet more controversy.

In his personal battle with Drogba, Vidić had come out on top and that in itself answered the pre-match jibes from Chelsea's striker Salomon Kalou, who had claimed the Serb was the weak link in the United team. Kalou had said: 'We still believe that there is some weakness in their defence and that we can exploit that and score some goals. They are like everyone – Ferdinand is a great defender, Vidić also. But Vidić has not played a lot because he has been injured, so that could be a weak point for them and it is up to us to play well and score a goal.'

Kalou, who arrived as a 92nd-minute sub for Florent Malouda, may well have felt pretty foolish afterwards when Vidić shook his hand and commiserated with him. Nemanja was big enough to forgive and forget, but then he had just won the biggest prize in club football, hadn't he?

When the teams were announced before the match, it was clear that United boss Ferguson had his concerns about Chelsea's physical prowess. He sent out a powerful three-man midfield, anchored by Owen Hargreaves and Michael Carrick, to counter Chelsea's own 'Big Three' in the centre of the park: Claude Makelele, Ballack and Frank Lampard.

The teams, and formations, read:

MANCHESTER UNITED (4-3-3): Van der Sar; Brown, Ferdinand, Vidić, Evra; Hargreaves, Scholes, Carrick; Ronaldo, Tevez, Rooney.

CHELSEA (4-3-2-1): Cech; Essien, Carvalho, Terry, A. Cole; Makelele, Ballack, Lampard; J. Cole, Malouda; Drogba.

After 26 minutes, United went ahead when Cristiano Ronaldo powered in to head home a cross from Wes Brown, the Portuguese winger's 42nd goal of a remarkable season. But Chelsea leveled with a killer goal on the stroke of half-time as Lampard ghosted in to hammer home a ball floated in by Michael Essien.

It would take the sting out of United's attack as they headed in for the break, but Ferguson would reassure them that everything was OK, that they could still triumph if only they kept their nerve and kept their heads.

Led by Vida and Rio at the back, they did just that – although even the usually solidly reliable Nemanja suffered a couple of surprise jitters as the clock wound down in the second half. In one two-minute spell, he superbly turned over a cross by Ashley Cole, but then, just a minute later, fouled Drogba 30 yards out. From the resulting free kick by Makelele, Michael Carrick was forced to clear a dangerous ball away.

Afterwards Vidić would admit that he was not immune to nerves, that the tension and importance of the occasion had got to him a couple of times. Like his team-mates, he was well aware that one false move could mean the vital difference between triumph and failure. And who wanted to be remembered as the man who had lost his team the Champions League final?

Another instance of the jitters came just 9 minutes from the end, when Vidić was booked for upending Nicolas Anelka. Fatigue was setting in along with the nerves, but fortunately for the Serb, Drogba would balloon the ball wide from the ensuing free kick.

The Ivory Coast hitman and the Serbian blocker had been scrapping for supremacy for 116 minutes when Drogba finally blew a fuse. Renowned for years throughout the English game for his petulance and temper, he saw red 4 minutes from the end – for slapping Vidić in the face.

Nemanja had pushed him to the limit, steadfastly refusing to stand off or to be intimidated and had finally come out on top.

Indirectly, by stoking up that moment of madness by frustrating Drogba, he won the Champions League for United. Now Drogba would be off the field for the vital penalty shootout – he had let his team-mates, fans and the club down at the moment they needed him most.

Who is to say that it wouldn't have been Drogba who would have stepped up to take the penalty missed by Terry? Surely, he would have done – and would also as surely have scored, which would have taken the Cup back to Stamford Bridge.

Before the final, Vidić had issued a warning about Drogba and now his words proved ominously accurate. He had told the *Daily Telegraph*: 'Sometimes he [Drogba] goes in very strong and sometimes he pretends he is weak. He plays with your mind and tries to make the defender think about the next tackle.

'He can pretend he fell down to win a penalty, but referees know that. The Champions League final is a big game and I'm sure the ref will know his job. He's a great player and he's a top scorer – it's a hard job to stop him.'

Nemanja had spotted that Drogba is a master of manipulation, by the way he 'plays with' defenders' minds and attempts to influence the refs, and so it had panned out just as he predicted in Moscow. The Serb had played him to perfection and Drogba had blown up simply because Vidić refused to bite at his antics.

Winning and losing on the world's biggest stages often come down to what initially appear to be minor details, but when examined more closely they usually highlight a fatal flaw in approach by one side. In this instance, one man's sending-off led to another team's glory. Yes, United owed much to Nemanja Vidić, that wonderful night in Moscow, for his authoritative display at the back and for lighting the fuse that led to Drogba's calamitous dismissal. Cometh the hour, cometh the Serbian hero!

Drogba's recklessness and the way clever Vidić frustrated him would resonate around the world. One man was to be castigated worldwide, the other congratulated. Journalist Sean Connolly summed up the situation as well as anyone when he said: 'If you're a Chelsea fan though, do not blame Nicolas Anelka for not going right, or John Terry for not being aware of the conditions of the field, blame Didier Drogba. Reminiscent of the 2006 World Cup final between France and Italy, where France superstar Zinedine Zidane head butted Marco Materazzi and was sent off, Didier Drogba lost his head in a confrontation and decided to slap Manchester United player Nemanja Vidić.

'And the worst part is, it wasn't even a good slap. If you're going to slap someone to get sent off in the Champions League Final, make sure you get him good. At least Zidane's headbutt was creative, I mean, who headbutts someone in the chest anyway? Instead Drogba barely glanced Vidić's chin right in front of the referee… To play for that long and get kicked out of the biggest game of your career over something so small and dumb is beyond me.'

In the tense shootout that followed United rode their luck to bring back the trophy to Old Trafford for the third time in the club's glorious history. Tevez scored to make it 1-0, Ballack made it 1-1, Carrick made it 2-1 to United, then Beletti made it 2-2. Ronaldo missed, Lampard put Chelsea 3-2 up, Hargreaves kept United in it at 3-3, Ashley Cole put the Blues 4-3 up. Then Nani had to score or United were dead and buried: he did so, but Chelsea still had the upper hand as the tension became unbearable. Luckily for United, Terry slipped and shot wide – when a successful penalty would have won the trophy for Chelsea.

Anderson then turned everything on its head by putting United ahead 5-4, only for Kalou to equalise. The legend that is Ryan Giggs now stepped up and, cool as a cucumber, scored to make it 6-5 to United.

Finally, when we could take no more, Nicolas Anelka unconvincingly sent his penalty straight at Edwin van der Sar.

The European Cup was on its way back to Manchester for the first time since 1999.

Afterwards, Vidić celebrated with the rest of the United boys back in their hotel as it finally struck home that he had become a European champion with the club to whom he had pledged his future 29 months earlier. The team had planned to visit a Moscow nightclub, but were exhausted and felt like keeping their celebrations in house. They had truly become a team who fought together, won together and celebrated together. United in every sense of the word after the Moscow triumph of 2008, they would continue to grow, develop and win more success as a unit.

A couple of days later Vidić would be publicly critical of

Drogba, accusing him of cheating, but also took the opportunity to confirm that he was delighted to be at United, whom he referred to as 'the best in the world'.

Nemanja said: 'Drogba likes to cheat and you need to be on alert about that all the time. His nerves let him down, which is hardly surprising since the pressure was colossal. The referee was close to the incident and was right.'

Then he added: 'Can anyone still doubt that I play in the world's best team? Or that the English club football is the best in the world? What happened in Moscow was the greatest success in my career – I'm still overcome with emotion. On Wednesday night we were so tired, no one could think of going to celebrate in a Moscow nightclub. Of course we celebrated for an hour or so at the hotel, but then went to bed.

'But I couldn't sleep because I was so excited after that great match. In the Luzhniki Stadium, I probably felt more comfortable than the rest after playing there for Spartak in front of their wonderful supporters. In fact, I met several friends from Moscow, who told me that all Spartak fans are now going to support Manchester United.'

He admitted the final was all the more special not only because he saw history being made, but was part of it. As United dug out a famous victory, it did not go unnoticed that Ryan Giggs came on as a sub to break Bobby Charlton's club appearances record. Already the club's most decorated player with, at the time, 10 Premier League titles and 5 FA Cups, Giggs had revealed that his one regret was that he had only won the one European Cup winner's medal in 1999. In saying that, he was very much singing from the same hymn book as his boss, Fergie, and both men were relieved and jubilant to make it two in Moscow.

Giggsy came on for Paul Scholes 3 minutes from the end of normal time to pass Sir Bobby's 46-year record of 758 appearances in the red of United. It had been claimed that the record was 759 until just weeks before the final when it was revealed that Sir Bobby had not, after all, played in a 1962 FA Cup tie against Bolton.

Giggs was rightly proud of his achievement, saying: 'What appearing in tonight's game proved is that I was right to remain at United throughout my career. When I first came through, Serie A was the place to be and the best players went there. Now all the great players are playing in England.'

Like Vidić... and Nemanja was one of the first to pay tribute to the wing legend. He said: 'Yes, I knew Ryan would beat the record of Sir Bobby if he came on and it was great to be part of it. Also, he played an important role for us in the penalty shootout.'

Indeed he did: as we have already noted, Giggsy coolly slotted home the penalty that gave United a 6-5 lead – the one that would prove the winner after Anelka's costly miss.

Vidić would not get time to see many of his old friends in Moscow for United were booked on a flight home the day after their momentous win, much to the disappointment of his former Spartak Moscow team-mates, who had hoped to meet up and congratulate him in his moment of triumph.

And if his old mates felt a bit put out to have missed him in

Moscow, Vidić himself – and his United team-mates – must have sighed in dismay when they were told there would be no victory parade back in Manchester to mark their win. Greater Manchester Police dismissed the idea on the grounds that it would risk public safety.

United chief executive David Gill described the decision as 'unfortunate' and Vidić admitted that he and the rest of the United squad had been looking forward to parading their Champions League trophy on an open-top bus. But the police stood firm, especially as the previous week Manchester had been turned into a no-go zone when hundreds of Glasgow Rangers fans rioted in the city after their UEFA Cup final defeat to Russian club side Zenit St Petersburg.

GMP Assistant Chief Constable Dave Thompson explained the decision in this way: 'It is right and fitting that MUFC's fans should have the chance to celebrate the club's success this year in the event of last night's win, but they should do this in safety.

'The last major homecoming event was in 1999, where there were serious safety issues raised regarding the risks of crowd crush. Manchester United is the biggest football club in the world and we believe any event would attract more people than in 1999.

'It was decided that a parade could not take place today, Thursday 22 May, because of the serious risk to public safety and major disruption to the rest of the community on what is a normal working and shopping day. GMP's primary concern is the safety of the people of Greater Manchester and the fans of the club.'

No one could argue with that, but surely the police and United might have got together to work something out? Certainly, the fans believed they could have done so, as exemplified by the comments from Sean Bones. Vice chairman of the Manchester United Supporters' Trust, Bones said: 'The supporters need the opportunity to show their gratitude to the players and the manager for their magnificent effort and achievement. If the cost is an issue, the Glazers have made enough money out of the fans – maybe they should step in and sort it.

'The parade in 1999 was hugely successful. This is very different from when Rangers came – this is a hometown team and hometown fans.'

But it was not to be. On *Talking Reds*, the club's official internet forum, one fan moaned: 'Am gutted and embarrassed that there won't be a victory parade tonight. "Something later in the summer" just doesn't cut it and Manchester City Council, GMP etc. are making themselves a laughing stock by telling the whole country that they aren't prepared for a victory parade.

'Can you imagine Chelsea doing this? Even Portsmouth. Portsmouth, for God's sake, managed to organise an event the day after they won the FA Cup. Have Manchester authorities just woken up from a winter hibernation or something? Why hadn't it been organised as a contingency? An absolute disgrace.'

At least one wisecracker lifted the mood by commenting: 'If Manchester City Council won't allow the parade, why don't we approach the London City Council for permission to hold it at

Stamford Bridge? It will be the only chance that the Chelsea supporters will get to see the Cup at close quarters. We could also load Chelsea's display cabinet on to the bus to save us buying a new one for our trophy overflow. They have no use for it anyway!'

Instead, just a few hundred fans congregated at Ringway airport to greet the team as they arrived back in Manchester at around 9pm on the day after the match. Vidić and Co. posed for photographs with Sir Alex and the European Cup on the gangway leading down from the aeroplane, but were then ferried away on the team coach.

It was an anti-climatic end to the greatest week in Nemanja Vidić's life and even the promise from the club and the police that there would eventually be a parade failed to lift spirits. For the fans, it should have been there and then – on 22 May 2008, the day after the final, and on the streets of Manchester.

Who knew when they might get the chance to acclaim their team as Champions League winners once again? It could be another decade before United even reached the competition's final. As fate would transpire, it would be just another 12 months. Remarkably for Nemanja Vidić, Moscow 2008 would not be the endgame in his glittering journey at Old Trafford. No, this was merely a staging post on the road to glory.

The following season would see Vidić and United lift the Premier League trophy once again, falling only at the final hurdle in the Champions League. But before we take a look at how the season of 2008–09 unfolded for the Stretford End's newest idol, let's examine just how highly Vidić rates in the cult hero charts at Old Trafford; just how much of a legend he had become on the terraces for his bravery and commitment to the United cause. How the struggling newcomer, eyed with certain distrust by some supporters, transformed himself to become one of United's most popular players ever by 2010.

Chapter 7

TERRACE IDOL

O F COURSE, there have been many heroes of the Stretford End over the decades. Georgie Best in the sixties, Jim Holton in the seventies, Bryan Robson in the eighties, Eric Cantona in the nineties and the likes of Gary Neville and Wayne Rooney in the noughties. United have always been a club rich in terrace heroes, often bad boys or mavericks, who the fans love to death.

But where does Nemanja Vidić fit into the list of legends? Well, with much thought and scratching of the head, I've come up with what I see as a fair assessment of the Serb's position in the vaunted line-up.

The legends in this list are not necessarily the best players to appear in United red (although some undoubtedly are), but the ones who developed the closest bonds with the club's incredible supporters, who were deified and came to stand for something more than mere footballers – much like Vidić from 2006 onwards, in fact.

So, here's my Top 10 terrace idols at United:

1. Eric Cantona – the King and fans' all-time favourite.
2. George Best – the 'fifth Beatle', and arguably United's greatest-ever player. The fans adored him and his popularity was highlighted by the state funeral that he received in Northern Ireland when he died.
3. Roy Keane – there's only one Keano... The all-action growling skipper who would have died for United.
4. Denis Law – the King before Cantona arrived and No. 1 with the fans.
5. Bryan Robson –the original Captain Marvel, he shed blood for United in the hedonistic days of Big Ron Atkinson.
6. Norman Whiteside – one of the so-called 'Three Musketeers' along with Robbo and Paul McGrath. Renowned for his boozing and wild life as much as his exploits on the pitch, but let's not forget he was the youngest-ever player in a World Cup final (at the age of 17). And he won the FA Cup for United with his cracker of a goal against Everton at Wembley in 1985.
7. Mark Hughes – the proverbial bull in a china shop. Won United the European Cup-Winners' Cup in 1991.
8. Wayne Rooney – Braved the Scouse hate mob and death threats to join United. Fans love him for that and for his 100 per cent battling and world-class skill.

9.   Les Sealey – a surprise in the Top 10, maybe but a hero for sure. He took the place of jittery Jim Leighton to help Ferguson keep his job by winning the FA Cup in 1990, then the European Cup Winners' Cup a year later. Died young, too young.

10. Nemanja Vidić – the Man of the Moment.

Yes, Nemanja makes the top 10 after just three years at Old Trafford – and could yet go higher depending on his exploits at the club in seasons to come. Already, he is vying with Wayne Rooney for the title of current No. 1 cult hero at the club and he may well surpass the boy-man known as 'Wazza'.

There is a remarkable video of Vidić on YouTube. It depicts the Serbian as 'The Terminator' amid excerpts from his best moments in a Manchester United shirt. Well worth watching, it was made by a United fan and shows how affectionately Nemanja is viewed by the people who matter most at Old Trafford, the vast army of supporters who help pay the players' wages.

As we have noted, they love him for his aggression and commitment to the United cause, the way he seems willing to die for United. He throws himself into tackles others might have shied away from, and often head first. In that sense, he combines the bravery of Bryan Robson with the never-say-die attitude of Roy Keane. Mixed in with his instinctive Serbian battling nature, which leads him to rush straight over to the United fans and salute them whenever he scores, he was always going to be an idol of the Stretford End.

One United fan, Matt, says: 'He's just great, a real leader – and we needed one after Roy Keane left.' According to him, several tongue-in-cheek Vidić 'hardman' sayings have been doing the rounds at Old Trafford over the past couple of seasons. These include:

- Guns don't kill people. Nemanja Vidić kills people.
- Nemanja Vidić does not sleep. He waits.
- The chief export of Nemanja Vidić is pain.
- In an average living room there are 1,242 objects Nemanja Vidić could use to kill you – including the room itself.

However, Emma, another Red through and through, wants it known that there is a different side to Vidić, more sensitive than the one portrayed on the pitch and which the fans loved to sloganise on their T-shirts and in terrace chants. She said: 'Yeah, those jokes just come from the way he is on the pitch – tough tackling, impossible to get past, solid as a brick wall. He's actually a lovely, sweet guy in real life, but he puts his body on the line on the pitch and gets more than his fair share of red cards, which gives people the impression that he's not to be messed with. Which is completely true on the pitch, but not off it.'

Even his boss Sir Alex can understand why the fans love Vidić so much. When the Reds beat Wigan 1-0 at home on 14 January 2009, Ferguson admitted Nemanja's performance that night was 'the best display at centre-half I have seen in years.' Why was this? Well, just as the fans acclaimed Vidić for his courage and defensive mentality, so the boss also appreciated the raw genius of his big centre-back. Ferguson said, 'He has the courage of Bruce. He would always stick his head in and ask the question of the forward. But we are the kind of club where they concentrate on the star players, not defenders. I used to say that Denis Irwin would give you eight or nine out of 10 every week and would never get mentioned, but we all knew the value of him. It is the same with Vidić.'

That he was a defender and not an attacker also helped to explain, in Sir Alex's view, why Vidić had not won any of the Player of the Year awards. The United boss felt aggrieved by that for in his eyes, Nemanja was his star man of the 2008–09 season, certainly his Player of the Year. Ferguson explains, 'The awards go to the entertainers. I have been to the sportswriters' dinners and looked up at the photographs of the winners and seen these great players, who put bums on seats. We have had great defenders, who have never got there.'

And former England boss Terry Venables too believes that Nemanja deserved to be Player of the Year – and he can also understand why he is a hero with United's fans because of his all-round talent as a defender. Venables told the *Sun* in March 2009, 'There has been an increasing clamour in recent weeks to make Ryan Giggs the Footballer of the Year, but I am going to give this award to his Manchester United team-mate, Vidić.

'The solid-as-a-rock Serb has had a super season in which he has continued his progression into the complete centre-back. He can pass, he can tackle, he is quick and he possesses an aerial threat that makes him a danger in both penalty areas.

'His sheer presence intimidates centre forwards and yet he maintains his aggression without recklessness. Just what you want from a defender in an age where referees' cards are dished out all too frequently.'

Venables also made this succinct point: 'He must go down as one of Alex Ferguson's best-ever acquisitions and is proof the Scot can be every bit as wily in the transfer market as Arsène Wenger.'

That is also true – Vidić rates as one of Ferguson's all-time best buys, a snip at £7.2 million in the days of over-inflated transfer fees. Nemanja also rates as being one of United's best-ever foreign stars. Only the great Cantona and keeper Peter Schmeichel immediately spring to mind as better buys. Cantona, of course, at just £1 million was probably the best buy ever at United, full stop. Surely his influence on the team and the club will never be matched. One man brought about a belief that United could finally regain the top-flight crown that had eluded them for an unbelievable 26 years.

His well-founded arrogance, optimism and wonderful self-belief opened the floodgates for every title that followed. Similarly, the great Dane Peter Schmeichel provided a foundation at the back that helped United to build on Cantona's legacy, and just as Cantona helped them regain the League title after so many years in the wilderness, so Schmeichel's brilliance as a stopper took United to Champions League glory in 1999 – 31 years since they had last claimed Europe's biggest club prize.

Set against those feats, Vidić will always struggle to be viewed as a better foreign buy, but already he has one Champions League medal more than Cantona, one more Champions League appearance than Schmeichel.

In December 2007, the *Observer* provided Nemanja with another welcome accolade – declaring him the No. 2 all-time best buy in the January transfer window. I would argue he was No. 1, especially when you consider their No. 1 was a package of three players. The *Observer* claimed the transfer of Pedro Mendes, Sean Davis and Noe Pamarot (to Portsmouth from Tottenham, for £7 million for all three in 2006) was the greatest because 'Mendes' goal against Manchester City six weeks after the window closed sent Pompey off on a run that took them out of the bottom three.' Hardly as awe-inspiring as leading Manchester United to several Premier League titles and two Champions League finals, is it?

A year later and Vidić would fall to No. 3 in Fleet Street's analysis of the best-ever January transfers. The *Telegraph* decided that not only was Pedro Mendes the No. 1 man (without Davis and Pamarot) because he was 'the catalyst in a successful battle against relegation', but a Birmingham player from 2003 deserved to usurp Vidić in the No. 2 slot.

Yes, step forward Christophe Dugarry, who signed for Brum for Bordeaux on a free in that year. According to the *Telegraph*, he 'galvanised struggling Birmingham and scored five goals in four games to ensure their safety.' Again, is that as big a contribution as Nemanja made in turning Manchester United into the European and World champions?

Certainly, United fans would disagree with those ratings. Diehard Red John Lane says: 'That's a load of rubbish! Vidić did much more than they did. He helped make United invincible at the back by plugging the holes and enabling Rio to become a better player. Let's not forget that: Vidić is a great player himself, but his talent freed up Ferdinand to improve.'

Vidić is grateful to the United fans for helping him settle down in Manchester after a stuttering start to his career at Old Trafford. He once remarked: 'I think the fans appreciate the way I play. I think they recognise I give 100 per cent all the time. I want to win and do my best, no matter what. I really thank them for their support.'

He also said that he never forgets that the supporters are the people who matter most – that is why he makes a point of saluting them first, before his team-mates even, when he scores and he is often seen applauding them for their support. He is glad to sign autographs and give the fans as much time as he can. It is a link forged from the days in 2006 when United supporters finally saw the true Vidić emerge – the battling superman they love to watch and urge on. Yes, Nemanja Vidić will always be remembered with great affection by the Stretford End. They came to realise that not only was he like them, in that he was a working-class boy made good, but that he was one of them – a United supporter, who played as if he would suffer for the red shirt.

For another view on the debate, I asked United fanatic and national newspaper journalist Andy Bucklow for his assessment of Vidić in the all-time book of United's legion of foreign legends – and about who else he rated right up there at the very top of the pile. Bucklow, who is a journalist on the *Mail on Sunday* and has followed the club religiously since the early 1970s, came up with some excellent, alternative observations about the men from abroad who most made their mark at the Theatre of Dreams.

He told me: 'When you're talking about the status of foreign legends at Old Trafford over the past two decades or so, it would be very easy to make two lists... one for Eric Cantona and one for everyone else. That may be a bit harsh on the other fans' favourites, such as Vidić, Solskjaer, Stam, and of course, last season's heroes, Ronaldo and Tevez. But you have to acknowledge that Eric's aura, self-belief and French swagger, combined with not a little talent, helped create not just an occasionally successful team, but also the ultimate winning mentality at Old Trafford way back in 1992 – when, although the first trophies under Ferguson were starting to trickle in – FA Cup, Cup Winners' Cup and League Cup, the squad which included mentally tough guys such as Schmeichel, Hughes, Bruce, Pallister, Robson and Ince were still battling the collective meltdown when it came to winning the League title for the first time in 26 years.

'You could say United would have won it pre-Cantona in 1992 when Eric was working his magic at Leeds, had it not been for the fixture pile-up of four games in less than a week. To this day Ferguson continues to espouse that view and undoubtedly that was the biggest factor in the end-of-season collapse. But it should not be forgotten that the fall-out from such a major disappointment had carried over big time to the start of the following season when, after a shocking start rising to mediocre, it seemed the welcome long-awaited progress under Fergie might come to a shuddering halt.

'Then Eric arrived and it's been well documented what happened next. He changed the mindset of the whole place just at a time when Giggs, Scholes, Butt and the Nevilles were coming through the ranks. He'd just won the title for Leeds. Now he was to help the experienced players in the squad conquer their demons on the way to what proved to be a glorious title run-in of seven straight wins in 1992–93.

'For that alone he is unsurpassed. He's still doing it, if now on the big screen... "I am not a man, I am Cantona", he says, enigmatic as ever in the movie *Looking For Eric*. But if Eric was the cornerstone of the new mindset at Old Trafford, he would not be around for ever. And when he walked away in 1997, it would take special players to carry it on, Roy Keane being the obvious name which springs to mind but I wouldn't class him as one of the foreign greats, as Ireland is a United home from home.

'Schmeichel was immense and his bolshy attitude to his

defence whenever an opposing striker got within five square miles of his penalty area won over the fans as much as his individual brilliance. He is, by some distance, the best keeper in United's rich history. Van der Sar has many of Schmeichel's big-game qualities and though he arrived at Old Trafford five years too late, he's extended his career at a level one doubts he'd manage to maintain if still at a club like Fulham. And, of course, his penalty heroics in Moscow will forever keep him in the fans' hearts as a true foreign legend.

'Similarly, Jaap Stam has to be right up there, despite the unfortunate circumstances of his premature departure from United in 2001. He'd been at the club for only three seasons when revelations about being tapped up by Fergie popped up in in his autobigraphy. This, and a bad day at the office on the opening day of 2001, when he allowed Louis Saha to stroll past him and through to score twice for Fulham, prompted a rare Fergie cock-up, when he shipped Stam out to Lazio to be replaced by the slow – and getting ever slower – Laurent Blanc.

'For three seasons Stam had been immense, was twice voted the Best Defender in the 1999 and 2000 Champions League and, whether alongside Johnsen or Berg, was a one-man wrecking ball who shattered the threat of Europe's elite strikers. It says it all that, even now, United fans still sing the Jaap Stam song, seven seasons after his departure. Equally as sweet for him is the sound of Fergie's recent admission that he sold Stam too soon... even if he did recoup £16 million for a 29-year-old central defender.

'But in the past couple of superb seasons, four foreigners in particular have encapsulated what it takes to inherit – or fall short of – the mantle of Eric. Four players, all of them highly talented world-class individuals. Four players, all from abroad, who ought to have no problem establishing themselves as prominent figures in the rich Manchester United history.

'Ronaldo, Berbatov, Vidić, Tevez... Yet in my opinion, for various reasons, two will always be cherished at Old Trafford and two fall short.

'Ronaldo's place in the record books and the legacy he left in terms of his unique ability and sheer weight of spectacular goals is already assured. He should be a shoo-in as an Old Trafford legend, as the first to rival – and in some eyes to even surpass – George Best. Yet you can have all the ability in the world, but show even an inkling of being less than 100 per cent dedicated to the Red cause and your legendary status is diluted.

'By continually flirting with and then signing for Real Madrid, Ronaldo was unfaithful to United. When you have the stellar season he did in 2007–08 it takes a bit of an effort to turn the fans against you. But Ronaldo managed it, almost before the champagne had stopped flowing in Moscow, with his lovesick teenager act.

'He partially recovered the affections of the faithful by staying, somewhat reluctantly, for another year but further similar, not very subtle entreaties to the Bernabeu eventually made the split permanent. Most United fans I talk to thought that £80 million was good business, and although he will be missed, none had the stomach for yet another "Will He, Won't He?" summer – even though it meant finally letting go of perhaps the most wonderfully natural footballer ever to grace Old Trafford, certainly in the modern era.

'Similarly, Berbatov has all the attributes to carve out his own niche at United, and finally in an under-achieving career, with the players he has around him guaranteeing a healthy haul of medals, no excuse not to do it. He makes the game look effortless, but that, sadly, is also the nub of his problem with the Red faithful. United fans will forgive most things if they think you're putting a shift in. Crikey, years ago the Stretford End was even cheering for Gary Birtles after 27 games without a League goal!

'But despite his sublime skill, and several crucial late winners in another title-winning season, the Bulgarian still sharply divides opinion and the manner of his penalty shootout miss at Wembley against Everton signalled the premature end of an ultimately disappointing campaign for him personally. The 2009–10 season will be crucial for him, both to win round the home support and, more importantly, find a more permanent role in the fabric of the team.

'Unlike Ronaldo, I actually thought Tevez was already assured of his place at the fans' top table, although the move to City and the laughable sky-blue "Welcome To Manchester" billboard might yet put paid to that. Plus, if you believe Fergie, it now appears he had the move stitched up for months.

'It was too simplistic to say that his popularity was because he "ran around a lot", but it has to be said that this didn't hinder his cause. He was a fans' legend after such a short spell at the club because the vocal support sees him as one of their own: a street-fighter. An Argentine Wayne Rooney, if you will... A craggy face, which shows every emotion, a never-say-die demeanour, which showed that defeat hurt him just as much as it hurt the 70,000 sitting in the stand. When you have that, as well as an abundance of skill, it's clear why Tevez's late winners in his first season will be talked about long after Berbatov's equally important strikes in his first.

'I happen to think this is a tad unfair on Berbatov, as he would become totally ineffective and look slightly silly, if he even considered adopting the Tevez style – which he won't – although there is little doubt he is not flattered by the comparison. So it says something for one Nemanja Vidić that in a season peppered by chants of "Argentina" and "Fergie, Fergie, sign him up" that it was he, and not Tevez, or any of the other glamour boys who won the players' and fans' Player of the Year award.

'It also says much for the man himself that he was surprised he got the plaudits ahead of Rooney, Ronaldo et al., though no one else at Old Trafford would be – least of all, Sir Bobby Charlton, who, during a generous end-of-season tribute to the Serb, went as far as to say that United are a club looked on "with envy" because they have Vidić.

'Since his arrival for what has proved to be a steal at £7.2 million in January 2006, after an uncertain start, Vidić has been part of arguably the best defence in the history of the club. For one thing, he's helped make even a world-class defender like Rio an even better player. Rio has always been a class act, but his occasional lapses of concentration were the only stain on his game... then Vidić became his regular partner and it's hard to remember a significant gaffe in the past three years.

'Sometimes you have to step away from the bosom of your own fanbase to get a perspective of a player's worth, and I have lost count of the number of rival fans with no particular fondness for United, who said to me at the end of last season: "After Ronaldo, if we could buy one of your players it would be Vidić. He's a proper defender, who doesn't take any nonsense." In other words, a proper defender who does exactly what it says on the tin: physical and brave in both boxes.

'I remember that in the Sixties, despite a team including Best, Law and Charlton, Matt Busby cited Pat Crerand as the key. "When Pat plays well, United play well," said Busby. I believe the same applies to Vidić in today's team. His very presence gives confidence to van der Sar and the rest of the defence and spreads through to the midfield. On the flipside, the reverse can also be true and the two off-key games he had last season proves this very point. By his own admission he struggled against Torres in the freak show at home to Liverpool and this uncertainty quickly spread to the rest of the team.

'Similarly, the 2009 Champions League Final turned after just

10 minutes when Vidić was uncharacteristically turned rather too easily by Samuel Eto'o for the opening goal. I believe it was the shock of how the goal was conceded, as much as the strike itself, which prompted the nervousness and uncertainty which affected seasoned battle-hardened players to succumb to the pressure of the occasion.

'But the big players learn and recover from their mistakes, and I've no doubt Vidić has the character and class to remain a central figure at Old Trafford for another decade – if he wants it. His authority in the air and threat at set pieces have been a cornerstone of United's three title successes since he arrived, and Champions League triumph in 2008. In today's money-obsessed world of Premiership football, no foreign import is likely to come even close to staying at one club like home-grown lads like Giggsy, Scholes and Gary Neville. But as fans, we really want to believe Vidić's agent Silvano Martina when he said his client would remain at United, despite reported interest from Barcelona, AC Milan and Inter: "There are no grounds for Vidić to leave. He is at a great club with high ambitions."

'If that really is the case, bearing in mind all agents' pronouncements need to be taken with a very large sack of salt, then there is no reason why the past three years could not be just the start of a stellar career at Old Trafford – which could end up with Nemanja being right up there with the likes of Eric when, say in 20 years' time, United fans come to re-evaluate their all-time greats.'

Thanks Andy, great stuff. Now let's move on to the start of the

2008–09 season – a season which would bring more glory and awards for the Serb, whom Manchester United fans had come to love as one of their own.

Chapter 8

LOVE AND EIGHT

THE START OF THE 2008–09 season saw Nemanja shrouded in an unlikely controversy over comments he made about Manchester. Rather than focusing on United's stuttering impact to the new campaign, Vidić was forced to answer questions on his allegiance to the club and to the English way of life. Much to his surprise, and eventual annoyance, it appeared his detractors were determined to make a mountain out of a molehill.

It had all begun when Nemanja spoke to a Russian football magazine as a favour. He knew the editor from his time at Spartak and agreed to a chat after the Champions League final win over Chelsea. Assuming he was with old friends, he spoke about his difficulties in settling in to a new country, at a new football club and with a new way of life. He was shocked and dismayed when the magazine's version of events appeared in print and denied having made the comments attributed to him.

In the magazine he was alleged to have said English people did not 'feel the joy of life' and that 'I will never stay to live in England, that's for sure. You get only a brief glimpse of sunlight before it's all cloudy again. The winters are mild, but in summer the temperatures seldom go higher than 20C. And it rains, rains, rains.

'In future, I would like to test myself in another top league. I'm thinking of Spain. At least there will be no reason to complain about the weather. In England, they say that Manchester is the city of rain. Its main attraction is considered to be the timetable at the railway station, where trains leave for other, less rainy cities.

'It's not only the weather that I'm not happy about here. In Russia and Serbia the people's way of life is similar. In England it's totally different. Here they just don't have time to feel the joy of life.

'Throughout the week they all work so hard. They only talk to people at lunch break. Then in the evening they come home and watch the telly, so they can get up early for work the next day. The only time to meet friends is at weekends, but for football players it's the busiest time of all. It was much easier for me to adapt to Russia than England. In England I had no one to talk to. The first month was especially hard. I lived alone in a hotel, which I left only for training. I thought I would go crazy inside those four walls.'

Naturally, the remarks did not go down well in Manchester. A spokesman for Marketing Manchester said at the time:

'Manchester continues to be a hugely popular place to live, work and visit. We welcome millions of tourists a year, visiting such attractions as the Lowry, the Museum of Science & Industry and the Imperial War Museum North.

'We are home to more than 100,000 students every year, Manchester is known for its diversity and the strength of its communities. It's vibrant and varied, with a compact city centre that offers a full range of bars and restaurants, theatres and live music venues. Whether you want to see internationally renowned plays, independent cinema, cutting-edge theatre, a West End blockbuster or an up-and-coming band, Manchester has it all.'

And a Serbian writer and Man United fan told the *Sun*'s Martin Phillips that he totally disagreed with Vidić's comments. Zoran Djordjević, 45, said: 'I think all those beautiful women and fast cars have gone to his head because he's obviously forgotten what it's like living in Belgrade. We have war criminals running around and neo-Nazi riots in the streets. I don't understand what has got to him.

'I think he should be happy with the weather there. I'd take Manchester's rain in a flash over the heatwave we are having here. The thought of cool rain is enough to make you want to get on the first flight to Manchester as it's over 40 degrees C here most days.'

As the furore over his alleged remarks grew, Nemanja felt obliged to comment publicly on them, saying he had been misquoted. In a statement, he said: 'I'd like to clarify I did not make these particular remarks. I spoke about the difficulty I had settling in to life in Manchester, but that does not reflect how I feel now. I have far too much respect for the people of Manchester, and England, to criticise them in this way.'

While some Mancunians felt insulted by the alleged comments, most – and most United fans, too – accepted Vidić's assertion that he had been misquoted. And, as the comments began to look less and less like a big deal, the national newspapers also started to look at the subject with more humour and less rancour. *The Times*, for instance, pointed out that even if they had been true, Vidić's words were nowhere near as bad as those of some other overseas footballers, who had readily bitten the English hand that fed them.

They pointed to a few lads from abroad as proof. Chief among them was Georgi Hristov, the former Barnsley forward. Certainly, he was in a different league when it came to the bristling criticism of his lot in South Yorkshire, back in 1998. The homesick Macedonian said at the time: 'The local girls are far uglier than the ones back in Belgrade or Skopje, the capital of Macedonia, where I come from. Our women are much prettier. Besides, they don't drink as much beer as the Barnsley girls, which is something I don't like at all. England is a strange country and I found it hard to adapt to living here. To be honest, I expected more of Barnsley as a town and a club.'

His comments led to the memorable headline in one red-top, 'PISTOV HRISTOV', and a series of angry reactions from locals. Indeed, one Barnsley girl, Michelle Dodson, 21, told the BBC: 'My reaction to his remarks is unprintable. He wants to look in the mirror before talking about us. He's no oil painting. Barnsley women are the best looking in the country.'

When *The Times* tried to put the boot in with what they considered an amusing look at how Manchester compared with Vidić's hometown, Užice, the fans hit back en masse, accusing the newspaper of xenophobia and stirring up a hornet's nest that didn't really exist.

One reader typified the fans' annoyance when he wrote in defending Vidić and condemning their coverage: 'What a silly article, one word of criticism quoted out of context and an article sniping at Vidić, how childish. I think Vidić was on the money, Brits work all day, drink or watch telly each night and go to work the next day.

'Not his fault he is from a ex communist country but through his talent and hard work he can now make choices that many cannot and he honestly said he was driven nuts sitting in a hotel room, as many would. Silly article deserves no further comment.'

It was clear that Vidić was building up a loyal following as his exploits at United continued to grow – he was becoming a major cult hero among the diehard who had season tickets in the Stretford End.

Meanwhile, on other websites, fans rushed to his defence – even though he had denied making the comments – and some claimed he had a point, anyway! They were very understanding of the man and the fact he was an eastern European trying to establish a new life in Western Europe.

One said: 'I think he enjoys and appreciates playing for Man

U, it's just that he'd rather the club was located elsewhere, preferably a warmer country. Bars and nightclubs don't appeal to all footballers, he probably wants to be part of the Continental way of life – where all family members go out together to places other than pubs or the cinema, and where cultural establishment are open in the evening, and people spend more time outdoors (not just the youths hanging about on the streets in the ASBO capital of the country and the smokers outside); and be able to visit a nearby beach frequently. Who'd not want this?'

Of course, some critics would not accept Vidić's apology and his claim that he had been misquoted. They were led by professional Mancunian Lesley Thomas, who slammed Nemanja in the *Daily Telegraph*, saying: 'How dare you, Mr Vidić. How very flipping dare you. Yes, it rains in Manchester. Did you not check the long-term weather forecast before leaving your last club in sunny Moscow? The joy of life passing us by? We're singing in the rain. Manchester is one of the planet's great party capitals... By yesterday afternoon, the no-nonsense defender was crying foul, stating that his comments had been misunderstood... He needn't have bothered. Mancunians are a stoic lot (something to do with all that rain) so there's no need, Mr Vidić, to pull on a flak jacket. I'd strongly suggest, however, that you take some of your 50k a week to Manchester's excellent shopping district and get yourself a decent raincoat.'

Indeed, the controversy raged on for days before finally blowing itself out, much to Nemanja's eventual relief. When asked about it later, he would smile and shake his head, baffled by the English and their love of a good controversy fuelled by a mischievous press. And the truth of the matter was that he had much more important things to worry about, come September 2008... like United's disappointing start to the campaign.

It began at Wembley in the FA Community Shield against Portsmouth – the FA Cup winners from the south coast who had triumphed over Cardiff the previous May, up against the Premier League champions. The traditional curtain raiser to the new season, but boy, was it a damp squib.

The teams fought out a 0-0 draw in the summer heat of 10 August 2008. Ultimately United emerged victors with a 3-1 penalty shootout win, but there was little to get excited about as they began the coach journey back to Manchester.

Vidić was booked – unusually for him for kicking the ball away – along with Gary Neville, and Pompey's Sylvain Distin as the Reds retained the shield they had won a year earlier against Chelsea. Carlos Tevez, Ryan Giggs and Michael Carrick scored for United from the spot while Lassana Diarra, Arnold Mvuemba and Glen Johnson missed for Pompey.

ITN Sport claimed: 'Manchester United will be the team to beat after this effective display', but Sir Alex Ferguson was not so easily convinced and later voiced his concern at the number of chances his men had missed, saying: 'We dominated possession and had some good chances, but it is this issue with scoring at the moment.' However, Fergie admitted he was pleased with the way Vidić and Ferdinand had begun the new campaign as they had ended the previous one: in dominant form. They snuffed out the threat from Pompey's top-notch centre forward partnership of new £11 million signing Peter Crouch and the always-dangerous Jermain Defoe.

Nemanja declared himself happy with his performance after the match, but made it clear that the team would, in his opinion, have to step it up a couple of levels if they were to keep pace with the team he feared most, Chelsea. The Londoners had brought in Brazilian World Cup-winning legend Luiz Felipe Scolari as their new boss and Vidić said he believed the man known universally as 'Big Phil' would prove a winner at Stamford Bridge.

He said, 'Chelsea are a great team with big players. This season they have bought one or two players and will want to win trophies under Scolari. They are hungry probably because last year they won nothing, but that desire is how we are.'

United would still be the team to beat when the new season got underway, a week later, and the influence of veterans Gary Neville, Paul Scholes and Ryan Giggs would prove vital, he felt. He continued, 'We've worked hard in the pre-season and I can see the hunger in the players' eyes. We are ready to win the trophies again. Gary, Scholesy and Giggs are players with experience who still want to win trophies. You saw yesterday that they fight for every ball. This is what pushes other players to play the same, this example to follow. We try to do that and keep going. We have a big squad, everyone has stayed and I see the boss speaking of maybe bringing in one more player.

'We will miss Wazza [Wayne Rooney] and [Cristiano] Ronaldo in a few games but, like you saw yesterday, we have players who can take positions. [Darren] Fletcher did brilliantly and so did Nani — I think we are ready for the new season.

'It is very satisfying to win. Last season we did the same. It is an important game and good to start the season with a trophy.'

But his boss's concerns about the impact on the club's strike force of losing Ronaldo for a month would prove well founded in the Premier League opener against Newcastle at Old Trafford on August 17. With Ronaldo injured, he had been forced to employ Ryan Giggs up front with Carlos Tevez at Wembley. Rooney would return against the Toon army, but appeared to still be suffering the after-effects of a virus as he teamed up with Frazier Campbell.

Tevez had to return home to Argentina because of a family bereavement, so he missed the match and United struggled to find their rhythm in his absence. Obafemi Martins put the visitors ahead on 22 minutes with a fine header, only for United to equalise 2 minutes later with a Darren Fletcher strike. Vidić too almost scored with a powerful header, but it rebounded back off the bar. Overall, though, it was an off day for the Reds, made even more disappointing when Michael Carrick and Ryan Giggs were forced out of the action with ankle and hamstring injuries respectively.

Boss Ferguson said: 'We played well in the first half and their goalkeeper made several good saves to keep them in the match. Our attacking play in the first half was good, but as soon as we lost Ryan Giggs to a hamstring injury and Michael Carrick with an ankle, which is swollen up badly – he'll be out for two to three weeks – we lost a bit of our experience in midfield.

'We had possession of the ball, but didn't make it count at times – but in light of the people we had missing, it was a creditable result for us.'

Certainly a glass-half-full way of viewing the outcome: against a Newcastle team who would go on to struggle against relegation, this was actually a poor start to the campaign and privately Fergie would admit as much.

A week later, United won 1-0 at Portsmouth with Vidić and Ferdinand again proving the key men as they kept a tight grip on Crouch and Defoe, who were combining upfront for the first time at Fratton Park. Darren Fletcher followed up his equaliser against Newcastle with the winner at Pompey.

Ferguson was pleased with the win and the way Vidić and Ferdinand had policed the Pompey 'Little and Large' pairing of Crouch and Defoe. He said: 'They are so solid and reliable, very little gets past them.

'We played some excellent football tonight. This is a difficult place to come, so it is a bonus to come here and win. We tried to play a system where the players would be comfortable. We wanted to have Anderson playing centrally, close to Carlos Tevez. We let Paul Scholes control the game and used Darren Fletcher's energy.'

Had United turned the corner? No, the stop-start nature of their early season continued when they blew their chances of winning the European Super Cup the following Friday in

Monaco. United, as European Cup winners, lost 2-1 to UEFA Cup winners, Zenit St Petersburg – the only consolation for Vidić being that he grabbed United's goal at the Stade Louis II. It was their second Super Cup loss in a decade – the previous one coming, of course, in the 1999 Treble year.

On that occasion, in the same Monaco stadium, the Reds crashed 1-0 to Italian outfit, Lazio. Juan Sebastian Veron was the man of the match that balmy summer night in 1999, giving a performance that would persuade Ferguson to sign him for a then club record fee of £28.1 million in 2001.

United had made their debut in the Super Cup in 1991 with a happier outcome. As winners of the European Cup-Winners' Cup (after beating Barcelona), they overcame the challenge of Red Star Belgrade (who had won the European Cup) to lift the trophy, thanks to Brian McClair's goal in a 1-0 victory. The match was due to be a two-legged affair (the permanent site of Monaco only came into being in 1998), but political unrest in Belgrade at the time meant only the Old Trafford leg was played.

A 10-year-old Nemanja Vidić was cheering on Red Star that night in 1991, watching the match on TV with his father Dragoljub, back home in Užice. He was upset when the team that he had supported as a boy lost, but would find consolation five years later, when Red Star signed him up for their youth team.

In the 2008 Super Cup, Vidić would again retain unhappy memories of the event. The Man of the Match in the clash against the Russians of Zenit was the Venezuelan midfielder

Danny, and it was he and second-half sub, Andrey Arshavin, who made life tough for Vidić, Ferdinand and United. Arshavin, who would go on to sign for Arsenal later that year, dribbled past Vidić on a couple of occasions, leaving him for dead. It was a tough night for the Serbian hero – not many players left him gasping for air as they raced past him, but Arshavin would do so in Monaco, just as Fernando Torres would do so in Manchester for Liverpool at Old Trafford, a few months later.

Ferdinand also struggled to contain the dynamite quick feet of Danny and United were glad to get out of the Principality with just a 2-1 defeat.

It says much about Vidić and his never-say-die attitude and commitment to the cause that he kept on battling despite the lesson he was given by Arshavin – and it was only right that Nemanja should be the man who brought some respectability to the scoresheet for the Reds.

Pavel Pogrebnyak had put Zenit ahead 6 minutes before the interval and Danny clinched the victory with the second goal just before the hour mark. But it was Vidić who came steaming in to save some face for United on 73 minutes, getting himself on the end of a pass from Carlos Tevez in the box and smashing the ball home from 6 yards. Afterwards, Vidić conceded: 'It was a great feeling to score in such a big match, but the outcome was not so good.'

United would lose not only the match, but also Paul Scholes to a one-match ban, after he foolishly tried to punch the ball into the goal from a Wes Brown cross just a minute from the end. The ref showed him a second yellow card and his sending-off meant that he would miss United's first Champions League game in September, at home to Villarreal. Boss Ferguson claimed he was more disappointed about the loss of Scholes in a big game than losing the match, although he had said beforehand that he wanted to win the trophy (it was one of the few to elude him in a glittering career). The defeat also ruined his dream of a 'Magnificent Seven' haul of trophies in the season. Now, he would not be able to win all the silverware available to United. Fergie did say that he had enjoyed Vidić's goal, but accepted his men had not been at their best.

He said: 'I think we played our best football at 2-0, unfortunately. It was a warm night and so I think my players did OK under the circumstances. I thought Tevez was outstanding – probably the best player on the park – and I thought we had chances to do something in the game. But Zenit are a very good team and have exceptional movement. They'll be a force in the Champions League, playing like that.'

Vidić's goal had been good for his confidence, but the fact that it had taken a defender to score after the two goals from midfielder Fletcher in the first two League games stressed United's urgent need for a striker who could put the ball in the net.

A few days later, Ferguson would remedy that by signing Dimitar Berbatov from Spurs on a four-year deal for a fee reported to be £31 million. Berbatov, 27, put pen to paper on his £100,000-a-week contract and said: 'Joining United is a dream come true. I look forward to playing my part in helping this club win more honours.'

Fergie admitted the deal had taken United close to having a dream squad. He said: 'This is a key signing. Dimitar is one of the best and most exciting strikers in world football. His style and ability will give the team a different dimension and I'm sure he will be a popular player with the fans.'

Certainly, the purchase was popular with Vidić. The way Nemanja saw it was that the more world-class players United had at their disposal, the more chances they had of becoming the greatest team on the planet.

He welcomed Berba to Old Trafford and did his best to help the Bulgarian settle in, inviting him to dinner with his family and looking out for him as he slowly found his way around the club. On and off the field, the two men became friends and allies, and it would be Vidić who jumped to Berba's defence at the business end of the season when he missed a penalty against Everton in the FA Cup semi shootout at Wembley, pointing out to the *Sun*: 'Look, anyone can miss a penalty and he was more angry about it than anyone. It was hard for him. But when John Terry missed in Moscow last season, no one said he was a bad player because of it. Everyone knows he's a great one and it's the same with Dimitar.

'I wouldn't be surprised if he got the winner against Tottenham on Saturday, because he's a very talented player with great qualities. Don't forget this is his first season here. It's always hard when you change clubs, especially going to one as big as United. Obviously, we know he can do much more, but he has still got 13 goals and done really well so far.'

The words of a loyal friend and team-mate, they summed up Vidić as a man you could count on in good and bad times.

Berba and Vidić would team up for the first time for United on 13 September 2008, in the crunch match against Liverpool at Anfield. Vidić had already revealed that the two encounters he most relished in English football were against Chelsea and Liverpool – the big grudge matches for United since games with neighbours City were viewed as little more than a slight irritant, and the hated Leeds were floundering in League One.

He particularly relished the tussles with Drogba and Steven Gerrard; the former had become his nemesis, the latter was a man he rated exceptionally highly and consequently enjoyed the challenge of trying to get the better of him. Of course, there was extra spice to Vidić v Liverpool as he had turned them down for United and had not been slow in criticising them in his first season at Liverpool, much to the delight of United's staunchly anti-Anfield fans.

This would be the season when Nemanja would add a third name to the list of rivals he most wanted to get the better of: Fernando Torres. As yet, the big Spanish striker had not troubled him much, but he would do so in the return fixture at Old Trafford in 2009. Yet for now, that rivalry would have to wait because the injury-prone Torres was kept on the bench and would sit out the clash at Anfield.

Having said that, Vidić's day would still be a highly charged, fiery one as he tussled with Robbie Keane and Dirk Kuyt. This would be a day that the Serbian would not easily forget as United crashed 2-1 to their biggest rivals and he was sent off for two bookable offences.

Months later, he would also be sent off in the return fixture in Manchester – red-carded twice in one season against Liverpool. It might give him nightmares, but would cement his status as cult hero with the United fans. In their eyes, a man who was sent off twice against Liverpool in one season was undoubtedly worthy of their adulation and total devotion!

The 2-1 loss was the first win in 9 attempts over United for Liverpool boss Rafa Benítez since taking over in 2004. And it hadn't looked as though United would be licking their wounds when Carlos Tevez had shot them ahead after just 3 minutes, when Berbatov had set him up.

But an own goal from Wes Brown and a late winner from Ryan Babel spelled despair for United and their fans. And things went from bad to worse in the last minute as Vidić was given his marching orders for fouling Xabi Alonso after an earlier, similar discretion against Robbie Keane. Nemanja could hardly complain – in fact, he was lucky not to be dismissed for the foul on Keane alone.

Afterwards, he was contrite, admitting it had not been his day or United's, but he promised there would be better times as the season progressed. He was right about that, but he and his team-mates might be forgiven for closing their ears as Kop boss Benítez crowed about the victory as if Liverpool had won the title for the first time in two decades rather than just a single match!

Benítez said, 'We knew we needed to improve against the top teams and after conceding the early goal, it was important for the points – and the confidence too. These games are more or less six-pointers and give confidence for playing the top sides. It makes people realise we can beat anyone.

'If you can't beat United, everyone will be saying you cannot be contenders. Now people will be saying maybe we can. Last season we started really well and this year we have done the same without playing to our level. If we can keep improving, it will be good for our results. We have shown we can beat United, so we have confidence.'

So it was left to Sir Alex to put the result into some sort of perspective. Yes, it was a setback, but it wasn't the end of the world – it did not mean United would not retain their League crown. It was, after all, just the third match of a long season! But he did express his disappointment about the slack defending that led to the goals and warned that the backline would need to improve, and fast, or they would find it tough in the next Premier League showdown at Chelsea in eight days' time.

Ferguson said: 'Liverpool were far the better team. They tackled us, got about us and harassed us, forcing us to make mistakes and we didn't cope with that well. The two goals were absolute shockers – the defending was very, very poor. People will think they are watching a Conference side when they see the highlights.

'It's going to be difficult at Chelsea and if we don't address the physical part of the game, then we'll struggle there too.'

Before that, United would begin the defence of their Champions League crown, with a home match against the Spanish side Villarreal. Vidić's sending-off at Anfield meant that he would miss the match at Chelsea four days after Villarreal, so Ferguson, astutely, decided this would be a good time to give Jonny Evans a run-out. He would replace Nemanja for both matches with the Villarreal group fixture giving him time to bed down for what appeared to be the tougher battle at Stamford Bridge.

A fairly uninspiring United drew 0-0 with the Spaniards and then 1-1 at the Bridge in Nemanja's absence. Damage limitation in that they had not lost, but the team lacked spark and Vidić's drive.

Ten days after his enforced absence, he was back in action for the home League Cup match against Middlesbrough as United sauntered to a 3-1 win.

He and United kept up the good work with a further five straight victories, including a 2-0 win over Bolton in the Premier League and Champions League Group E wins over Aalborg (away) and Celtic (at home), both 3-0.

For the Reds, the season was beginning to open up, with Vidić playing a key role again. His personal dream of winning the Champions League for a second time was taking shape as a 1-1 draw in Glasgow with Celtic on Bonfire Night kept United bang on target for qualification to the knockout stage of the competition.

Four days before that commendable result, Nemanja also proved what an asset he also was in scoring goals for the club as he grabbed United's final one – slotting home with a half-volley – in their 4-2 Premier League win over Hull at Old Trafford.

Everything was looking rosy in the garden, but then came a real body blow for the club and the Serbian as they slumped to an unexpected low at Arsenal on November 8. Before the match, Nemanja publicly boasted of how United were coming into top form and how Arsenal should be very wary of them, yet he was to be silenced and embarrassed afterwards.

Beforehand, he said: 'We started badly in the League this year, but things are slowly falling into place. The United defence is now as hard as a rock.

'We have played together for a few years now and are a tight-knit unit. Sir Alex Ferguson always demands total concentration and a fighting approach, and all the players know their duties.'

He had also warned the struggling Gunners to beware the threat of Dimitar Berbatov and Ronaldo, saying: 'We are getting better with every game and we will reach our peak very soon. The arrival of Dimitar Berbatov has given us even more firepower going forward. He's a great player and he always caused us a lot of problems when he was with Spurs. Fortunately, he's with us now. I think we got something different with him, another option up front. With Berbatov, Carlos Tevez, Cristiano Ronaldo and Wayne Rooney, we have four players who can change the course of the game singlehanded.

'Cristiano was injured at the beginning of the season and has not reached his best yet, but he's getting there and I'm sure he will deliver for the team like he did last season. The club expects a lot from him, but he's a good guy, a great player and I'm very happy he is still part of the side.

'Cristiano didn't really want to leave for Real Madrid in the summer, even though the media went crazy with the story. Fergie has a special relationship with all of his players and Cristiano is no different. He will be a massive player for us this year.'

But the comments and warnings would come back to haunt Vidić as United slumped to an unexpected 2-1 defeat at the Emirates on 8 November 2008 – and he himself suffered a nightmare of a match.

Normally, he and Ferdinand would deal easily with hopeful crosses punted at them from all angles, but against the Gunners they were unusually inept and United paid the price. Nemanja and Rio rarely looked at ease and played too far apart to cope with the crosses Arsenal pumped in at them.

Samir Nasri led the home side's charge, scoring both goals and proving a constant thorn in the side of United's backline – so much so that the man he mauled most, Gary Neville, was eventually substituted.

The 21-year-old Frenchman's first goal came just before the half hour – a shot that deflected off Neville's leg and into the net past Edwin van der Sar. His second goal, just after the second half restart, saw him lash home a fine volley.

United's young Brazilian fullback Rafael grabbed a 90th-minute consolation, but it was not to be the Reds' day, even with 6 minutes of injury time to pull the game back. Vidić and Ferdinand were down after the match – the team had only let in eight goals beforehand – but both vowed to get back on their game, and quickly.

Even boss Fergie was downcast, admitting: 'It is a big blow to us. We needed to win the game. Our results against the other big clubs are a big concern – we have got to get above 85 points to have a chance of the title, so we must keep going for it. Having every game away after a European tie is not easy.'

His assistant Mike Phelan tried to inject some sense of optimism into proceedings, by claiming United could have taken something from the game. He said: 'We are disappointed. We made enough chances to score a couple of goals, but that wasn't to be. It was an open game and very end to end, but we came out the wrong side of it. It was too open and we suffered from that.

'We put a lot of pressure on their goal and created about 20 chances. We were chasing the game at 2-0 down and it is always difficult. We didn't get the luck that we needed. Cristiano Ronaldo created a great opening for himself when we were 2-0 down, but he put it wide of the post. If we had got back to 2-1 then we could have gone on to get something from the game.'

Despite his attempts to boost morale, Vidić and United crept away from the Emirates disconsolately, knowing they had blown a chance to put the boot in on one of their biggest rivals.

The win had lifted the Gunners into third place in the table above United and set the alarm bells ringing at Old Trafford. After all, they had now lost to title rivals Arsenal and Liverpool, and only managed to draw at Chelsea. Would they be able to pull themselves up off the floor and reignite their domestic and European campaign? Or would they slump and throw it all away? The pundits who dared suggest the latter would, of course, be proved wrong. It was not in the tradition of Manchester United FC to fall away just because of one bad result, one setback. This was the club renowned for fighting until the last minute, and for turning things around when all looked lost. As proof, consider the tumultuous comeback in the 1999 European Cup Final, when they came back from the dead to defeat Bayern Munich in Barcelona in injury time.

Understandably, it was Arsenal boss Arsène Wenger who felt the result was good for his team, that it was the turning point they all had been waiting for after disappointing results against Spurs, Stoke and Fenerbache. He said, in rather triumphal, told-you-so terms: 'It was difficult to understand why everyone had become so critical. I didn't speak much, though – the best thing is always to show what you can do on the pitch and show how much we want it. We showed quality. It was a big game for the future of this team and for the club, and a very important result.'

Even his new skipper, Cesc Fabregas, was caught up in the tidal wave of optimism that now engulfed Arsenal. Asked if he thought they could outdo United over the season and win the Premier League title, he smiled breathlessly and gushed: 'Oh, yes! We have shown here we have the qualities to do it. We've had a tough week, but we couldn't have dreamed of a better result. Maybe we don't have the experience of Liverpool, Manchester United or Chelsea, but this was a great answer to show how mature we've become.

'Yes, we are back in it. But we always thought we were in it anyway, even before this game. We know what we can do and we can definitely achieve the title this season.'

In the event, both he and his boss Wenger would be proven wrong; it would be Arsenal who would slump and United who would prosper and flourish. It was just as that brilliant old-timer Edwin van der Sar had predicted after the defeat when he refused to join those who were now clambering off the United bandwagon and on to the Arsenal one. He said: 'If we had won or drawn, we would have kept them below us in the table. Now we've let them back in. But Chelsea, Liverpool and Arsenal all have to come to Old Trafford. We have to make sure we get maximum points from those games.

'Am I concerned? No. I think we have been unlucky in all three of the games against the big teams. The belief is still strong.'

And Vidić backed van der Sar's optimism and defiance, adding in true Arnie Schwarzenneger-style: 'Yes, it is just one defeat. We know we didn't play well – we can play much better, especially me and Rio at the centre of the defence; we'll be back.'

And he wasn't wrong about that. United was about to embark on an amazing unbeaten run in the Premier League and become world champions. The Vidić story was soon to take in yet another awe-inspiring twist.

Chapter 9

SWEET SIXTEEN

A FTER THE DEFEAT at the Emirates Stadium on 8 November 2008, Manchester United would embark on one of the most remarkable runs in football history. They would go 16 matches unbeaten in the Premier League – until 14 March 2009 – as they marched unrelentingly towards retaining their title.

And, with Nemanja Vidić and Rio Ferdinand solid in front of him, keeper Edwin van der Sar would also set a new British record for keeping clean sheets. Van der Sar would pay tribute to Vidić's role in the brilliant feat, saying: 'I have not played behind a better centre-half partnership than Nemanja Vidić and Rio Ferdinand. The understanding between them is great.'

It was a scenario no one had envisaged after the demoralising defeat at Arsenal that dark November day. Most pundits had predicted it would be the Gunners who would now go on a roll and that United may need time to regroup. Yet we should all have known better than to doubt the fortitude and strength of Sir Alex Ferguson and his troops. As the boss would remark later in the season when United needed to win in Porto: 'We at United are good at making firsts.'

That 16-match unbeaten run would take in some fine results, too. Straight after the loss at the Emirates, they would pummel an ever-improving, tough-to-beat Stoke City 5-0 at Old Trafford and then win 1-0 away at Manchester City.

A fortnight after the win at the City of Manchester Stadium, United beat Sunderland 1-0 at Old Trafford; that triumph on 6 December would see Vidić score the killer goal – and declare afterwards that it was 'my most important goal ever.' The injury-time winner was greeted so enthusiastically by Nemanja and his team-mates that anyone would have thought they had won the title again. Certainly, they had gone a huge way towards that aim. The win would fill them with optimism and the belief that they could pull it off again; Vidić's goal was that important at the time. His eighth goal since joining United, it couldn't have come at a more vital moment, arriving as it did in the slipstream of setbacks for Liverpool and Chelsea.

After a shot from Michael Carrick deflected into his path, Nemanja smashed the ball home. And he himself was in no doubt as to the importance of his goal in rallying the troops. He said, 'How important was it? Just look at my reaction. It is not my favourite goal, but it is my most important ever. At this time in the season, you need to win every game. Sunderland did not make it easy because they defended with 11 men all the time.

'We didn't have that many clear chances, but we never gave up and in the end we got our reward. This win could be a big moment in our season.'

Midfielder Carrick also believed that Vidić had set United up for what would be a barnstorming crusade to retain their crown. Carrick observed, 'It was a case of knocking on the door for the whole match and luckily Nemanja was there for us when we most needed him. He and Rio have been brilliant for us at the back over the last year, but they both also present a threat at the other end for us.

'We deserved the win – you can't argue with that. It's a lot better feeling when you score late, but we should have killed it off earlier. It was important for us to win the game; we want to keep the run going that we've started. It's a tough challenge winning the League, we've done it from the front and now we'll have to try and win from behind.'

United also beat Chelsea 3-0 at home and won 5-0 at West Brom in January.

The demolition of Chelsea – with Vidić on target yet again for the Red Devils – signalled the true beginning of the end for Luiz Felipe Scolari's short, troubled reign at Stamford Bridge. Chelsea's defeat in Manchester meant that they had taken just 10 points from their last eight games and this set alarm bells ringing for owner Roman Abramovich, who was now worried they might even miss out on a Champions League spot.

Just a month after Vidić pulled the trigger in the match at Old Trafford, the Russian did the same with poor Scolari – a legendary World Cup winner who, it has been argued, had been given neither the resources nor the support to succeed at Stamford Bridge.

Before the match, Nemanja was asked if he thought United might struggle against the Blues because of the hangover from their shock 1-0 loss to Championship outfit Derby in the League Cup semi-final first leg, four days earlier. He laughed off the question, pointing out that United had played the kids against County, but would be treating the visit of Chelsea much more seriously, saying: 'The Premier League is different. It will be a great game and we will be doing our best to win. Maybe in the back of our minds we recognised we would have a second chance against Derby when the second leg comes around. We didn't perform as we can and Derby took advantage.'

He was right in his analysis: it was a very different United that emerged against the Blues. And it was Vidić who scored United's first goal just before the interval to move them within a point of second-placed Chelsea.

Vidić said: 'It was an important weekend because Liverpool only drew at Stoke and we beat Chelsea, but we don't look at our opponents. We just have to concentrate on ourselves. We have needed to score more.

'The problem is to score at the right time, because if you get one in the first half the other team has to open up a bit more to chase the result. Once we get into that situation, our attacking players mean we are very dangerous. That is what we have finally managed to do. That early goal is crucial because so often this season the opposition have pulled 11 men behind the ball and we have found it hard to break them open.'

Confidence was flowing through the veins of United's determined stars as the end of January loomed. The previous month they had become world champions (more of that shortly) and now they felt sure that they could knock Liverpool off the top of the Premier League. Vidić and his team-mates were right about that, too.

The 5-0 win at the Hawthorns meant United leapfrogged Liverpool and went 3 points clear at the top of the table. The momentum was theirs and, like a dog with a bone, they would not let it slip now.

Only recently, Liverpool boss Benítez had claimed his United counterpart Ferguson was receiving preferential treatment from the authorities and that he had too much power over referees and Premier League officials. He recounted his grievances by reading them from a sheet of paper and ended each one with the word 'Fact'. Now the tables were turned and as United coasted to the top of the League, the fans revelled in making the most of his misery. As the goals went in at the Hawthorns, they chanted, 'Top of the League – and that's a fact!'

The facts after the 5-0 romp were these: United had taken a maximum 21 points from their last seven games, compared to 13 for Liverpool. The last time United had dropped points was in the 0-0 draw at Tottenham on 13 December. And the last time they had conceded a goal in the Premier League was the previous year: in the 2-1 defeat at Arsenal, on 8 November 2008.

The 5-0 win also meant United kept a clean sheet for an 11th successive Premier League match, which was a new record. It also opened the way to another record – Edwin van der Sar had not conceded a goal for 1,032 minutes, beating Chelsea keeper Petr Cech's previous best of 1,025 minutes.

Vidić enjoyed the occasion as much as his team-mates, celebrating the plethora of records with his sixth goal of the season. He grabbed United's third on the hour, heading home powerfully from a Ryan Giggs' corner.

Boss Ferguson expressed his delight at the way his defence had put together that record. He said: 'I am proud of them; they have been fantastic in this run. Edwin van der Sar has had a fantastic career, but he was really pleased to get this record. You look at him and what happened has really thrilled him.

'The scoreline was important. We showed a ruthless streak about us, possibly for the first time this season. It has been a long time coming and we needed it because I think goal difference could play a part. It is a satisfying result in that respect.'

Van der Sar broke the record after he kept West Brom at bay for 84 minutes. After collecting the match ball, he remarked: 'The most important thing is the win, but of course it is great for the team to get the record. I just needed to keep the concentration levels high and fire up the defenders and midfielders.

'We are delighted with the record because we haven't even had a settled defence, with players injured and others coming in and out.'

Apart from himself and Nemanja Vidić, that is. They had

been the only ever-presents in defence during the 11-game run. Nemanja declared himself also to be delighted and 'honoured and humbled' to be part of the record-breaking defensive shield.

Four days later, United chalked up a 12th League shutout in the 1-0 win over Everton at Old Trafford after they thrashed Albion. Everton boss David Moyes paid tribute to the effectiveness of the Reds' defence, but insisted that it was down to the world-class pairing of Vidić and Ferdinand, as much as van der Sar. He said he knew of no better combination at the back and added: 'I think that after Ferdinand and Vidić, our [Joleon] Lescott and [Phil] Jagielka, as a partnership, are the next best.'

Jagielka endorsed his manager's comments about the quality of United's defence, adding that he thought they would now be unstoppable. He said: 'United have been there and done it. There is a phrase about winning ugly. I'm not saying they were ugly tonight, but they have done what they needed to do. The other teams aren't quite used to doing that and it could be crucial. If you are keeping clean sheets and have attacking options, you're always going to have a chance. They are always going to score goals. If I was a gambling man, I would put my money on United.'

Vidić was delighted by the support of the Everton manager – and even prouder when van der Sar went on to claim the British record for clean sheets. The United keeper managed that one when the Red Devils won 1-0 at West Ham, eight days after the Everton match.

The shutout at the Boleyn Ground on 8 February meant the Dutchman surpassed the achievement of Bobby Clark, a former Scotland international, who went 1,155 minutes without conceding between the Aberdeen posts in the 1970–71 Scottish First Division season. Ironically, Clark also played a part in the Dons side managed by Sir Alex Ferguson that would win the Scottish First Division in 1980. Van der Sar had beaten his record after walking away from East London with his goal still not breached for 1,212 minutes.

Clark told *The Times* that van der Sar deserved great praise, but that centre-backs Vidić and Ferdinand should also share the accolade. Without them, the record would not have been possible, just as he could not have achieved such a wonderful run without his two stoppers at Aberdeen. He said: 'I love watching him [van der Sar]. He does so many things very well, but he's got two very good centre-backs in front of him as well. It was the same back in 1971 – Martin Buchan was in the middle of the defence alongside a big lad, Tommy McMillan.'

Former United star Arthur Albiston also paid tribute to the marvellous achievement of the Dutchman and his defence. Albiston told Sky News online: 'I don't think I'll see this kind of run again in top flight football – in my lifetime, anyway.'

Thirteen days later, United would finally concede in a Premier League match. Unlucky for some – a 2-1 win over Blackburn at Old Trafford – but not van der Sar. He missed the game, with Tomasz Kuczcsak deputising. The goal came after 32 minutes and it is worth noting that our man Nemanja was not on the pitch at the time; he would come on as a sub just after the hour. Yes, without van der Sar and Vidić the defence was at last breached.

Two weeks later it was breached again in the League, but this time both men would play from the start and for van der Sar it would mean the end of a remarkable record. In the match at St James' Park on 4 March, Vidić and his fellow defenders could not be blamed for the goal that cost the keeper his remarkable run of 1,311 minutes. No, big Edwin himself was at fault for the Newcastle goal – fumbling a shot from Jonás Gutiérrez and setting up Peter Lovenkrands to knock in his first goal for Newcastle.

The consolation for him was that United still went on to win 2-1, with Rooney and Berbatov finding the net, and that the victory established a seven-point lead at the top of the table. And you could argue that the keeper was hindered by a lottery of a playing surface – slippy, wet and treacherous as the snow swirled on the Tyneside turf. Little wonder Vidić earned the unwanted accolade of becoming the first man booked for lunging into Martins as the conditions worsened.

The result also meant that United had notched up 11 straight wins – not a bad way to lose a record, and some record it had been, stretching all the way back to the previous November in a brilliant sequence of results in the Premier League. A brilliant set of performances from the keeper, but just as importantly, a brilliant set of performances from Nemanja and Co. Without them, van der Sar would not have been lauded in the first place:

Vidić and his men provided the cement that produced such a solid foundation for the Dutchman to build his feats upon.

Some overexcited pundits claimed that Edwin had beaten the world record for clean sheets when United triumphed 3-0 over Fulham, a few weeks earlier – when he bettered Atletico Madrid goalkeeper Abel Resino's 1,275 minutes. But they had not got their facts right in their rush to grab the back-page lead. It transpired that he had not even beaten the European record, let alone the world one.

In fact, the European record had been set by Danny Verlinden of Club Brugge: 1,390 minutes in the Belgium League of 1990. And the world record was way beyond that, standing at 1,816 minutes and set by Brazilian goalkeeper Mazaropi with Vasco Da Gama in 1978.

After losing the chance of beating those records van der Sar, typically of a perfectionist and a dream professional, held his hands up in the dressing room, admitted his error and asked for his team-mates' forgiveness. Vidić was one of the first to commiserate and tell him he had nothing to apologise for – a gesture which the Dutchman appreciated. The two men hugged – both appreciated the other's worth to the cause: a cause which had seen van der Sar shut out all Premier League foes since Arsenal's Samir Nasri beat him twice in the Gunners' 2-1 victory at the Emirates, the previous November.

Alex Ferguson also brushed aside any criticism of van der Sar's gift to Lovenkrands and was stoical in his assessment. He made the point that records were all very well, but it was the bigger picture alone that concerned him and his team were on their way to another Premier League crown because of his defence's heroics. Fergie remarked: 'It wasn't a great performance. We got off to a terrible start and Newcastle were pumped up for it. We expected that and we should have dealt with it better, but coming from 1-0 down was a good result for us; it required a lot of grit.

'Edwin says himself he made a mess of it [the goal] and they had a couple of near things after that. It was going to happen some time and it is out of the road now.'

Indeed it was, but there would be a few jittery moments for Vidić and van der Sar as the League programme now hotted up. It was as if the loss of the goalless record had hit their confidence – none more so than in the devastating 4-1 loss at home to arch rivals Liverpool that would follow just 10 days after van der Sar finally conceded. But there would also be happier results in Europe as Nemanja and United headed to a second successive Champions League final appearance.

More of that later... First, let's turn the clock back a little and examine how Nemanja earned two more medals to add to his ever-growing list of honours at United. Both came in between that magnificent run of clean sheets in the Premier League: one would be in Japan just before Christmas, as Vidić became a world champion; the other at Wembley at the start of the following March as he added another Carling Cup medal (a second after winning one in 2006) to his packed trophy cupboard, back home in leafy Cheshire.

Chapter 10

WORLD CHAMPION

'I want to emulate my boyhood heroes in Japan'
— *Nemanja Vidić , 16 December 2008*

PARADOXICALLY, the pre-Christmas trip to Japan in 2008 would prove both a dream and a nightmare for Nemanja Vidić. As Manchester United officially cemented their position as the best club side on the planet, he would become a world champion. He would also be sent off in the very match that determined their elevation and forced to miss the next match in the Red Devils' bid to retain their Champions League crown: a tough-looking clash in the San Siro in Italy, with José Mourinho's Serie A toppers and Italian champions Inter Milan as hosts.

However, Vidić would later admit that he was happy to take the suspension if it meant winning the World Club crown – which it did. The competition was seen by many pundits in the UK as a non-entity of a sideshow: a junket around the other side of the world that benefited only FIFA, and could distract United from their aim of retaining their Champions League and Premier League titles.

The *Daily Mail* summed up the general feeling among Fleet Street when it stated that the competition was 'Sepp Blatter's worthy, but flawed, attempt to get the best club sides on the planet together in a mini version of the World Cup.'

TV pundit and former Liverpool player and manager Graeme Souness led the sceptical chorus as United headed out to Japan on Sunday, 14 December, the day after the 0-0 Premier League draw at Spurs. Souness had played for Liverpool in the competition's predecessor, the Intercontinental Cup, held in Tokyo in 1981, when they lost 3-0 to Flamengo. He described it as being like playing in a friendly match, akin to the Community Shield, and said that the team didn't care about winning.

He told the *Daily Mail*: 'We treated it as a testimonial and were told not to get injured. Sir Alex Ferguson can't say he'd rather not be going because it sends out the wrong message to his players, but it's something he can do without. Given a choice between being crowned the best team in world and winning the Premier League again, I know which he'd choose.

'You spend goodness knows how long on a plane, allowing your body to get into another time zone and then back again. We didn't take it that seriously. You can't sleep the first night because of jet-lag. We didn't know what to eat and were ordering hamburgers in the middle of the night. At 3am the night before the game all the players were on the floodlit golf range because we couldn't sleep.'

Even among United fans there were fears and apathy about the journey to Japan. One supporter summed up the feeling of many when he said: 'Sitting 6 points behind top-placed Liverpool [with a game in hand], you wouldn't think jetting off to Japan to play in the World Club Cup would be a priority for last year's Premiership champs, but this is where United are – but why?

'The time it takes to get to Japan, not forgetting the inclusive jet-lag, the possibility of injuries to key players and most of all, interest factor – does anybody actually care – is this whole tournament a waste of time?'

And evergreen United star Paul Scholes summed up the belief that even the players weren't really up for the trip when he admitted the day before they left for Japan: 'It's a big club competition and we want to win but obviously, we'd probably rather be here in England, playing our League game and not have so many fixtures in January, like we've got.'

That was the rub as far as most who had United's welfare at heart were concerned: would they pay a heavy penalty for competing for what many football people saw as a worthless trophy? Would the travel leave them exhausted and would they lose the rhythm they had picked up in their League games? Would it cost them the two titles that really mattered?

But for Nemanja Vidić, this was a no-brainer – in his eyes the event meant everything and he wanted to win it more than anything. Certainly, he was more eager to win it more than any other United player. This was no tin-pot trophy and no extravagant jaunt that should have been avoided at all costs, as far as the big Serb was concerned.

No, it was one of Vidić's biggest ambitions to lift the trophy because seeing his countrymen lift it, some 17 years earlier, had been one of the defining moments that inspired him to become a top-class footballer. The idea of winning it had driven him on. That determination to secure the trophy would perhaps explain why he was eventually sent off in the final, but more of that shortly.

Nemanja was gushing with enthusiasm for the nine-day trip and admitted as much the day before boarding the plane for Japan from Manchester. He explained how his love for the competition went back to 1991, when his boyhood heroes, Red Star Belgrade, were crowned world club champions after beating Colo Colo 3-0.

He said: 'I remember the Intercontinental match in Japan very well. The game was played early in the morning, and my brother and I asked my father if we could get up and watch it. He woke us up and brought us downstairs so we could see it.

'Yugoslavia was a small country and we didn't become world champions at anything that often, so that was a big year for football in Yugoslavia and Serbia. It also sparked my dreams of playing for Red Star, even though I never thought at that time that I could eventually play in a Club World Cup final, like they did.'

But his dream would soon come true – he was part of the 23-man squad chosen by Sir Alex Ferguson for the trip. The squad indicated how seriously the manager was taking the event, too:

Goalkeepers: Van der Sar, Kuszczak, Foster; Defenders: Neville, Evra, Ferdinand, Vidić, O'Shea, Evans, Rafael; Midfielders: Ronaldo, Anderson, Giggs, Park, Carrick, Nani, Scholes, Fletcher, Gibson; Strikers: Berbatov, Rooney, Tevez, Welbeck.

The squad was full-strength, with all the top men making the journey to the Far East.

Of course, a United side managed by Ferguson had won the tournament's forerunner – the Intercontinental Cup, a one-off match between the champions of Europe and South America – with a 1-0 win over Brazilian side Palmeiras in 1999. But now the event had a new name – the World Club Cup, – and a new format. For Fergie, that meant it was a different tournament – and one that United had never won.

United knew they would enter the competition at the semi-final stage in Yokohama on Thursday, 18 December – and that their opponents would be Japanese outfit, Gamba Osaka. The final, if they made it, would be three days later at the Yokahama Stadium, the venue for the 2002 World Cup final between eventual winners, Brazil, and runners-up, Germany.

United touched down at Tokyo's Narita airport at 4pm on the Monday – and Sir Alex got straight down to business. Hours after the boys had booked into their hotel, he had them out training! The idea was to shake off the stiffness in their joints from the flight and to acclimatise locally. Partnering Vidić, Rio Ferdinand, in particular, appreciated the workout – he, more than any other in the squad, suffers when he is cramped for hours on a plane or a coach, his back often in agony.

Vidić couldn't stop smiling: he was just delighted to be out in Japan for the competition. It was a dream come true and he was determined to enjoy every minute of the expedition. He also loved it when the squad went on a tour around Tokyo, taking in the sights and stopping off at the shops for souvenirs, buying gifts for his family. But United were there essentially for business, not as idling tourists, and he and his team-mates would fit in two more training sessions and then it was time for the first match: the semi-final against Gamba Osaka.

It was the sort of opener the Red Devils had prayed for: a match that would be a gentle test, but one that would help them get used to the heat, the humidity and the playing surface at the Yokohama. Gamba had won the Asian Champions League, but they were not of the same calibre as the teams United had met in the later stages of the European Champions League. Indeed, they were not as good as the teams at the top of the English second division, the Championship.

Gamba, who finished 8th in their last J League campaign, had beaten Adelaide United in Sunday's quarter-final to earn the right to meet the only United that counted, and although they never expected to beat Vidić and Co. No, it was an honour to play the world-famous champions of England and they would do their best to make the match a memorable one. Which it certainly was, as United ran out 5-3 after a spirited display by the Japanese who, far from disgracing themselves by being on the wrong end of a thrashing as many had imagined, actually did themselves proud.

Wayne Rooney was the big name missing from the starting line-up – he had suffered a knock in training – but the team that Ferguson put out was a strong one: van der Sar, Neville, Ferdinand, Vidić, Evra, Nani, Anderson, Scholes, Giggs, Ronaldo and Tevez. Rooney was on the bench, along with Michael Carrick and Darren Fletcher, among others.

Sir Alex had told his team that Gamba's main threat would probably come from Japanese international midfielder Yasuhito Endo and Brazilian forward Lucas.

United, who knew victory would bring them face to face with Liga de Quito in the final (after the Ecuador outfit's 2-0 win over Mexico's Pacucha, the day before) – would strike first and, appropriately really given his affection for the competition, it would be Nemanja Vidić who scored.

He rammed home a pinpoint cross from Ryan Giggs's corner to put United 1-0 ahead after 28 minutes. Vidić wheeled away in absolute delight: this was euphoria for the man who had dreamed of playing in the tournament since he was a boy. Not only was he involved, he had scored the first goal for his club.

Gamba had been showing promising attacking touches, but the goal by Nemanja seemed to deflate them, albeit only temporarily. It was almost inevitable that United would hit them again while they were down – and so it proved, with Ronaldo making it 2-0 with another fine header from an amazing Giggs corner, just on the stroke of half-time.

Eleven minutes into the second half there was alarm on the United bench – and in Vidić's mind as well – as Nemanja pulled up in agony when he lunged in to clear a cross from the opposition. For all the world it looked as if he had pulled a hamstring and Alex Ferguson signalled for him to come off for treatment as the physio raced onto the pitch.

'I was worried sick that might be the end of my involvement in the match and the tournament,' Vidić would admit afterwards. 'I feared I would miss the final – and everyone knows how important winning the trophy was to me.'

Fortunately, it proved a false alarm – and 3 minutes later Nemanja was back on the field, smiling and joining Ferdinand in the heart of the defence. 'I was mighty relieved,' he conceded later. He was also happy when Sir Alex decided to bring him off after another 10 minutes of action. There was little chance that United would now squander their lead, so he was definitely booked in for the match of his life: the final on the Sunday.

It emerged that Ferguson had taken his key defender off as a precautionary measure – as we have noted, he wanted to have his big players out there on the pitch for the final. No point gambling, especially as Vidić might have picked up another knock that could have aggravated the initial problem.

Just 5 minutes after Vidić pulled on his tracksuit to watch the match from the bench, United's backline was breached, with Masato Yamazaki pulling one back for the hosts with a fine shot. 'Typical,' Nemanja would joke, 'As soon as I'm off the pitch, they fall apart!'

But sub Wayne Rooney made it 3-1 a minute later and Darren

Fletcher headed home the fourth not long after that. Rooney then grabbed his second and United's fifth. The Red Devils were coasting at 5-1 and it showed as they allowed Gamba to grab two goals in the following 15 minutes as the game descended into a showcase of skills.

United had enough in the tank to run out 5-3 winners and Ferguson and Vidić were both confident they would now go on to take, what was in their eyes at least, the coveted trophy against Quito. Sir Alex praised his team for their entertaining display and said he believed tighter defending – which would have been easier to achieve against Gamba, had Vidić not been substituted – and the talent of Wayne Rooney would prove decisive on the Sunday.

'I think Wayne can be a number nine,' said Ferguson after the match. 'We are trying to develop him that way. We have tried to play him there for most of the season. His movement, strength and penetration are very good.

'For the third goal that really killed them he made two runs: across and back, and across and behind. They were really clever. It marks out the quality he can give you in that position and he will improve from there.'

By Friday morning United were not only preparing for the final on the Sunday, but also the Stoke match that would follow on the following Friday. It was all part of the club's insistence on doing things right so that they had the best chance of winning every game they played. From 9am that Friday morning in Japan, the players, management and staff started to switch back to UK time so that their minds and bodies would be in sync for the return to England and the build-up to the Stoke match at the Britannia Stadium on Boxing Day.

Tokyo was eight hours ahead of Manchester, so although it was 9am there, it was only 1am in United's world. This meant an upside-down existence for Vidić and Co. for the next three days. They would start their day at 3pm in Tokyo, as that was the equivalent of 7am in England. After breakfast, they would go out training under floodlights as it was almost dusk in Tokyo. Then they would have their lunch at 9pm in Tokyo (1pm in England) and take dinner at 3am in Tokyo (7pm back in England). Finally, they would retire to their rooms for a good night's sleep at 7am, the equivalent of 11pm in England.

This was repeated on Saturday and Sunday, which meant that when they arrived back in England on the Monday, they were fresh and alert, their bodies in tune with local Manchester time. All this was possible because the club had their own chef travelling with them, as well as a nutrionist and a medical adviser. Plus, everyone on the trip was keen for it to work – they knew the importance of the Stoke match, a potentially tough, bruising encounter against a team made up of dogs of war battlers. United needed to win at Stoke at whatever cost, if they were to put the pressure on table-topping Liverpool.

Of course, it raised the question of how the final against Quito at the Yokohama on the Sunday fitted into the regime. Were United saying it was less important than the Stoke match? And were they saying that of the two games, it was the one they felt they could win more easily and so it was more worthwhile gambling with this than Stoke away? Probably, yes, to both questions – but wasn't it a fair enough gamble? If you agree with that, you also agree that the World Club Cup is a less important – but easier to win – event than a Premier League encounter.

United diplomatically dodged the questions, saying both matches were of equal, vital importance in the minds of the club and anyway, it was hardly as if they were playing Quito in Tokyo at an unreasonable hour by either time zone, UK or Japanese.

The match kicked off at 6.30pm local time – 10.30am GMT, so Vidić and the boys did not have to play in the middle of the night in their own peculiar time zone! It meant they missed what would have been their evening meal, but United's nutrionists supplied them with energy bars and drinks to make up for it – although some of the squad later admitted they had felt a bit confused about kicking off in the early evening when their bodies believed it was morning.

The gamble paid off. United beat Ecuadorians Liga de Quito 1-0 in the final to lift the World Club Cup trophy, thanks to a late winner from the irrepressible Wayne Rooney. But the match turned into a disaster for the man to whom lifting the trophy meant the most.

Yes, Nemanja Vidić was sent off 4 minutes after the break for elbowing striker Claudio Bieler.

Rooney won the game with his fine shot low into the net after 75 minutes. It meant United became the first English club to win the event in its revamped format of semi-finals and final. Also, remarkably, United were now champions of England, champions of Europe and champions of the world. And Vidić was an English champion, a European champion and a world champion despite his red-card shame in the final.

Sir Alex refused to be too hard on the Serbian hero. He knew that Nemanja had put himself on the line for him many times over the past couple of years and now it was payback time. He was determined to stand by his man, to show him the same loyalty as Vidić had always given him. Ferguson said: 'The sending-off made it difficult for us. It's a soft sending-off, but he swung an elbow. When you do that in front of the referee, you've got no chance – he gave the referee no option.

'Half an hour to go is a long road with 10 men, but Wayne scored a magnificent goal. After Vidić was sent off, it was important that we didn't lose the ball. It was important to keep passing and hope Ronaldo or Rooney did something special.

'The collective spirit of the team won the day. With 10 men, we played with great expression and tried to win. It is a measure of the players' ambition. In 30 years you'll look back and see Manchester United's name on the trophy, although I won't be around to enjoy it.'

Rooney, who was named Player of the Tournament after the final and won a Toyota car for the accolade, also had sympathy for Nemanja, declaring he too did not believe the offence merited a red card. He said that he had sought out Vidić and given him a hug, as had others within the squad, and assured him that he had still played a big part in United becoming champions of the world.

Wayne said: 'We're the best team in the world and that's a great achievement for the team and something we're all really proud of. It's been a long road. To score the winning goal in a match like this is a great feeling.'

Certainly, the win finally put to bed any lingering bad memories from 2000, when United played in the inaugural tournament in Brazil. Then, they were criticised for pulling out of the FA Cup to take part and did not play to their true ability in the heat of Brazil, returning home early, beaten and despondent.

This time they arrived back in England as champions of the world, with both their reputation and bank balances profiting. And, thanks to the meticulous planning of the time zones, they were up and ready for the next League match at Stoke, five days later, and would also compete in the FA Cup.

Only Nemanja's sending-off clouded what had been a successful, well thought-out venture. As he walked off, he looked dejected and his mood did not lift as he watched his team-mates' triumph. He accepted their hugs, commiserations and sympathy for the sending-off, but was very hard on himself. Afterwards he told reporters: 'This is not a good time for me.'

The dream he had nurtured since boyhood had turned sour and even the victory did not truly soften the blow of disappointment and melancholy that fell upon him. Vidić knew that he had blundered, and felt that he had let his team-mates down. He had been having an easy night and had elbowed his rival instinctively, annoyed at the player's physical approach. This was a moment of madness, pure and simple.

Of course, the consequences might have been worse. United could have lost and he might have been banned for two Champions League matches. Indeed, directly after the game, a FIFA official announced: 'He will get at least a one-match ban. A FIFA commission will have to meet to decide if they will recommend any more to UEFA.'

Even Sir Alex was not optimistic, saying: 'It depends how FIFA interpret it and how UEFA act. Vidić is disappointed, but the referee was correct to produce the red card.'

No, it didn't look promising although, in the event, Nemanja would miss just the away leg in the tie against Inter Milan.

'I don't think they really wanted to play,' remarked Edwin van der Sar, who was one of the first to comfort the man who had held things together in front of him for most of the season thus far. 'When they broke, only four players came out, and for our part we were disappointed we didn't score and punish them earlier. Even in the second half, they were not coming out of their shell. We were still playing the best football and had the best possession with 10 men.'

The last word went to Rooney, who summed up the importance of the victory in terms of helping United kick on with the rest of the season. He said: 'If we hadn't won, it would have been difficult going back home. We would probably have been on a downer and it would have had a knock-on effect.'

United's skipper in the final, Rio Ferdinand, seconded those words before also making sure Vidić – his partner in the heart of the United defence – was OK.

'Unbelievable!' he roared. 'We're elated. It's been a hard trip, but winning softens any feelings of tiredness.'

On the plane home, Vidić was quiet, alone with his thoughts. He was glad to return to the sanctuary of his family and to have a few days to get the disaster out of his system. The one bonus for him was that he still became a world champion: he still took the medal home, but being a perfectionist and a man who took pride in his work, it would be some time before he forgave himself for losing control in what he viewed as one, the biggest matches of his career.

In his own eyes, his own standing and reputation of the man from Serbia had taken a knock, but not in the world of football. A clear indication of the importance with which he was now viewed at Manchester United came just a fortnight after he returned from Japan when former Chelsea boss, José Mourinho, called for him to be banned for two matches for his sending-off in the final.

The Portuguese was now in charge at Inter Milan and said that he believed Vidić and Wayne Rooney should miss both legs. He might as well have said that he had been praying they might do so, such was his fear and respect for the two men.

Mourinho said he was surprised England forward Rooney had been cleared of allegedly stamping on an Aalborg player in a previous round – and then got in his dig at Nemanja. 'I was amazed that Rooney was not banned,' he told Italian sports paper *La Gazzetta dello Sport*. 'And I would be amazed if Vidić did not get at least two matches, which could be too little for a gesture like that in a match seen by the whole world.'

It was typical Mourinho hyperbole and it did not influence the decision makers at FIFA. Nemanja missed the first leg – a 0-0 draw in the San Siro on 24 February 2009 – but was back in business for the second, the 2-0 win at Old Trafford, a fortnight later. He put in a convincing shift, shackling Inter Milan's danger man, Zlatan Ibrahimović, and provided a rock-solid base with his partner-in-crime, Ferdinand.

He was also on hand to power United in front with a brilliant header from a Ryan Giggs cross – a goal that broke the deadlock and Inter's defensive confidence. Another header from Ronaldo then killed off the challenge from the demoralised Italians.

Afterwards Sir Alex was surprisingly subdued and critical of his men, saying: 'After Vidić scored the first goal, I thought we'd kill them off. I thought we could score a few goals, but then we started doing flicks and back heels. We can play better than that, but I am happy to get through it.'

But Mourinho was honest enough to admit that the return of the Serbian powerhouse had been the difference in the teams during the two legs. He said: 'Vidić is a great player, not only in defence, but how he gets forward and scores such big goals. He is a handful and we didn't cope with him when he came up for the corner.

'United have experience, quality, great physical condition and intensity in their game, that's why they're European champions. United have worked together for five consecutive years. They were a young side, but are not young anymore.

'They have basically the same team as when I was at Chelsea.

Only Dimitar Berbatov is new. United are a quality team and showed against us exactly why they are European champions. You have to say they deserved to win – they can win anything.'

The self-styled 'Special One' was right about that: Vidić and United had already secured two trophies that season and it was only the start of March.

Sandwiched in between the two-legged tie against Inter, they added the League Cup, or as it is better known in the modern era, the Carling Cup, to the trophy cabinet that already housed the World Club Championship and the Champions League crown.

The victory came on the first day of March 2009, as United battled to beat a spirited Spurs team at Wembley. Nemanja had been looking forward to the trip to football's spiritual home in London and said he even hoped to score one of his trademark headed goals. Already he had scored six goals that season, including two vital ones against Chelsea and Sunderland, and planned to mark his return to the side after suspension in Milan with another.

Vidić said: 'I love that feeling when you score. It's fantastic as a defender because it is not one of your main jobs. I always try to score when I can by taking up good positions in the box and going up for corners. If you get lucky, it is brilliant.'

And he admitted that he was delighted to take the plaudits that were coming his way in a fabulous season. The Serbian said: 'Why not enjoy the limelight? You play football to do the best you can and try to improve yourself in every game and training session. The aim is to do well and get the team flying high.'

Yet on the day of the final Nemanja was stunned to learn that he wouldn't be starting. Instead he was named one of the substitutes. Sir Alex explained the decision by saying that he had wanted to stick with a settled team after the 0-0 draw at Inter Milan. That meant Jonny Evans continued in the team alongside Rio Ferdinand in central defence.

A few days after the match – which United won 4-1 on penalties after the game fizzled out to a 0-0 draw after 120 minutes – Fergie would, remarkably, admit he had made a mistake in leaving Nemanja out of the starting line-up. He explained that he had done so because he wanted to reward those who had played in the competition in earlier rounds – and that it had slipped his mind that Vidić was one of those players! The Serb had been involved in three previous rounds and Sir Alex said: 'With the League Cup, it was simple – the ones who started the competition would play throughout. The only mistake I made on Sunday was Vidić. I didn't realise he'd played three games in the competition. But the reason I played Rio was because he's missed so many games since December with his back problem; I needed to get him back – big defenders need to play games. Rio and Vidić will be a solid partnership now until the end of the season.'

Nemanja still earned his medal after coming on as a late substitute because the match went into extra-time and later he told friends that he had been as puzzled as anyone at the time when Sir Alex left him out. 'In the end I was just grateful to be involved and earn another cup winner's medal,' he admitted.

He would take his place in the United team after 76 minutes in the Wembley showpiece, replacing John O'Shea. That was 7 minutes earlier than he had arrived on the pitch at Cardiff's Millennium Stadium, almost three years to the day. Then, he had replaced Wes Brown on 83 minutes – as fellow newcomer Patrice Evra took over from Mikael Silvestre at the same time. It had been boss Ferguson's way of showing they had a big future at United, a treat that enabled both to take home silverware just a couple of months after they joined the club.

Now winning honours was becoming a way of life for the Serbian, who had left Spartak Moscow and Russia to do just that. His second Carling Cup winner's medal would sit nicely in his trophy cabinet alongside his two Premier League medals and a Champions League winner's gong.

United had struggled to break down a resolute Tottenham, but the better, more enterprising team would eventually emerge triumphant. It was a more experienced team than many had expected that started the match – Foster, O'Shea, Ferdinand, Evans, Evra, Nani, Gibson, Scholes, Ronaldo, Welbeck, Tevez – and would later be strengthened by the introduction of Vidić, Giggs and Anderson. In the end, it would be reserve keeper Ben Foster who won the day for the Red Devils, with a brilliant save when one-on-one with Aaron Lennon in normal time and another memorable stop from Jamie O'Hara's penalty kick in the shootout. When David Bentley also missed from the spot and

Anderson scored for United, the match was decided. Giggs, Tevez and Ronaldo also scored from the spot for the Red Devils, with only Vedran Corluka doing so for a devastated Spurs, who had been the holders of the trophy.

Afterwards, United assistant manager Mike Phelan congratulated Foster on his part in securing the trophy. He said: 'In the end it came down to the goalkeepers and our one made a great save. Ben has been unlucky with the odd injury this season, but we know he's got quality and he can be a Manchester United goalkeeper.

'It is important he gets games for us and what happened can only help us. It was a hard game and both sets of players were shattered at the end – they were cramping, but they kept going – and it's a good feeling when you win on penalties.'

And Foster, who had studied Spurs players taking spot kicks on an iPod as he waited for the shootout, commented: 'I felt good from the start. I haven't played many games, which isn't great, but it was great of the gaffer to give me a chance. All the lads are heroes, they had to knock in the penalties and they looked super-cool; they all looked like they were going to score. If they hadn't, we wouldn't have our medals. I'm delighted we managed to win.'

Vidić told friends that it had been another great day in his career at Old Trafford. He let his hair down with the other lads as they celebrated their win in London before heading back to Manchester. But the celebrations did not last long. After all, Nemanja and co. were hardly going to go overboard at winning the Carling Cup, the least awe-inspiring of trophies when set against the likes of the Champions League and the Premier League. No, our boy had much bigger fish to fry – and with almost three months of the campaign still remaining, he would put major celebrations on ice. It was as he had done so the year before, funnily enough.

Even defeated Spurs boss Harry Redknapp said he could see United going on to win the Champions League, the Premier League and the FA Cup. He said: 'They have got a big chance - they are the team to beat. They have a fantastic squad…it looks as if the League is going their way and you wouldn't bet against them in the Champions League and the FA Cup.'

Yes, the Carling Cup triumph would prove just a staging post as Vidić and Co. retained their Premier League title and only lost their Champions League crown in the final itself against Barcelona.

Let's now take a look at how they kept their nerve in the heated run-in to the end of the Premier League season of 2008-09 – and how Vidić's role as cult idol and hero of the Stretford End was officially confirmed by the fans themselves as he became their Player of the Year, and also notched the Barclays Premier League Player of the Year Award.

Chapter 11

MAN OF THE PEOPLE

NEMANJA HAD ALWAYS made a special point of showing the United fans how much he loved them and appreciated their support. At away matches, he was invariably the first player to walk over to United's army of visiting supporters to applaud them for their efforts – and the last to head down the tunnel. This was a man of the people, a man who understood how important the supporters were; that without them there would be no club.

He knew that he enjoyed a privileged lifestyle as a modern-day footballer and that most fans earned less in a year than he did in a week. Also, he never forgot how patient those fans had been during his early, jittery days at the club. Despite his public image as an on-field, footballing Rambo, he is an intelligent, thoughtful man. In short, Vidić and the United faithful enjoyed a special relationship and by the end of the 2008–09 season, this would be officially confirmed as he walked off with two prestigious Player of the Year awards at United's annual awards ceremony at Old Trafford in mid-May.

He won both the fans' award and the players' award, showing how valued he was by those who helped pay his wages, as well as the men with whom he played in the first team, week in, week out. This was no mean feat, given he held off support for Ryan Giggs, who had already collected the PFA Player of the Season honour.

The stars of United stepped forward to pay tribute to Vidić – and were led by the club's president and a man who should know a bit about opposing centre-backs, legendary former centre forward, Sir Bobby Charlton.

Sir Bobby said: 'It's normally the glamour players who get these prizes, but Nemanja deserves this. He has been such an influence – a brilliant, brilliant player for us. He is unbelievable in the air and wins absolutely everything. He is so powerful and brave, and has a fantastic leap to get above the strikers.

'And he also comes up for set-pieces and scores goals. As a defender he makes the full-backs, the goalkeeper and the midfielders in front of him all feel secure. He is a player you can depend on and put your trust in, and that's important. I like that he doesn't try to do too much, he sticks to his task of defending, and does that job very well.

'It's hard for me to imagine that Manchester United would be congratulated and lauded for our defensive capabilities. We're not supposed to be defensive! But alongside Rio

Above: Nemanja celebrates with team-mate Rio Ferdinand after scoring against Inter Milan on 11 March 2009.

Below left: Nemanja rues a wasted opportunity in United's Champions League clash with Porto in April 2009.

Below right: Vidić is certainly never one to shy away from an important challenge – here, he clashes with Arsenal's Emmanuel Adebayor during the 2009 Champions League semi-final.

Nemanja in training before Manchester United's Champions League final appearance against Barcelona.

Nemanja in action for Manchester United in the 2009 Champions League final. Unfortunately things didn't go to plan, with United going down 2-0.

Nemanja clashes with (*above*) Thierry Henry and (*below*) United team-mate Patrice Evra during Serbia's World Cup qualifier with France on 9 September 2009. Serbia, appearing in World Cup qualifying for the first time as an independent country, won their group ahead of favourites France.

Nemanja is extremely proud of his role in the Serbian team, and relished the opportunity to play in his first World Cup in 2010.

Above and below right: Nemanja takes on CSKA Moscow as United launch another bid for European glory.

Left: Vidić in friendly action for Serbia against Northern Ireland in November 2009.

Nemanja in action for Serbia against South Korea on 18 November 2009.

Proud to play for his country and now Manchester United's team captain, Nemanja Vidić certainly has a lot to look forward to in the coming years.

Ferdinand or young Jonny Evans, Nemanja has dominated our area this season.'

Winger Giggs added his own tribute, saying: 'Consistently throughout the season he's been brilliant. So many players have had a good season, but it has to be Nemanja for me.'

Vidić then admitted that he had not expected to win the double honour – and asked forgiveness on account of this for the quality of his acceptance speech! He said: 'It's a great night for me. I'm honoured. It has been a really good year. It's amazing to get these awards when I consider the quality of the players I play alongside. I'd like to say thank you to the fans and to my team-mates.

'I enjoy being here every day and playing with these players and working with the coaches. I'm very happy here at United. Since I came here three and a half years ago, I have progressed every year and I'm proud of that. To be honest, I don't have so many individual awards, that's why I am a bit confused and my speech is not the best. Next time, my speech will be a bit better.'

Then, after clinching the Premier League title in May 2009, Vidić received a further accolade when he was named Barclays Player of the Year, with his boss Sir Alex winning the Barclays Manager of the Year award. It was the ninth time Ferguson had received the honour, while Vidić collected his for the first time in his career and it was an appropriate recognition for the club as a whole for winning their third successive Premier League title.

Vidić, who had also won the January Player of the Year award from Barclays and was named in the PFA Premier League Team of the Season for the second consecutive year, had made 34 appearances in the League over the season, scoring four valuable goals.

The Barclays citation proclaimed that the Serbian had 'been instrumental at the heart of the United defence', while in response Nemanja said: 'I feel honoured to receive the award, it is a good feeling.'

To balance the Vidić story, it must be said here and now that it was not all to be gushing award ceremonies and lavish praise. There were some brickbats – two major ones over the whole season – but a bandwagon would form among some pundits, claiming they served to prove he wasn't as good as had been suggested.

Two blunders out of a nine-month season, in two matches: against Liverpool in the Premier League and Barcelona in the final of the Champions League. These would provide ammunition for Nemanja's critics, who would claim that Vidić could cut it in the bread and butter of the League against the likes of Hull and Stoke, but not against world-class strikers – in this case, Fernando Torres and Samuel Eto'o.

We will look at the Eto'o incident in more detail later in this chapter, but it is fair to say that against Barca – and the other main blot on Vidić's copybook in Europe, the Champions League semi against AC Milan in 2007 –it appears that he was not fully fit. He had rushed back against Milan after suffering a collarbone injury and suffered a niggle in training before United's showdown in Rome with Barca. The Reds' management tried to keep the incident under wraps as Rio Ferdinand had also been a fitness doubt and they did not wish to boost their rivals' hopes. But a United insider revealed that neither man was fully fit, hence Vidić's struggle to keep pace with Eto'o when the Cameron striker turned him for the first goal.

However, against Torres on 14 March, when Liverpool thrashed United 4-1 at Old Trafford, there are no excuses. It was a bad day at the office, pure and simple, but to deride one man's otherwise consistently top-notch career on the back of a bad day seems rather cruel and unreasonable. Maybe this was a case of critics tired of United's relentless success gleefully enjoying a chance to put the boot in when a man was down?

Vidić's moment of hell against Torres came almost on the half-hour as both battled for the ball after a long clearance from Martin Skrtel. Nemanja was hassled by the Spaniard and the ball bounced away from him. Torres collected and embarked on a dazzling solo run before dispatching the ball. He left Vidić for dead with his pace and strength.

It was a sickener and a sight few had anticipated. The defender could usually look after himself, whatever the opposition, but Torres was a different proposition. Minutes later, he almost compounded his error when he was lucky not to have a penalty awarded when Torres again got the better of him.

His afternoon of misery – certainly his worst in English football – was cemented on 76 minutes when he was sent off for pulling back Steven Gerrard. It was his second sending-off against the Scousers in one season and traditionally it would have been viewed as a badge of honour by United fans, but given the thrashing their team was receiving, and the fact that his foul led to the third goal, it was the last thing on their minds at that moment. United fan Dave Moore said: 'Yes, we would normally have seen him as a hero, but it was such a goddamn awful afternoon. But when we'd gotten over it a few weeks later, there is no doubt that Vidić had kept his special place in our hearts.

'OK, he had a stinker against the Scousers, but he still showed he would die for United. He only hauled Gerrard back to stop him scoring, didn't he? The great thing about Vidić is that, in our eyes anyway, he hates the Scousers as much as we do. That will always endear him to us!'

Fabio Aurelio punished United for Vidić's sending-off – smashing home a 25-yard free kick to make it 3-1 for the visitors.

Yet there had been no inkling of the upset that would cloud the afternoon when Ronaldo put United ahead on 23 minutes from the penalty spot. Kop keeper Pepe Reina had fouled Ji-Sung Park and Ronaldo gratefully accepted the invitation to add to his goals tally for the season.

Then came Vidić's faux pas – and Torres' moment of glory as he lashed the ball home beyond the despairing van der Sar. Skipper Gerrard put Liverpool 2-1 up from the spot almost on the stroke of half-time after he was tripped in the penalty area by Patrice Evra. Then Vidić's second faux pas, as he was sent off for holding back Gerrard – and his second punishment as Aurelio fired the ball home from the free kick.

United's misery was not over yet – Andrea Dossena made it 4-

1 in the final minute, chipping van der Sar after latching on to the ball from Reina's clearance. It was a bitter pill to swallow for Manchester United FC and their fans – hammered and humiliated by their biggest, most hated rivals.

Vidić was disappointed by his performance and the result – he is a perfectionist and blamed himself for the defeat, holding his hands up in the dressing room afterwards. But his team-mates were quick to console him and to tell him he had no need to berate himself. 'They said they were all to blame,' I am told by a United insider. 'Everyone had a nightmare, not just Vidić – but this was the first time he had been skinned by any opposing striker, so the spotlight fell upon him.

'He was honest enough to admit that he had fallen short of his very high standards, but he also said he would do everything to make sure it didn't happen again when he next faced Torres. He didn't like being made to look a fool by him.

'The United lads and the manager told him to forget it. It was just one of those days when everything that could go wrong, did. It was a freak result that probably won't happen again in our lifetime.'

Certainly that seemed to be the way Sir Alex was viewing it in public, too. Before the showdown clash there had been much talk about his Liverpool counterpart Rafa Benítez 'cracking up' – that Fergie's mind games had got to him and left him in a state. However, after the defeat you had to wonder if United's boss was losing it, too!

His comments were staggering, considering his men had

been given a true lesson. Fergie said, with no hint that he was having a laugh, 'It is a hard one to take because I thought we were the better team and the score does not reflect that. Now the thing is to respond. It always is at this club – you lose a game and you respond. We always do.

'There is no complacency on our part. It was a bad day in terms of the goals we lost, but I couldn't argue with the quality of play that much. One or two players were a little bit short in terms of what we expect of them but I do know the football was good. We kept driving on and they showed good energy, even though we only had two-and-a-half days to prepare for the match.'

It had been Liverpool's biggest win at Old Trafford since 1936, when the match had ended 2-5 and it also meant the visitors had closed the gap on United at the top of the Premier League to 4 points, but the Red Devils still had a game in hand. So the damage had been mainly to the team's morale – there was still a comfy cushion between them and their nearest rivals.

Indeed Sir Bobby Charlton espoused the view that the defeat could be good for United, telling BBC Radio 5 Live: 'There was a little bit of stress because we kept on winning matches. It helps to maybe turn the gas down a little bit, and a lot of pressure has maybe eased. I'm hoping we're going to do better because of this result.

'It wasn't a result that anyone at Manchester United could be proud of, but nevertheless you have to say that Liverpool really played well and they deserved to win.'

Sir Bobby predicted that the Reds would get back on track quickly – and that they would win away at Fulham in their next match. He would be proved to be no Mystic Meg as United also foundered at Craven Cottage, a week later. With the suspended Vidić missing, they crashed 2-0 with Fulham's goals from Danny Murphy (from the penalty spot after Paul Scholes used his hands to stop a Bobby Zamora effort from going in) and a late killer from Zoltan Gera. United also had Scholes sent off for his indiscretion and Wayne Rooney joined him for an early bath 3 minutes from time when he earned a second yellow card for throwing the ball aggressively.

Afterwards Fergie admitted his team had missed the towering presence of Vidić at the heart of his defence, but refused to be too downhearted. He said: 'I was disappointed with the first half, we didn't get started at all and that cost us the game. In the second half they responded to the half-time talk and we were unlucky not to get something out of it. If we'd have got the goal, we could even have won it.

'If you lose games in March and April then it can cost you, but fortunately we have a little slender lead at the moment.'

And he was not even convinced that Rooney should have been sent off: 'Did Rooney throw the ball at the referee? The ball was thrown direct to where the free kick was taken and did it hit the referee? No, the ball didn't hit the referee. Was it thrown in anger? Yes, because he wanted the game hurried up, he threw with pace to get the game going.'

Despite the second defeat on the trot, United were still in the driving seat as far as winning the League went. They were a point ahead of Liverpool and still had that precious game in hand. Skipper Ryan Giggs followed up that very theme when he remarked: 'We've got to do our own job, not worry about the teams around us. It's still in our hands.'

It certainly was, and after that slight wobble United would pull together and go unbeaten in the remaining eight League games. That would be enough, despite the admirable fight to the death from Liverpool, to earn them their third consecutive Premier League crown. Of course, it was Vidić's third as well – not a bad return from three-and-a-half years in England. And it was his ninth honour in total since joining United, assuming two Community Shields are bracketed in that worthy list.

After the defeat at Fulham, Nemanja also sat out the jittery – but vital – 3-2 home win over Aston Villa (which saw the emergence of another overseas cult hero in the making in Federico Macheda, the Italian 17-year-old, who grabbed a wonderful winning goal).

But the big Serb was back for the 2-1 win at Sunderland, when Macheda again stole the glory with another late winner. Vidić kept his place in the side right up to the 0-0 home draw with Arsenal, which secured the title. Then, along with most other key first teamers, he was rested in the final Premier League game of the campaign – the 1-0 victory at Hull City.

'It is a great feeling to win the League again,' he said, when the stats made it impossible for Liverpool to catch United after the draw with the Gunners on 16 May. They had made it with a game to spare, doing it perhaps not in style, but certainly with conviction in the nerve-racking fixture. 'I am very happy here at United and cannot imagine playing anywhere else,' Nemanja added. 'It is a very proud moment for me and for the lads.'

After the title was secured and back in the trophy room at the Theatre of Dreams, it was time to focus on the final challenge of the season: retaining the Champions League trophy. There had been hopes that they might win the so-called quintuple, but that dream died when they lost on penalties to Everton in the semi-final of the FA Cup at Wembley.

It had been one of those days when boss Fergie had one of his Mr Mad moods – he had decided that the chance to reach the final of the most coveted domestic Cup competition in the world merited United fielding… a team of kids and reserves! OK, Nemanja was in the starting line-up alongside Rio, but the rest of the team lined up like this: Foster, Rafael Da Silva, Ferdinand, Vidić, Fabio Da Silva, Welbeck, Gibson , Anderson, Park, Tevez, Macheda.

It hardly seems as if he was taking the tie that seriously, does it? No Rooney, no Ronaldo, no Giggs, no Carrick – no joy, ultimately. After extra time, the game finished goalless and United went out in the penalty shootout, losing 4-2. To his great credit, Vidić took one of the penalties, the third for United, and was the first man to score for them; efforts from Dimitar Berbatov and Rio Ferdinand were comfortably saved by former Reds keeper Tim Howard but Nemanja's scurried in off the post. Later, he would admit that it had been one of the most nerve-racking moments of his career, and that he was in raptures when it sneaked in.

Anderson also scored for United, but Phil Jagielka ended their hopes of another Wembley appearance when he slotted home his penalty.

Sir Alex had gambled high stakes – and lost big-time. Afterwards he would bemoan the refereeing, claiming United had been denied a surefire penalty when Jagielka brought down Danny Welbeck on 68 minutes. He was probably right to be angry, but the tie was also lost on his selection policy. Quite simply, it was asking a lot of such a vastly changed, less experienced line-up – eight changes from the match at Porto, four days earlier – to gel swiftly and wondrously against a settled, determined Everton side. Having said that, the boys did well and deserved to have won, but surely if Fergie had put out his big attacking guns, United might have been lining up for a final against Chelsea?

Afterwards he blamed everyone but himself, starting with David Moyes for suggesting pre-match that ref Mike Riley was a United fan. Fergie said: 'It might have got to him. I'm not saying for certain, but all that nonsense about him being a United fan – it can prey on a ref's mind. I don't know if the ref's totally sure and if he'd given a penalty in such an important game, he has to be. When he sees it, he will probably realise he's made a mistake.'

And finally, he blamed the pitch – claiming this was the reasoning behind his decision to send out the reserves in such a big match: 'It seemed a bit spongy and difficult to move the ball around. Berbatov would have started, and Paul Scholes definitely, with possibly Patrice Evra [if it had not been a bit spongy].'

On to the European Champions League: United progressed to the final after seeing off Porto in the quarter-finals (3-2 on aggregate) and Arsenal in the semis (4-1 on aggregate). The Porto two-legger witnessed a jittery United in the first leg, which ended 2-2, but commanding in the away leg, which they won – thanks to a Cristiano Ronaldo wonder goal. Well, that and a truly excellent defensive showing from Vidić and Co.

United, as holders, were the scalp every club wanted – none more so than Arsenal, who awaited them in the semis after they had finally put Porto to bed.

In the first leg at Old Trafford on 29 April, United squeezed home with a 1-0 win, courtesy of John O'Shea's 18th-minute goal – a close-range strike. With Vidić and Ferdinand dominant in defence against the menace of Adebayor and Nasri, Arsenal were never a real threat and United should have won much more comfortably. Cristiano Ronaldo hit the bar with a brilliant shot after the interval and Gunners keeper Manuel Almunia was the Man of the Match.

After the win, Vidić was concerned. His partner-in-crime Rio had been forced off with a rib injury and the Serb fretted he might not be fit for the return at the Emirates, the following week. He would have had no qualms about lining up with young Jonny Evans as his partner, but he liked it best when he was working with Rio.

Meanwhile, Arsenal were on something of a high even though they had lost the first leg. They felt they had escaped lightly at 1-0 and that their turn would come to show their mettle in London.

Sir Alex agreed they should have suffered a bigger beating, but warned that United would score in the return. He said: 'We played at a good high tempo and maybe we should have scored four goals, but before the game I wanted to win without losing a goal. We know we can go there and score, and that is the big problem Arsenal have.'

And so it proved to be as Arsenal shipped another three goals and could only reply with a single effort. Vidić grinned with delight when Ferdinand was declared fit for the test and both men performed strongly as a unit, generally coping well with the new examination of their partnership brought about by the return, after injury, of prolific goalscorer Robin van Persie.

The Dutchman did manage to get on the scoresheet on 75 minutes, but it was in controversial circumstances. He netted from the penalty spot after Darren Fletcher was wrongly sent off for bringing down Cesc Fabregas. TV replays showed the Scotland skipper had won the ball fairly. It was a travesty that he would now miss out on the Champions League final against Barcelona.

There was equal disappointment in the Arsenal camp that they had fluffed their big chance. Boss Arsène Wenger called it 'the most disappointing night of my career' and added, 'I felt the fans were really up for a big night and to disappoint people who stand behind the team so much hurts.'

The Frenchman would then go on to add: 'The most difficult

thing is that we do not have a feeling that we played a semi-final of the Champions League.'

It was a telling comment and a prophetic one if applied to United and their own destiny in the final of the competition, a month later. For just as Wenger had said the Gunners had not shown up for the semi against United, so too the Red Devils did not show – apart from a rousing opening 10 minutes – against Barcelona in Rome.

The critics made a big thing of Vidić's misfortune against Eto'o – when the Cameroon centre forward turned Nemanja and shot home past van der Sar – but it might be contended that the Serb was only as much to blame as his team-mates for the defeat. As a group, they were dismal and seemed to lose confidence and belief as the match progressed. Vidić was turned by Eto'o and could have done better, but as we have already mentioned, he had taken a knock in training (which was kept secret) and at times struggled for pace during the final. Also, where was left full-back Patrice Evra? He should have been on to Eto'o as he turned, not Vidić, but the little Frenchman was nowhere to be seen.

Nemanja was extremely self-critical about his failings against Eto'o. On the coach to the airport, he was silent and fell asleep on the flight back to Manchester. He admitted that it had been 'my worst moment in football' and must have been relieved when he got home to the sanctuary of his family in Cheshire.

But he should not have taken the weight of the defeat on his shoulders alone. This was a collective loss of form and nerve on a humid night in the Eternal City. And with no solid midfield to battle against the wondrous Andras Iniesta and Xavi, United's backline was always going to be in for a busy day at the office. Given the way United were overrun in the centre of the park, it was a result – and a credit to an exhausted Vidić and Ferdinand – that they escaped with only a 2-0 loss.

After suffering a calf injury, Ferdinand had been wrapped in cotton wool for three weeks before the final. Vidić had admitted that he hoped Rio would be his partner for the Rome showdown on May 27, saying: 'I don't want to think that he will not play. He is an important player for us and I think he will make it.'

He did make it, but just as Vidić was at fault for the opening goal so too was Ferdinand equally culpable for the second, allowing Lionel Messi to escape his clutches and rise to powerfully head home.

Before the final, Nemanja had predicted that United would pull a goal from nowhere, if they were in trouble. He said: 'When we need the goals, we score the goals. A few games we were one or two goals down and won the games. Our attackers have shown that when we need goals, they can deliver. We are not a team that is just going to go there and defend – we want to attack.'

But he was wrong about that in Rome and also in his belief that United would win, even if they had to win ugly. He had said: 'All that matters is the result, you'll quickly forget about the style. Football is not about the style – it's about the winning and we have the confidence and belief to do it.

'I don't think we are arrogant – we respect Barcelona, but we believe in ourselves and in the players we have. We won the League and have reached the Champions League final, so we have to believe we can win it. We know it's going to be a hard game and have big jobs to do, but we are excited and we will try to hurt them.'

Well, it proved to be a hard game, but United did not hurt Barca. The dream of everyone at Old Trafford of becoming the first team to defend the Champions League crown lay in tatters, destroyed by a rampant Barca, who demolished a nerve-ridden, out-of-form United.

Both Ferdinand and Vidić expressed their disappointment at losing in such limp fashion – and both admitted Barca were by far the better team on the night. 'We didn't come here and give a good account of ourselves,' Rio admitted. 'We have played better 99 per cent of the time this season, but saying that, we created four or five good opportunities to score, but they scored two goals at crucial times and two bad goals on our part.

'We have no arguments, they were the better team on the day; you have got to do it on the day – if we played better or played to our strengths it would have been a different game, but if you don't do it on the day, you don't deserve to win.'

Nemanja agreed with those sentiments, saying: 'We didn't play well. They had a good game and scored at the right time – then we chased the game and they had space to counterattack us. They deserved the win.'

Sir Alex also stood up and admitted his team had been outplayed, saying: 'I think the first goal was a killer for us – it was their first attack and they scored. We had started brightly, but we got a bit nervous after that and of course with a goal lead, they could keep the ball all night.

'In fairness we were beaten by a better team. We weren't at our best – after the first goal, it was very difficult for us. They defended quite well actually; we thought we could get at their back four better than we did. Losing is the best part of the game, because in adversity you always move forwards quicker.

'Of course we are disappointed, but we are a young team and we can improve.'

Fergie pinpointed that first goal as the killer, but he was not picking out Vidić as a scapegoat. Indeed, when asked about his player, the boss would always go out of his way to stress what a brilliant campaign the Serbian had enjoyed, and that without his fortitude and talent, United would have shipped many more goals over the season.

The fans also stood fully behind Vidić despite the press onslaught over his part in the Eto'o goal.

Stretford Ender Jude said: 'It's not right, the man makes a mistake and he is suddenly no good. The truth of it is that Vidić has been one of – if not the best – players this season. Give him a break, for God's sake!'

James, a long-time United supporter, remarked: 'It's just a shame that despite all Barcelona's good play, their two goals could have easily been avoided. No one tracked Iniesta's run for the first, while Vidić was turned too easily and Ferdinand did not pick up Messi for the second. I won't blame them, though – they have been outstanding for the last three years.'

Another Red, Paul, added: 'Rio and Vidić ensured the damage was far less than it could have been. They are rock solid and ever ready for big, big games. It's just one of those days.'

As Nemanja's third full season in English football now inevitably fizzled out into anti-climax after the loss in Rome, an unlikely ally emerged to say that, for him, the Serb had been the outstanding player of the season despite the setbacks he had suffered.

Step forward Steven Gerrard, captain of arch-enemies Liverpool, and the man who beat Vidić to the second major individual honour of the English season. While Ryan Giggs scooped the PFA Player of the Year Award, Gerrard lifted the Football Writers' Association version – the honour bestowed by journalists.

The 28-year-old topped the poll ahead of Giggs and Wayne Rooney to win the prestigious accolade, which had been running since 1948.

Gerrard said: 'I'm delighted, but I'm a little bit surprised. When you look at the quality of the players there are in this League, it's a great privilege to win this kind of award. It's not just the Manchester United players. When you look at the players the likes of Chelsea and Arsenal and other teams have got, they all have fantastic players throughout their squads now. The quality is getting better and better each year, so to win this award is a great achievement for myself.'

He then went on to lift the lid on his secret admiration for Vidić – and revealed that he himself had voted for him in the PFA Awards: 'Every time I watch Manchester United, being a Liverpool player, you want them to lose. But Vidić has been a rock. He and Rio Ferdinand have been superb and they have saved United so many points this season, and for me, United owe those two big time.'

Gerrard accepted that his team might have been responsible for Nemanja missing out on the awards front; that the Torres runaround that depressing day for Vidić and Co. in March 2009 might well have contributed.

The Kop skipper told the Sunday People: 'Maybe it's been a bit harsh on Vidić. I still voted for him in the PFA Awards and, if I'd had a Football Writers' vote, I would have voted for him again, because he has had a magnificent season.

'Possibly, he's been judged because of the incident against us at Old Trafford when he didn't deal with the ball and Fernando [Torres] scored. Maybe that's gone against him for both awards. He's still had a great season and it's just unfortunate – but maybe I have to thank Fernando for this award!'

Vidić was still headline news even as he prepared to leave Old Trafford for his summer holidays in June 2009. Real Madrid, under new president Florent Perez, were willing to splash out major sums as they set about rebuilding after a period of ignominy. The Brazilian Kaka, of AC Milan, and United's Ronaldo, were clearly their main targets.

But someone mentioned to Perez that it wasn't just in attack where Real had been suffering: no, the defence wasn't much cop either. Perez, the man responsible for the Galactico days at the Bernabeu (when he tried to sign all the biggest names in world football) simply shrugged, scratched his head and said: 'Well, maybe I should try to sign Vidić, then? After all, he is the best defender in the world, isn't he?'

He discussed the idea of offering United a world-record fee for a defender of £35 million, but was shot down immediately by Nemanja and his agent Silvano Martina. The agent – who also represents Juventus keeper Gianluigi Buffon –, when quizzed over the possibility of a move to Real or Inter Milan, who were also courting the Serbian, stressed that Vidić would definitely be staying with United.

Martina said: 'There are no prerequisites for Vidić leaving Manchester. Despite the Champions League final loss, he is at a great club with much ambition, and which has reached the final of the greatest European competition for two consecutive years. This season, he also won the Premier League.'

And there you have it: Nemanja Vidić, red through and through. A United idol, terrace hero and defender supreme. The man who, with Rio Ferdinand, put the heart of steel back in Manchester United's defence – but the new Steve Bruce? Well, let's tie up some loose ends now by taking a look at how he and Ferdinand measure up as a partnership to the revered Bruce and Gary Pallister.

Chapter 12

RIO GRAND

BY 2009 Vidić had grown accustomed to being hailed as one part of the best United central defensive pairing since the halcyon 1990s era of former skipper Steve Bruce and his solid as a rock partner Gary Pallister. But just how good was the Vidić-Ferdinand partnership? Was it as good or better than the Bruce-Pally link-up, perhaps the best of all-time at Old Trafford? Well, we'll take a closer look and try to find some answers.

First, let's put forward the candidates who could rival Rio and Nemanja. After consultations with United 'anorak' and fanatic Andy Bucklow – who has followed the Red Devils since the sixties and is a renowned commentator, thanks to his work on *The Mail on Sunday* – we whittled the list down to four partnerships, from the 1970s to the present day: Martin Buchan and Jim Holton in the seventies, Kevin Moran and Paul McGrath in the eighties, Pallister and Bruce in the nineties and Jaap Stam and Henning Berg in the early noughties.

Trying to pick out a partnership prior to the Seventies is nigh on impossible for the simple reason that they didn't really have them. You would, of course, draft the likes of Jackie Blanchflower, Mark Jones and Duncan Edwards into your list of top centre halves of the fifties and Bill Foulkes in the sixties, but they never played in defined partnerships as such. Indeed, the legendary Jones and Blanchflower would battle each other for the right to be known as United's centre-half from 1950 to 1958. It was one or the other in the team, not both together.

You might argue that either man, when selected, would win the ball and lay it off to the great Duncan Edwards or Eddie Colman – with either of the two half-backs then taking play forwards – but they weren't solid defenders lumped together at the heart of the defence.

The case of Jones and Blanchflower was all the more interesting as it threw two of the closest friends imaginable into a direct rivalry for the one starting line-up spot. Indeed, Blanchflower was the best man at Jones' wedding. But that did not stop them from competing fiercely for the one centre-back role in the team. Blanchflower won the nod from Matt Busby to start in the 1957 FA Cup Final, but Jones had regained the No. 5 shirt in the game against Red Star Belgrade in the former Yugoslavia – which directly preceded the Munich air disaster – a year later.

Jones, who was born near Barnsley in South Yorkshire in 1933, signed for United in 1948 and made his debut in the home League game against Sheffield Wednesday on 7 October 1950. Initially, he was understudy to Allenby Chilton, but became a fixture in the first team in United's 1955–56 Championship season. In the next campaign, he lost his place to the emerging Blanchflower but reclaimed it for the 1957–58 campaign.

The big stopper died in the Munich air disaster of 6 February 1958 – one of the eight players who would lose their lives as a result of the plane crash at the German city airport, having played his last game in that European Cup quarter-final draw against Red Star.

Blanchflower, like Jones, was born in 1933, but he was Northern Irish, from Belfast. His first appearance as a pro for United was in November 1951, against Liverpool, at Anfield. He helped the club to two League titles during the 1950s. Blanchflower was also in the squad against Red Star that fated February day in 1958. When the plane crashed after stopping to re-fuel in Munich, he was trapped inside the wreckage and owed his life to team-mate Harry Gregg, who dragged him out to safety.

He had survived, but his career would not. His injuries – fractured pelvis, broken arms and ribs and crushed kidneys – meant that he would never play again. His short career was over at the tender age of 24. He left United in June 1959 and became an accountant, dying in 1998 of cancer – the second of the players to have survived the Munich tragedy to pass away, the first being Johnny Berry in 1994.

Ten years later, United would achieve a kind of redemption

for Busby when they won the European Cup for the first time, beating Benfica 4-1 at Wembley Stadium. The manager had felt a personal sense of responsibility for the tragedy as it had been he who insisted United needed to be British pioneers by playing against European opposition when the English FA had not been enamoured with the idea. After the match, Busby would admit: 'The moment when Bobby [Charlton] took the Cup cleansed me. It eased the pain of the guilt of going into Europe [brought about by the Munich air disaster]. It was my justification.'

Similar to Jones in Belgrade in 1958, big Bill Foulkes would have no defined central-half partner as United roared to glory over the Portuguese outfit in 1968. Foulkes and Bobby Charlton both starred at Wembley – they were the only survivors from Munich to play in the match.

Foulkes himself was as adept at playing right-back as centre-half. He would always declare himself happier when he was in the heart of the defence, but equally would knuckle down at full-back, if that was Busby's particular request.

Big Bill, who was born in 1932, had been at the club for 18 years when United finally lifted the European Cup. He made his debut away at Liverpool in 1952 and would go on to make 688 appearances before leaving in June 1970. Like Jones and Blanchflower a decade earlier, he was a one-man rock and stopper at the heart of the defence – and like them, he also enjoyed keeping it simple, passing to one of the half-backs so they could take up the play.

By the seventies, football tactics were evolving and teams

started to play with four defenders across the back as the 4-4-2 system came into being. I followed United at every match home and away from 1973 to 1978, and it was during that time that my own favourite centre-back pairing was established: Jim Holton and Martin Buchan. Of course, I am not arguing that they were in any way the best – in fact, they would probably not get into the top five. But for sheer entertainment mixed with brute effort (Holton) and classy mopping-up (Buchan), they were the business – a true beauty and the beast pairing.

Buchan joined the club in 1972 and made 456 appearances before leaving in 1983. He was skipper of the emerging Tommy Docherty team that was relegated in 1973–74, but won promotion a year later and secured the FA Cup in 1977. In doing so, Buchan became the first man to captain a side to both FA Cup and Scottish FA Cup success – he had also won the cup north of the border with Aberdeen in 1970, who, eight years after that cup win, would eventually be managed by Alex Ferguson.

Buchan was such a cultured centre-half and he reminded me of a sergeant major as he kept his troops in line – once cuffing winger Gordon Hill's ears for not marking on a throw-in. Disciplined and articulate, he did not suffer fools gladly – on another occasion when asked for a 'quick word' by a journalist, he answered, with a straight face, 'Velocity'.

He was United's most influential player as he helped Docherty set up a team that was both swashbuckling in its entertainment and, another essential prerequisite for Old Trafford fans, winners. His vision on the pitch allowed the Doc to rip apart an ageing bunch to replace them with a young, hungry group, who wanted to win – and win in style. He was the backbone that enabled the Doc to carry out such aggressive surgery on a United that had fallen into disarray at the fag end of the Busby/McGuinness/O'Farrell era. True, he was signed by Frank O'Farrell, but it was under the Doc that he blossomed as a United great.

No wonder Doc made him his captain. I loved watching Buchan as he swept up any loose balls and then sprayed passes all over the park. He was like United's Beckenbauer in those giddy days under Docherty.

In Buchan's 11 years at Old Trafford he made 458 appearances, scoring four goals, and played 34 times for Scotland, including two World Cups, in 1974 and 1978.

Big Jim Holton would be his centre-back partner for a relatively short time at Old Trafford as injury devastated what had looked like being a great career in the red of United. Buchan would also go on to establish reputable centre-half pairings with Brian Greenhoff and Gordon McQueen – the latter another fine Scottish defender. But it was with Holton that I will always remember Martin and I am convinced had injury not struck him down, Big Jim would have become a true Old Trafford legend instead of just a Stretford End cult hero.

'Six foot two, eyes of blue, big Jim Holton's after you,' United fans would sing as the huge, raw-edged lad from Scotland roared on to the pitch on Saturday afternoons. After a period of uncertainty and instability at the club, he was just what the Doc ordered. There he was, larger-than-life and full of character and charisma – and one of Doc's first signings. Holton had a toothless, innocent smile that would have charmed yer gran, but a thundering, raw aggression that would scare the opposition to death. He helped Doc wipe away the cobwebs of despair and complacency that had built up around the club: he was a big, fresh, tough new beginning. Just what United needed – a real tonic for the troops.

Born in 1951, Holton joined United from Shrewsbury Town for £84,444 as part of Doc's dramatic surgery plan. He made his debut at home to West Ham on 23 January 1973 in the 2-2 Division One draw and scored his first goal for the club, just two matches later, in the 1-1 League draw at Coventry. On 17 March 1973, he scored another in the 2-1 home League win over Newcastle and grabbed his third goal in his first season at United in the 2-0 triumph away at Southampton.

He was bedding in well alongside Buchan and helped United beat the drop as they finished 18th that season.

The following campaign he developed his partnership with the skipper but this was not enough to stop United crashing through the relegation trap door as they finished 21st – with only 10 wins and 38 goals scored. In the League Cup they had reached only the second round and their FA Cup campaign ended in the fourth round.

Big Jim claimed another two goals that season – in the 2-1 home Division One win over QPR on 1 September 1973 and the

3-3 League home draw with Burnley on 3 April 1974. In that match he grabbed the second goal, in between successful efforts from Alex Forsyth and Sammy McIlroy.

In the summer of 1974, he went on to play a stirring role in Scotland's World Cup campaign. Big Jim played in all three Group games for his country and helped them stay unbeaten. They would win 2-0 against Zaire and draw twice – a fabulous 0-0 against then world champions Brazil and a 1-1 with Yugoslavia. But bad luck would cost Jim and Scotland dearly: they were eliminated from the competition on goal difference.

It was a cruel quirk of fate, but Holton – who would win a total of 15 caps with Scotland – was raring to go for what would turn out to be his second and final full season at United. He did not get on to the score sheets in the 1974–75 campaign, but success was his and United's as they stormed back to the top-flight. Yet it was all tinged with fear and darkness for in December 1974 he broke his leg against Sheffield Wednesday, his future club. The match was a belter – a 4-4 draw with end-to-end action – but it would be remembered for Jim's misfortune, too.

Previously in that campaign Holton and Buchan's partnership had been a marvel to behold as they propelled United towards the Second Division crown. Jim threw himself into every challenge as if his very life depended upon it, like a prototype of Vidić, while Martin was tidying up after his excesses.

United won the title with 61 points from a campaign in which they had suffered just seven defeats, and scored 66 goals in 42 matches. Docherty continued to strengthen his new team by bringing in Stuart Pearson from Hull and Steve Coppell from Tranmere Rovers.

United would build on their promotion-winning season. In 1975–76, their first season back in the top flight, they would finish third behind champions Liverpool, losing nine matches, but scoring 68 goals. They would also reach the final of the FA Cup, where they would surprisingly lose 1-0 to Second Division Southampton.

But Jim Holton would not enjoy the season at all. He had been hoping to cement his position alongside Martin Buchan and push on to further honours with United and Scotland – yet by the end of the campaign his career at United was effectively over.

It was a remarkably cruel turnaround for the man who was on the brink of becoming an all-time United legend. For Jim, it all started to go wrong with that broken leg in December 1974. Then, in perhaps what would be an omen of the tough times ahead, he was sent off in United's 3-0 1975 pre-season win over Danish side Halskov as Lou Macari scored two goals and Gerry Daly grabbed the other.

Worse would soon follow, with what was certainly an unlucky 13 for Holton. On the comeback trail in the reserves – on 13 September 1975 – he broke his leg again and this time, it was all over for him at United.

In his absence, a homegrown youngster would prosper and take his place. Brian Greenhoff was to go on to form a new partnership with Martin Buchan and when he had recovered from his broken leg, Holton could not displace him. Big Jim had made 72 appearances for United, scoring six goals.

Unable to command a first-team place, Holton left the club to join Sunderland in 1976 and then Coventry, but more injury setbacks wrecked his hopes of carving out a career elsewhere. By the time he had arrived at his final club, Sheffield Wednesday, his fitness was so dubious that he never played a senior match.

It was a rotten end to a career that had promised so much and so cruel to a man who had become a hero on the Stretford End – and looked to have a glittering, trophy-laden future in front of him. In the end, he was beaten by the bell as the injuries destroyed him.

Tragically, Holton died at just 42 in 1993, after suffering a heart attack at the wheel of his car. But he would never be forgotten for his exploits at United. He would be remembered with fondness by the club's fans and, with hindsight, it is easy to see why some view him as an early version of Nemanja Vidić – such was his outstanding bravery, commitment and ability to nip in with vital goals.

As we have noted, Martin Buchan would also go on to forge effective partnerships with Greenhoff and Gordon McQueen, but let's now look at the key centre-back pairing of the eighties, Kevin Moran and Paul McGrath.

For me, their most memorable outing was the 1985 FA Cup final – when United beat Everton 1-0 after extra-time, with an 110th-minute winner from Norman Whiteside. As well as celebrating victory, it was also the infamous match in which Moran became the first player to be sent off in an FA Cup final. TV footage later proved that he had gone for the ball, not Peter Reid, in the offending tackle and he was then presented with the winner's medal that had at first been withheld.

He and McGrath repelled everything that a spirited Everton attack – spearheaded by Andy Gray and Graeme Sharp – had thrown at them, and it was an inauspicious end to proceedings for Big Kev. The Irishman had joined United in 1978, after an outstanding career as a Gaelic footballer. Like Holton and Vidić, he became renowned for his bravery at Old Trafford and was known as 'Captain Blood' because of the head wounds he suffered.

Coincidentally, in 2008 the former Arsenal and Scotland striker Charlie Nicholas, now a TV pundit, would offer a modern-day version of Vidić as a 'Captain Blood', saying he 'had more scars than Al Pacino'! Nicholas would add: 'Vidić has got more scars than any other centre-back in the country – that's why he is the finest.'

Like Vidić and Holton, Moran was a fearless stopper and a blocker, who would think nothing of putting his head in where others would have put their feet. He also helped United win the FA Cup in 1983 – partnering McQueen at the back – when they crushed Brighton 4-0 in a replay, after drawing the first match 2-2.

Moran made 290 appearances for United, scoring 24 goals before joining Spain's Sporting Gijon in 1988.

As he played the warrior Vidić role in the 1980s, so was his partner, Paul McGrath, a less polished version of Rio Ferdinand. Ultimately, neither as talented nor as successful as Rio, nonetheless he had the ability to play football with the ball – rather than merely launch it into the stands, as was sometimes Moran's way. McGrath joined the club in 1982 and left seven years later as part of new boss Alex Ferguson's 'clean-up'. Renowned for his drinking exploits, he did not fit into the strict Scot's philosophy of how footballers should live their lives, but Ferguson would be one of the first to admit the boy had a sweet left foot. He instinctively knew how to keep the ball, how to play it and how to punish the opposition with it – not bad attributes for a centre-half.

Like Moran, he learned his trade in Ireland, eventually being signed by the then United boss Ron Atkinson in 1982. For a time, Big Ron played him in midfield – which also explains why he was so cool on the ball when he moved into central defence. Indeed, in that FA Cup final of 1985, he was named Man of the Match for his excellence in limiting Everton's strikers after Moran was sent off.

After his fallout with Ferguson he was shown the door in 1989 – and went on to prove the United manager was wrong to say he was finished by playing some of the best football of his career over the next seven years at Aston Villa. In all, he made 163 appearances for United, scoring 12 goals – but went on to play 252 times for Villa.

To rub salt into the wound, at Villa McGrath won the PFA

Player of the Year Award in the 1992–93 season and his first Villa trophy a year later as they won the League Cup final 3-1 by beating... Manchester United!

On to the next decade, and the arrival of another great central defender, the brilliant Jaap Stam, commonly known as a one-man defence, such was his 'thou shalt not pass' talent. So strong, a natural ball-winner and with a top footballing brain, he earned the 'one-man defence' accolade from fellow Dutch legend Johan Cruyff.

Stam joined United in 1998 from Dutch club PSV Eindhoven, becoming the then most expensive defender in the world at £10.6 million. Over the next three years at Old Trafford, he was also arguably the best defender in the world. Certainly, in my opinion he is, along with Vidić and Ferdinand, the best defender to grace Old Trafford in the modern era. He would prove his worth by helping the club to three Premier League crowns, one FA Cup, the Intercontinental Cup and the Champions League.

During his tenure, he had two main partners at the back – Ronny Johnsen and Henning Berg. Boss Ferguson did not seem bothered who played with Stam, as long as the Dutchman played. Describing how he chose the United central-defence pairing, he once said: 'Jaap Stam – plus another.'

I rated Berg the better of the two – and the most effective with Stam – but it would be Johnsen who would line up with the big Dutchman in United's defining match of the nineties, the 1999 European Cup final against Bayern Munich. That unforgettable night in Barcelona, Stam proved to be the veritable rock as United triumphed 2-1 after being 1-0 down at 90 minutes.

Johnsen joined United in 1996 and stayed for six years, making 99 appearances and scoring eight goals. Berg spent three years at Old Trafford from 1997 – he was the more natural defender than Johnsen and seemed to me to link better with the Dutchman.

In 2001 Stam joined Lazio for £16 million, winning the Italian Cup, before moving to Milan. In 2006 he returned to Holland with Ajax, winning the Dutch Cup and two Dutch Super Cups. He had made 79 appearances for United and scored one goal.

It was claimed Sir Alex had sold him because he was angry at allegations made by Stam in his autobiography, Head-to-Head, about himself and the club. Laurent Blanc was signed as his replacement – a terrible folly... how could a burnt-out, over-the-hill man replace the best defender in the world? Of course, he couldn't and United would suffer as a consequence.

In fairness to Ferguson, however, he has since admitted he made a big mistake in selling Stam. In January 2009, he said with regret: 'At the time he had just come back from an achilles injury and we thought he had just lost a little bit. We got the offer from Lazio – £16.5m for a centre-back who was 29. It was an offer I couldn't refuse, but in playing terms it was a mistake.'

And so on to the pairing rated best at United before Vidić

and Ferdinand – the rock-solid, rock-steady combo of Dolly and Daisy, better known as Steve Bruce and Gary Pallister. In terms of individual talent and skill, I would contend that neither is in the same league as Jaap Stam, or even Martin Buchan from the seventies, but as a bread and butter combo they were simply outstanding.

Both were hard men, who went into battle without a moment's thought for their own welfare. Brucey, in particular, suffered several bloody noses for his contribution to the United cause. They did not have the finesse of a Ferdinand or a Stam, but they knew each other's game inside out and knew what they both needed to do and when they should do it. Their success was built upon hard work and application to a winning formula devised between themselves and United's coaches.

For eight years, they played together as a partnership and won three Premier League titles (1993, 1994 and 1996), plus the 1992 League Cup, the FA Cup in 1990, 1994 and 1996, and the European Cup Winners' Cup in 1991.

Steve Bruce arrived at United for £825,000 in December 1987 as a raw, rough and ready centre-back from Norwich City. In all, he would go on to make 414 appearances for the club, scoring 51 goals. He is similar to Vidić in terms of the vital goals he scored – and 51 in 414 games for a centre-back is not bad going! Like Nemanja, he had that ability to pop up and head the ball home when the team needed it most.

Probably his most famous goal – certainly my favourite and the one myself and thousands of others always tend to associate with him – was the winner against Sheffield Wednesday in 1993. On 10 April that year, United were within striking distance of the first top-flight title in 26 years but with just four minutes to go, they were 1-0 down against the Owls at Old Trafford.

John Sheridan's goal just after the hour sent the partisan crowd into silence. Would the long, long wait for that title continue? Cometh the hour, cometh the power – in the shape of two thunderbolt headers from skipper Bruce, the man who had taken the captaincy in the absence of the lionheart who appeared constantly injury-jinxed: Bryan Robson. Famously, Bruce's second arrived seven minutes into injury-time (and sparked the even more memorable touchline celebrations from then assistant manager Brian Kidd).

It was a defining goal and a forever-defining image in the history of Manchester United FC – and it was all down to the heroics and vision of Stevie Bruce.

He had made his Manchester United debut in a 2–1 win over Portsmouth on 19 December 1987 and played in 21 of United's remaining 22 League fixtures – helping the club to a top-two place in the First Division for the first time since 1980.

The following season, the team could only finish mid-table, however, and boss Ferguson decided more new blood was needed to turn United around. In particular, he wanted a partner to bed down with Brucey at the back and so he turned to Middlesbrough's towering centre-half Gary Pallister to solve the problem. It had taken 18 months for United's network of scouts to identify Pally as the man who could best compliment Brucey – he was a big, powerful, no-frills, traditional English centre-half and would go on to make 438 appearances for United up until his departure from the club in July 1998.

But the man who would finally steady a rocky Reds defence with Bruce would not come cheap. Boro were reluctant to part with him at all and it took a then British record fee of £2.3 million for them to let Pallister walk away.

He was a top-class defender and even his fellow players realised as much – voting him their Player of the Year in 1992. With Brucey, he formed such an effective partnership that in 2006 United skipper Gary Neville felt strongly enough to claim it was United's best ever. Neville told The Times that he knew he would never make it as a first-choice central defender at the club because of their combined talent, saying: 'I switched from midfield to centre-back, but we had United's best-ever partnership in Steve Bruce and Gary Pallister.'

Though Pally would not be as prolific a goalscorer as Brucey, he would also grab one that he would one day be able to tell the grandchildren about: it came in the 1992–93 season – just a month after Brucey's brilliant double against Sheffield Wednesday.

In the final home game of the season against local rivals Blackburn, Pally made his mark in stoppage time, slamming a free kick into the bottom corner of the goal from the edge of the penalty area. That was his first goal of the season and it couldn't have come at a better time. It made it 3-1 to a triumphant

United – who could now go about the business of celebrating their first title since 1967 in front of their own fans.

While Pallister would play for England on 22 occasions, Brucey was never picked for his country, much to the amazement of Alex Ferguson and his United team-mates. True, he did gain eight England youth caps and, in 1987, was selected to captain England B against the full national team of Malta, but he never made the first team. Pallister, meanwhile, had even represented his country when at Middlesbrough, one of the rare occasions when a player did so while plying his trade outside the top-flight.

Bruce has since been rightly described as one of the best defenders of his era never to be selected for the full England team and he would admit his disappointment, saying: 'I bumped into former England manager Bobby Robson at Benfica. He came up to me and said, "I should have capped you." It was nice to hear, but it still didn't get me one... I'll always be a little disappointed I didn't get one.'

As has been pointed out already, neither Bruce nor Pallister were as good as Vidić or Ferdinand individually, but as a partnership they were of a similar level. Each covered for the other and encouraged the other – just as Nemanja's arrival helped Rio become a better player because he was able to concentrate on his own game rather than worrying about his co-centre-half – and both Bruce and Pally had a similar solid, dependable and honest nature.

Brucey, in particular, had the same heart and bravery as Vidić

– he was willing to similarly suffer for the United cause (indeed he even returned to the team at short notice in 1992 while struggling with hernia problems).

In December 2007 Sir Alex summed up the beauty of the beast that was Stevie Bruce when asked about whether Wayne Rooney had leadership qualities that might one day propel him to United's captaincy. Ferguson said: 'Some of the qualities he has are similar to two or three of our captains in the past. Like Steve Bruce, Bryan Robson and Roy Keane, he has got determination and heart and sometimes these are the qualities that can influence the team.'

Determination and heart – those are most certainly two characteristics that link Steve Bruce and Nemanja Vidić as central defensive bedfellows, even a decade apart from each other. As is the way they forged such a successful partnership with their respective co-centre-halves, Pallister and Ferdinand.

Since hanging up his boots, Bruce has become a top-class manager in the Premier League while Pallister has tried his hand as a TV analyst.

Brucey knows a good thing when he sees it, as shown by his comments on the Ferdinand-Vidić partnership. He said: 'Defensively, they are rock-solid. It would be wrong for me to make comparisons – I'll let other people do that – but you can see they are two excellent, excellent players and they do look as if they complement each other.

'You need a goalkeeper, too, and van der Sar's not bad. But looking from the outside, the thing that helps them is that they play every week, and you want that from your goalkeeper and centre-backs. They are a really good pairing.'

Rio joined United from Leeds in July 2002 for £29 million, a world record fee for a defender. It did not seem good business as, like Vidić, he struggled to settle in at Old Trafford and justify the massive outlay but by the time this biography went to the printers, he had turned that around dramatically – as emphasised by the honours he has since won at United: four Premier Leagues, one Champions Leagues, two League Cups and a Club World Cup.

Yet it is undeniable that he also suffered from errors of character and judgement. Most famous was the missed drugs test in 2003 – when he claimed he 'forgot' and went shopping instead. But that would not be the end of it: he was banned for eight months by the FA and missed out on Euro 2004 with the English national team.

Then he blundered further by following up a worthy campaign against knife crime by saluting a United goal by pretending to fire a rocket launcher into the crowd. And, just before the 2006 World Cup, he hosted Rio's World Cup Wind-Ups on TV, in which he played silly pranks on team-mates like David Beckham and Wayne Rooney. But since Vidić settled in at United – he admitted he didn't feel 'part of it' until the start of the 2006–07 season – Rio seems to have also settled and grown up.

Maybe even he would admit the man from Serbia has had a profound effect on him, both on and off the pitch. The two are undoubtedly good for each other. There is no doubt at all that

Vidić has helped Ferdinand become a better player at United. Rio is exceptional; classy, intelligent with his use of the ball and with a wonderful sense of defensive anticipation but he had been prone to losing his concentration over the years – he can be a bit of a daydreamer at times. It is as if he is thinking about something else, maybe worrying about something other than football when he sometimes gets caught napping by a surprise ball floated in or an unannounced attacking solo foray by an opposing forward.

Before Vidić, those lapses often proved costly – but since Nemanja's arrival, not so much. Why? Because of Vidić's ability to mop up and prevent the opposition from profiting from the lapses – he is a wonderful sweeper in that sense; he sweeps up Rio's (admittedly, less frequent nowadays) mistakes.

United goalkeeping legend Peter Schmeichel puts it this way: 'Vidić's displays in the last two years are second to none. Ferdinand is the best defender in the world but he's learned a lot from Vidić.'

The Danish giant, who played behind Bruce and Pallister, also reckons Vidić and Ferdinand could prove a better partnership, if they stick together over the long-term. 'I definitely see similarities,' said Schmeichel. 'I loved playing behind those two, and Rio and Vidić are on a par with them. Brucey had great heart and Pallister was superb on the ball. You can see similar traits in Rio and Vidić. For me, Vidić has been the key to the defence and he's made Rio into a top-class player.'

It helps that Nemanja and Rio are good friends off the pitch, as well as on it. They frequently dine together with their families and room together when United play abroad. In fact, Nemanja has admitted it was to Rio's native neighbourhood that he turned when he wanted to better his mastery of the English language – but with hilarious results.

Vidić said: 'Rio and I have a great partnership and we are good mates. It was difficult when I first came here because my English was not so good, but now it's much better. I didn't learn English at school. I learned from movies and TV programmes with Serbian subtitles – but I listened to the English. That meant I already had a few words when I came here.

'I watched all kinds of shows, like Only Fools and Horses, which was so funny but it helped me to understand the language. It was funny to learn that Rio was from the area where the programme is set.'

He also watched English games on TV in Serbia, which meant he was well aware of the history of Manchester United – and what their demanding fans expected of the players who donned the famous red shirts.

He added: 'I used to watch the games on TV back home so I know all about the players who have been at United for the past 15 years. I am proud to follow those players. Of course I heard about Pallister and Bruce, and I know it was a big partnership that won trophies here. But I didn't watch them especially and I only found out how much they were appreciated when I came to the club.

'I'm very glad when people compare me and Rio to such good players. It's obviously a very big compliment. We have such a great team here, but my first priority is to make sure we do our best to defend properly as we have good players up front.

'Last year I scored maybe five goals, this year just one, so I want to continue improving that part of my game and score more. Rio has done well and scored more this season in Europe and the Premier League and we need the goals from defenders.'

Vidić is the first to admit he owes much to Ferdinand – that the England international helped him settle after a tricky start at United and that he has helped him improve his own game. And he believes their partnership is now so good it is almost on a telepathic level. Nemanja said: 'Rio is a great player and I am really glad to be in the same defence as him. He is such a cool player, such an instinctively great defender. We know each other really well – we know where each other are on the pitch and we know what movements the other one is going to make. That has to be important and so far things have gone really well.'

Of course, the opinion that most matters on the relative worth of the Rio-Nemanja axis as opposed to Pallister-Bruce lies with the man who bossed them all. Of Vidić, Sir Alex Ferguson says: 'As I keep pointing out, good defenders win you things. In my time, we've had people like Bruce, Pallister, Paul Parker, Denis Irwin, Ronnie Johnsen and Jaap Stam. Vidić is really natural and really athletic.

'I know you need good defenders and that is exactly what this lad is. He is a quick and aggressive centre-half.'

Fergie was quick to point to Vidić's bravery after a pre-season trip to Ireland in 2007. During the match against Glentoran, Nemanja had to leave the field after an accidental clash of heads with an opposing forward. Ferguson had been amazed by the fact that as he walked toward the dugout, his player was smiling and laughing. The boss said at the time: 'Five stitches. Smiling. Aye, he was delighted. Big Pally [Gary Pallister] would have been crying. Pally was always concerned about ruining his "good looks". Then, in his last season, he broke his nose for the first time – he said he was going to sue me.'

Ferguson said that Pallister reminded him of Ferdinand and that Vidić was almost a double for Steve Bruce. 'He's got qualities like Bruce,' said the United manager. 'Brucey would stick his head in and ask the question of the opponent, "Do you want to get hurt? I'm going to put my head in there. If you want to get the ball, you're going to have to put your head in front of mine." Of course he'd lost his looks long ago. He's like Bernard Cribbins now! The hair's going white.'

Great stuff from the boss man, but perhaps we should leave the final word on the Vidić-Ferdinand partnership to another Scot, a man who is arguably the finest journalist of his generation and one of the few to have unfettered access to Sir Alex. Hugh McIlvanney is my colleague at *The Sunday Times*. Certainly, he is one of the best analysts of footballers and their various faults and attributes. He described the partnership in these terms: 'The Londoner's swift fluency of movement, calculated positioning and technical range give him a graceful mastery of the arts of containment and frustration that scarcely any contemporary centre-back can rival. But all that sophistication increases dramatically in value if it is complemented by the simpler (though unmistakably exceptional) skills and physical power, the combative bravery and threat-devouring energy of Vidić.

'Whereas Ferdinand invariably presents the appearance of a comprehensively gifted footballer who happens to have developed his career as a defender, Vidić looks like somebody born with a love of defending, with a temperament that finds fulfilment in repelling sieges and surviving crises. He is one of a rare, but recognisable breed. Jamie Carragher has long been a classic representative and so is John Terry, although there are worrying signs of diminishment through wear and tear on his body.

'As with Terry, Vidić's innate commitment to defending doesn't prevent him from being notably capable of scoring the occasional goal, usually, again like Terry, by dint of fearless competitiveness in the air. But such men leave us in no doubt that at heart they are gamekeepers, and we should cherish their enthusiasm for jobs which, like that of the goalkeeper, too often involve exposure to lop-sided apportioning of blame and acclaim.'

Beautifully put, Hugh – a fine summary of how the two men

at the heart of United's defence so wonderfully compliment each other. Vidić and Ferdinand: the new Bruce and Pallister. Only better...

Let's now conclude our examination of Vidić the footballer and Vidić the phenomenon by taking a look at his international career – one that would be full of hope, typical aggression and determination, but also one that would be surprisingly underachieving as 2010 dawned.

Chapter 13
NATIONAL SERVICE

A S A BOY, Nemanja Vidić's dream was to play at the very top of world football – at both club and international level. He told his brother Dusana that he would one day be captain of a big football club, and also of the national side. By the time this book went to press, he had, of course, achieved the first part of his dream – by skippering Red Star – but the second was still to materialise with Serbia.

Yet, he had been tantalisingly close to achieving it in what would have been the most remarkable circumstances... in the first-ever international match for Serbia as an independent nation. Previously, the country had played under two different banners in its history – as part of Yugoslavia and Serbia and Montenegro.

Known as Yugoslavia until 4 February 2003, and then as Serbia and Montenegro until 3 June 2006, it became known simply as Serbia when independence as the successor state to the former union of Serbia and Montenegro was declared. The team was officially renamed the Serbia national football team on 28 June 2006, while the Montenegro national football team was created to represent the new state of Montenegro.

It was sheer bad luck that prevented Vidić from collecting the honour of leading out Serbia in their debut national match against the Czech Republic in Uherske Hradiste on 16 August 2006. Nemanja missed out with injury and Dejan Stanković of Inter Milan profited, leading the team to a 3-1 win in the international friendly.

Spaniard Javier Clemente had just been appointed boss of Serbia and he explained how he had been hoping to put Vidić in the skipper role – and how he understood the importance of the match for the new nation, despite his Spanish heritage. Clemente said it was a brand new start and that he wanted to celebrate that with the introduction of new players and a new impetus.

He revealed that he would need a new captain as former skipper Savo Milošević had declared he no longer wanted to be part of the international set-up after collecting 101 caps. Clemente – who also told how the team would be wearing a new kit of red shirts, blue shorts and white socks and would sing a new anthem to celebrate independence – said: 'I know every Serbian is proud and I am too. It is normal to be excited at these moments and we will try to make a good impression.

'I had planned to make Vidić the leader of this team and I was planning him to be the captain of this representation, as he has experience from Manchester United. Unfortunately, he is still recovering from his injury.'

It had been as part of the previous national football regime that Nemanja had really started to make his name. He was an integral player in the Serbia and Montenegro so-called 'Famous Four' defence that conceded just one goal during the 10 matches the team played to qualify for the World Cup of 2006. Vidić played alongside Mladen Krstajić, Ivica Dragutinović and Goran Gavrančić in the Scrooge of a backline that set a new record for the fewest goals conceded as they finished above Spain to top their group. Cruelly, having done the hard work in helping his country get to the finals in Germany, Nemanja then missed out on the finals through injury, but more of that and the qualifying campaign itself later.

A Yugoslavian youth international, Vidić also starred for the Under-21s. In 2002, aged 20, he came up against England for the first time as the Yugoslav U21s played at Bolton's Reebok Stadium that September. It would be an interesting introduction to football English-style for Vidić – he and his team-mates would come away from the North West with a 1-1 draw.

They had gone ahead after 41 minutes, thanks to Danko Lazović's brilliant solo effort. The Partizan Belgrade striker took the ball in his own half and raced through to lash it past Chris Kirkland into the England goal.

Shaun Wright-Phillips equalised with 10 minutes remaining for his first international goal, but Vidić and Co. left with their heads held high. Nemanja had dominated the compact, but dangerous England forward line of Jermain Defoe and Francis Jeffers and the visitors had demonstrated much more flair and imagination.

Vidić also showed his skills at the opposing end of the pitch, almost scoring with just five minutes on the clock. In what would become a common sight when he joined Manchester United four years later, he got his head on the end of a cross from Igor Matić, only to be denied by a wondersave from Kirkland.

It would have been a sensational goal and he was disappointed afterwards, but not downcast. No, he said the effort had settled him down early in the match and had given him the confidence to believe in himself as a player of international stature. To earn a draw against an England team, which included 10 players with Premier League experience, was not to be sniffed at.

Clearly, he had made a major impression, for just two months after his powerful showing against England, Nemanja made his debut for the full Yugoslavian national side in the Euro 2004 qualifier against the Italians on 12 October 2002. The match ended 1-1 – an encouraging result in Naples and Vidić would now become a regular in the side.

Initially, he would suffer disappointment as they failed to reach Euro 2004, finishing third in Group 9 behind winners Italy and runners-up Wales. Four days after the draw in Naples,

Yugoslavia played as an international team for the final time, beating Finland 2-0 at home.

Their next Euro 2004 qualifier would see Vidić turning out for Serbia and Montenegro on 12 February 2003, but it would bring a poor result: a 2-2 draw at home in Podgorica with minnows Azerbaijan. It typified their campaign – topsy-turvy results with no stability or sense that they were settling down into a team who could be feared. The very same Azerbaijan had already lost 2-0 at home to Wales and 3-0 away in Finland.

Yet worse was to come in the sequence of qualifying games in 2003 after the changeover from Yugoslavia to Serbia and Montenegro. The team would lose 2-1 in Azerbaijan and 3-0 in Finland.

The loss in Azerbaijan was a crushing one, and the setback in Finland, on 7 June 2003, was also particularly disappointing for Nemanja and his team-mates as they had been determined to show the fans back home that the dire 2-2 home draw with Azerbaijan had been a one-off shocker.

It looked anything but that as the Finns set about them with a vengeance, bringing to an end their unbeaten record in the group. For Nemanja, it was especially painful as he was to blame for the final goal. In Helsinki's Olympic Stadium first-half strikes by Liverpool's Sami Hyypia and Joonas Kolkka, plus another after the break from Chelsea's Mikael Forssell, left the Serbians demoralised.

They also had Lazio midfield enforcer Sinisa Mihajlović sent off just before the half-hour mark for pushing Forssell in the back.

Vidić's misery was compounded when he allowed Forssell to turn him for the final goal, the hitman lashing the ball home low into the net. 'It was a bad day,' he would tell reporters after the defeat, 'We never looked like winning, we were not good enough.'

Four days earlier, he had stepped out on English soil as Serbia and Montenegro took on England in a friendly at Leicester in preparation for the Finland match. Again, he would suffer the bitter taste of defeat – but England, and Joe Cole and Wayne Rooney in particular, would not forget the abrasive, tough-tackling central defender in the opposing shirt. Vidić certainly left his mark at the Walkers Stadium.

England took the lead on 34 minutes when Steven Gerrard burst through from midfield, exchanged passes with Frank Lampard and Michael Owen, and then hammered the ball home. On the stroke of half-time, the visitors equalised, thanks to a toe-poke from Nenad Jestrović. But Sven Goran Eriksson's team won 2-1 after Joe Cole fired home a curling free kick with just 8 minutes remaining. Cole himself had won the free kick, teasing Vidić into hauling him down 20 yards from goal.

Some pundits claimed it was sweet revenge and just desserts on Vidić after he had snapped at the then West Ham star's heels all night. In fact, Cole was one of a staggering 21 substitutions during the 90 minutes.

Nemanja also had a rough-and-tumble introduction to the man who would become a valued team-mate at United, three years later: Wayne Rooney. The 17-year-old had emerged from the tunnel as a substitute and he and Vidić squared up almost from the start.

Nemanja later admitted he had 'very much enjoyed' the duel with the boy who was then a tough rival – and who would, three years later, became a valued team-mate at United. England boss Eriksson believed Wayne had handled himself well against such a tough, determined opponent as Vidić, saying: 'Of course Wayne has a lot to learn at 17 and maybe he has to look at his temperament, but the quality he has is incredible. You can't expect a 17-year-old boy to be a young man and be perfect in everything. When he gets the ball, things happen. I know he's a big hero with the fans. You never know what's going to happen, physically or mentally, and it's not easy being that famous when you're so young.

'But Wayne Rooney seems very confident and has kept his feet on the ground. I've not seen him change. We do talk, but not for very long – I think he's quite shy. If you're 17 and your national manager comes and wants to talk to you, it's not easy. I would never force him to do something like that.'

When asked about Vidić, the Swede smiled and said simply: 'Tough, never gives in, but fair. I like him.'

It was a nice compliment, one that made the journey back to the Continent a little more pleasant for Nemanja as he and his national team-mates headed for Finland. To lose to England in a friendly was not too bad – although he hated losing full stop – but the loss a few days later in Helsinki would go down as one of his worst experiences when playing for the national team.

One interesting sidenote of the defeat at Leicester was that among the England substitutes in the second half another big defender made his international debut that night... a certain John Terry. It is worth noting that Terry, who, of course, went on to captain his country and who is widely regarded as one of the best centre-backs in the world, was only just being introduced to the international stage.

In comparison, Vidić – who is 10 months younger than Terry – had already made a handful of international appearances since his debut the previous October. Comparisons would readily be made between the two players as the years went by, with many pundits considering them of equal worth and some viewing Nemanja as a Serbian version of Terry.

Indeed, respected Belgrade journalist Zoran Panjković would famously claim that he was a mixture of Terry and Rio Ferdinand. I would agree with Zoran's analysis, but believe Vidić is a better all-round player than Terry – and, crucially, much quicker to intercept and read the play.

Showing the other side of their inconsistent nature, Vidić and Co. would follow their defeats to England and Finland with much more respectable performances in their Euro 2004 qualifying campaign – namely a 1-1 draw at home with Italy and two fine wins over the Welsh at home (1-0) and away (3-2). But the late rally was not enough to get them to the finals of the tournament. Nemanja was understandably disappointed at missing out on what would have been his first major international tournament, but consoled himself with the fact that he was now a regular in the team and that, slowly but surely, the side was coming together.

After all, those creditable results in the 2003 section of their Euro 2004 qualifiers – the two wins over the Welsh and the home draw with the Italians – had been the final three results of the campaign.

Surely better times lay around the corner?

Of course they did – but, as we have already mentioned, with a cruel twist to the tale. Let's now take a look at how Vidić helped his country to the 2006 World Cup finals, only to be hit by a heartbreaking injury once they got there.

The story of Vidić's 2006 international odyssey began two years previously, when Serbia (then still Serbia and Montenegro) opened their qualifying campaign with an emphatic 3-0 win in San Marino on 4 August 2004. Given the terrible record of the country they were facing, nothing less might have been expected but hiccups often occur in the unpredictable world of football. Vidić and Co. were more than happy with the result, especially as they knew it was the start they needed, if they were to win the group outright. Before the match, boss Ilija Petković warned his players that they had to win – and win comfortably – as much tougher encounters awaited them against Spain, Bosnia and Herzegovina and Belgium.

There were six teams in Group 7 (Lithuania being the other) and Petković knew that his men would have to emerge as winners if they were to qualify automatically for the finals in Germany. Only the winners went through: the runners-up would be thrown into a play-off and wily Ilija did not fancy the lottery of pinning his hopes on a two-legged encounter that, given the nature of knockout football, could go either way.

No, he would much prefer going through in the comparative comfort zone of the group stage.

Zvonimir Vukić fired them ahead in San Marino and a brace from Nenad Jestrović ended the resistance of the part-timers. Vidić was booked: he had been his usual winner-takes-all self and received his caution for one tough tackle too many. Just because he was turning out against a group of part-timers did not mean he would take it easy! That was hardly part of the make-up of the man who was a born winner and a born perfectionist.

Petković's warning that there would be much tougher times ahead proved correct just five weeks later, when his men were held to a 0-0 draw in Sarajevo, the home of bitter rivals, Bosnia and Herzegovina. Nemanja had been injured playing club football and did not make the trip.

Petković declared himself happy with the result – two away matches to begin a tough campaign plus a draw and a win. 'That's a good start,' the manager said. 'If we maintain that form

– and win our home matches – we will be in contention to win the group.'

His theory seemed to be on the right track as the previous month their biggest rivals in the group, Spain, had also begun their campaign with a draw at the same venue (1-1). The Bosnians were clearly nobody's fool and, like Belgium, had no plans to simply make up the numbers in the group.

Nemanja was still not fit enough for the next match, four days later – what would turn out to be a walk in the park against San Marino in Belgrade. The hosts won 5-0 and it might have been more against one of the whipping boys of European international football. Savo Milošević opened the scoring and a goal by Ognjen Koroman and a brace from Dejan Stanković completed the inevitable rout.

The same night Spain dropped two valuable, and unexpected, points in Lithuania. It was starting to look good for Vidić and his team-mates – and, as the campaign continued, it would get even better.

In November 2004, they approached what would be the first real defining match of the campaign with a certain caution, but full of optimism and determination. Petković was grateful to have his big centre-half return for the clash in Belgium – and Vidić was to enjoy an immense game in the No. 5 shirt, repelling waves of attacks by the hosts. In a game that brought five cautions and might have had more, given the intensity of the commitment and the tackling, Nemanja was not even booked as the Serbs stormed to a 2-0 triumph.

The prolific Zvonimir Vukić and Mateja Kežman scored the goals emphasising that they and their countrymen meant business: no matter how good and highly-rated the Spaniards were, they were coming for them and they expected to pip them to top place in the group.

Four months later, the two would collide for the first time in Group 7 at Red Star Belgrade's ground. Though billed as the clash of the giants, it did not quite live up to expectations. Perhaps too much had been expected with another seven months and numerous games to go before qualification was assured or denied.

The match was a cagey, cautious affair with both defences coming out on top in a 0-0 draw in front of almost 49,000 partisan fans urging on the Serbs.

Nemanja performed well, keeping Fernando Torres – the man who, with Didier Drogba, would become his biggest adversary in the English Premier League, a couple of years later – at bay.

Over the years, Vidić and Torres would enjoy titanic struggles and this embryonic one proved to be no different, with Vidić just coming out on top as he prevented the big Spaniard from hitting the back of the net. Boss Petković declared himself happy with the outcome and praised his backline. He said: 'We did well against a team who are very good offensively. The defenders did their job and stood their ground. We are happy with the result – it keeps us on track for qualification against our biggest group rivals.'

It was Serbia's fifth match of the campaign – they were exactly halfway through. They had won 3 and drawn 2, but the goals for and against showed just how efficiently and effectively Vidić and his team-mates were going about their business. They had scored 10 and conceded none.

Whichever way you looked at it, Petković had created a team that was a force – both at the back and up front. At the time, Nemanja said: 'I am proud to be part of this team – we are hard to beat and solid at the back, but also dangerous up front. We believe we can beat Spain to the top spot in the group.'

Three months after that draw with the Spanish, the Serbs were back into battle again, this time against Belgium at home. Confidence was high, the team convinced to a man that they would collect another three points on their way to Germany. After all, they had already beaten the Belgians 2-0 in Brussels the previous November, hadn't they?

Such optimism sometimes leads to complacency and so it was in Belgrade on 4 June 2005. The match would end with the same result that the Serbs had achieved against Spain: 0-0. It was a letdown for the Serbs, but boss Petković refused to criticise his men. He knew they were still in the hunt for the single automatic qualification spot for Germany as the Spaniards had also dropped points along the way – drawing in Bosnia and Herzegovina and Lithuania.

But they would have to step up a gear for the remaining four games and would probably have to get a result in Spain in the group's crunch match in September, win their other matches and hope the Spaniards slipped up. After six games, both teams were neck-and-neck at the top with 12 points, although Serbia and Montenegro had the better goal difference.

Vidić had shone again against the Belgians, keeping the tricky Mbo Mpenza from causing any damage. Indeed the diminutive Mpenza would get so frustrated by his inability to get past Nemanja that he would be booked on 83 minutes and withdrawn a minute later.

Just four days after the demoralising draw with Belgium, Vidić and Co. earned themselves a vital breakthrough. The Spanish messed up, drawing 1-1 at home to Bosnia and Herzegovina. It was a shock result and, although Spain now topped the group by a point, they had played a game more. The scales were beginning to tilt towards Serbia, but they would need to beat Lithuania at home the following September, if the result in Valencia really was to mean anything.

The Serbs kept their nerve and won their game in hand 2-0 in Belgrade, with goals from Mateja Kežman and Saša Ilić. They were now in the driving seat and Vidić and his team-mates celebrated after the win that put them two points ahead of their nearest rivals at the top of Group 7. But they did not toast their good fortune with alcohol – no, that would have to wait. Just four days later, they were heading for Madrid and a final showdown with the Spanish in what would turn out to be a winner-takes-all clash.

In a stormy encounter Spain took the lead after 19 minutes, thanks to a goal from Raul. But Kežman hauled the visitors level on 68 minutes, much to the joy of the estimated 5,000 fans from Serbia and Montenegro, who had travelled to cheer on their heroes.

The headlines and the glory would go to Kežman, who until recently had been playing his club football at Chelsea, but it would be at the heart of the Serbian defence that the game's outcome was really decided. Vidić was a colossus as he stayed firm in the face of an onslaught from the Spanish, ably assisted by his partner at the back, Igor Duljaj.

He and Vidić were the equal of most everything Raul and Torres could throw at them, but Duljaj would be dismissed in the final minute for one fierce tackle too many, as he struggled with tiredness.

His red card was a blow, but the Serbs, with the full backing of coach Petković, celebrated after the draw. After the win over Lithuania, they had abstained but now enjoyed a few well-earned beers and a singsong following the terrific result.

Petković had told them: avoid defeat and we will be knocking at the door of the finals, and they duly obliged. Now the heat was off and onto the Spanish, who had been expected to top the group as a matter of course. Unless the Serbs slipped up in their final two matches, it would be Torres and his team-mates who would be the ones heading for the nightmare of the play-offs to keep their hopes alive.

It was a time to salute their achievements, but Petković – confident as he was – knew work was still to be done and there were two tricky fixtures to negotiate, if he and his men were to complete the job.

Both would come a month later as the campaign drew to its conclusion. The first was away in Lithuania and the final match was a potential powderkeg fixture at home against bitter rivals Bosnia and Herzegovina. At the same time, Spain had two away games to complete their programme – first in Belgium, and then in San Marino.

On 8 October 2005, the Serbs won 2-0 in Lithuania. Vidić was the man of the match as they kept their nerve and eventually coasted home with goals from Kežman and Vukić. That same night Spain won by the same scoreline in Belgium, with Fernando Torres grabbing both goals.

So it was all set for the grand finale with Serbia and Montenegro knowing that they would be in the finals in Germany, if they beat the Bosnians. They were two points ahead of Spain and four goals better off (14 to 10 being the goal difference). But Spain's final match would surely bring them a glut of goals – the minnows of San Marino were hardly renowned for their clean sheets.

It meant the Serbs had to win to ensure qualification. A draw could have seen them level on points, but out on goal difference. Sure enough, on 12 October, Spain thrashed San Marino 6-0 away – Torres helping himself to a hat-trick – and that put them ahead of than Serbia.

As the Serbs aimed to complete qualification with the win they so desperately wanted, a rowdy crowd of over 46,000 turned out in Belgrade. Tensions were running high, but they would scrape home by a single goal – from Kežman. It would be a game that would live long in Vidić's memory... and not just because of the win.

No, he would be sent off for the first time amid chaotic scenes as the home crowd and the small group of Bosnian fans pelted each other with flares and plastic seats, forcing police to keep them apart as the legacy of the 1992–95 war lingered in the air.

On the pitch, the Serbs dominated and kept their nerve, even after Nemanja was dismissed for two bookable offences, to seal top spot in Group 7. The result meant Spain would be the ones battling for survival in the play-offs.

And Vidić's sending-off meant that he would miss the first match when Serbia's World Cup finals campaign began in earnest the following summer. Two months after clinching qualification – and two weeks before Christmas 2005 – coach Petković was to learn of his country's fate when the draw was made for the finals.

It was bad news – they were plunged into the toughest group, Group C, with Argentina, Holland and the Ivory Coast. This was quickly dubbed 'the Group of Death' because of the quality of all four teams, but Petković did not let it dampen his spirits. He said: 'I have emphasised many times that the most important thing is that we are in Germany. My first impression is that our group is the hardest, but we had the hardest group in qualification as well.

'I was optimistic then, and I am optimistic now. We are a small country, we are poor and we are in transition, but in the qualifiers we fought with big countries like Spain and Belgium. We fought with our hearts, with knowledge and with a desire to prove people wrong. We are not afraid of anything or anyone. Our mentality is like this: we are a small nation, but we can be great out of our stubborn spirit.'

It was a rallying battle-cry, and one that might have come from Vidić himself, the defender also saying that he and his team-mates would not be going out to Germany worrying about the opposition. He told friends that they would go there to 'enjoy ourselves' and 'to do our best for our country'.

Petković said he also based his optimism on the fact that the team he had created had become so powerful and unbeatable. Of course, they had gone through the qualifiers without defeat and only conceded one goal in 10 matches.

He purred as he spoke about his wonderful backline of Mladen Krstajić, Nemanja Vidić and Goran Gavrančić, but also pointed out that his team could score goals as well. He had been criticised in some quarters for sometimes omitting the popular Mateja Kežman in favour of Nikola Zigić, but used that talking point to back up his claim that his side possessed arguably the best spirit of any that would be heading for Germany.

He said that he had brought Kežman back for the vital games against Spain and Bosnia-Herzegovina, and that there had been no dispute between him and either player. 'There were no angry words,' he said. 'There were a lot of stories about a disagreement, but I was a friend to everybody.' Clearly, Kežman had no hard feelings – he did his best for Petković and was the team's top scorer, with five goals in qualifying.

The last time a team featuring Serbs qualified for a major tournament had been 14 years earlier, in 1992. But Yugoslavia had been expelled as war broke out in the Balkans, and their replacements, Denmark, went on to win Euro '92. Petković said the finals in Germany gave his nation a chance to put right the disappointment of missing out back then: 'This time we are not sending any substitutes – we are going ourselves.'

As 2006 dawned, Nemanja was as excited as the rest of the squad at the year that lay ahead. Within days, he was a Manchester United player – his move from Spartak Moscow eventually being confirmed in the first week of January – and by the summer, he was happy and confident that he and his Serbian team-mates would not let their nation down.

Before arriving in Germany, Vidić and the team played two important friendlies – one against African opposition, to prepare them for the Ivory Coast match, and another against South Americans to give them an idea of what they might expect against Argentina.

On 1 March, they won 1-0 in Tunisia, with a goal from Kežman and on 27 May, they drew 1-1 with Uruguay in Belgrade, Dejan Stanković grabbing their goal.

Everything was going to plan as the Serbs arrived in Germany a few days before their first game – against Holland on 11 June – to acclimatise and settle. They were based in the Münsterland area of Nordrhein-Westfalen. The region's capital is Dusseldorf, its largest city Cologne.

The team checked into the plush Hotel Weissenburg in Billerbeck – it was a base used by Schalke 04 to prepare themselves for home games. Just an hour from Gelsenkirchen, it was ideal for the Serbs, who would play their second group game in that city against Argentina.

Vidić and Co. certainly enjoyed the hotel's facilities – a four-star establishment in which they had the use of a swimming pool, sauna and solarium, plus fine food to match. It was an idyllic scene, but the next few days would see it change dramatically for Vidić as his World Cup ended before it got started... in heartache. At the time, he would call it his 'most disappointing moment in football' and one of the biggest disappointments of his life. He had toiled for perfection with his defensive partners to get Serbia to the finals, now that dream would be taken from him in the cruellest of fashions.

Nemanja missed out on the first group match against the Dutch in Leipzig, a legacy of that sending-off against the Bosnians in the final qualifier. Puzzlingly, given the absence of his No. 1 strongman, coach Petković decided to sit back and defend – and try to catch Holland on the break. It was a decision that would backfire badly.

Winger Arjen Robben caused all sorts of problems and panic

in the Serbian defence and it was the little magician who put them 1-0 up in the first half. After the break, Petković brought on Nikola Zigić for Savo Milošević up front and immediately the Serbs looked a much more potent, powerful attacking entity.

They should have scored, but the Dutch had luck on their side and the match fizzled out at 1-0.

It was a disappointing start, but not the end of the world – not yet anyway. If the Serbs could draw with Argentina and beat Ivory Coast, they would still be in with a shout.

Back at the hotel, Petković tried his hardest to cajole his players and to instill belief in them that they could still progress. It seemed to be working for there was a spring in their step at training and they were laughing and joking again. The famed spirit that the coach had spoken about the previous December was again apparent – they were going to have a go and they wouldn't give in until they were absolutely beaten.

But then out of the blue came the blow that crushed their hopes and extinguished their light: a blow from which they would not recover. A blow that effectively killed off their World Cup dream and made all the hard work they had done in qualifying an irrelevance.

One of the things that Petković had been keen to drum home to his men was that. They had lost to Holland, but they hadn't been at full strength. One of the key components of that brilliant defence – the defence that had gone nine games out of 10 without conceding a goal in qualifying – had been missing in Leipzig. Yes, the rock known as Nemanja Vidić. But, as Petković was keen to point out, Vidić's suspension was for one game only and after the Holland match, he would be back with a vengeance and on a mission: to ignite Serbia's faltering campaign in Germany.

Pure and simple, he was a leader and their key defender. Without him, Serbia were not so effective, but with him they had a chance of beating anyone.

With that in mind and following his pep talk, Petković upped the ante at training, two days after the defeat by Holland. The match had taken place on the Sunday; the Monday was a rest day, a day to take note of what had happened and why it had happened – and to learn from it – and then on Tuesday, 15 June, they were back on the training pitch, trying to blot out the memory of the loss by sheer hard work and purpose.

Vidić was in the thick of it, tackling ridiculously hard and getting on the end of headers at both ends. Everything was going well – the cobwebs of disappointment being blown away, the faces of the players full of hope and Petković sensed a new determination and steel from his squad. Out of the blue, disaster struck.

Nemanja Vidić's World Cup was over after he pulled up injured, halfway through the training session.

It was quickly confirmed that he had suffered a knee ligament injury that would keep him out for several weeks. Serbia spokesman Aleksandar Bošković made it clear there was no way back for Vidić in Germany – and that he would also face a race to be fit for the start of Manchester United's Premiership season in August.

Bošković said sternly: 'Our national team will have just 22 players for the rest of our games in Germany as Nemanja Vidić is sidelined because of a serious knee injury. During training yesterday, he went to block a shot but, unfortunately, rotated his knee too much. His yell was horrendous and we knew immediately something bad had happened. He was taken to hospital and we discovered he had damaged his medial collateral ligament.

'He must rest for several weeks, according to our national team doctor, Ilija Asanin. Nemanja will remain with us here in Germany. He is in a stable condition and is psychologically good, as much as a youngster who dreamed about the World Cup can be after suffering such a thing.'

The words were poignant and true: Vidić had dreamed of playing in the World Cup finals; now that dream was over and all that was left was a bleak landscape. He cheered on his team-mates in their next two matches, but without him they were shot: his exit had punctured their hope and belief much as a nail punctures a tyre.

It certainly showed in the next match. Without Nemanja, the Serbs crumbled in Gelsenkirchen, slumping to a devastating 6-0 defeat to Argentina. This was followed by another humiliation – a 3-2 loss to the Ivory Coast in their final match.

The Serbs had arrived in Germany with such hopes and

aspirations, but with Vidić absent from all three matches, they collapsed like a pack of cards, ending their campaign in disarray and despair, bottom of Group C, having scored just two goals – and shipping 10. Not what you might have expected from the meanest defence in the competition, but then again it was a defence deprived of its kingpin.

Vidić was a strong character and eventually accepted the cruel quirk of fate that cost him his World Cup dream in 2006. Surely there would be many more tournaments as he was only 24 during the one in Germany.

The first one was Euro 2008 – and this time he planned to play his part through qualifying and the finals themselves. The only snag was this: the Serbs somehow bungled their qualifying campaign and did not even make the finals in Austria and Switzerland. Serbia was making its first entry in an international tournament as an independent nation and hopes ran high, but the team could not click as it had done during the World Cup qualifiers.

In a group of eight, they finished third, behind group winners Poland and runners-up Portugal. They actually finished joint third with Finland, on 24 points, but were adjudged third because they had the better head-to-head record.

The highlights of their campaign were two 1-1 draws with Portugal and a 2-2 draw with Poland, but they came up well short against the so-called minnows in the group. In particular, one result exemplified the uncharacteristic chaos and unreliability that would cost them so dearly.

On 24 March 2007, the Serbs travelled to Kazakhstan, the former Russian satellite state that won its independence in 1992. Everyone connected with Serbia expected them to stroll to a win – a win that would have taken them to the top of the group and would probably have given them the confidence to get their act together on a regular basis and make it to Euro 2008.

But, in one of the shock results of world football, Vidić and Co. came an almighty cropper in Almaty. The team lost 2-1 and on a night no Serb would appreciate you ever mentioning, striker Nikola Zigić received his marching orders – an absolute, unadulterated disaster.

Previously, Kazakhstan had been most famous for being the home of Sacha Cohen's comic character, Borat. They had never won a competitive match, but claimed victory, with goals from Kairat Ashiberkov and Nurbol Zhumaskaliyev.

Ashirbekov fired them in front on 47 minutes with a powerful shot that took a deflection before ending up in the back of the net. Zhumaskaliyev then sent the crowd wild when he headed home what turned out to be the winner. It was also the first time they had scored at home in a European qualifier since joining UEFA in 2002. Vidić went close with a header that flew inches over before Nikola Zigić pulled one back for the visitors, but Serbia's night of misery was complete when Zigić went from hero to zero as he was sent off for elbowing.

It was a shocker and coach Javier Clemente would only shake his head and apologise after the match. Vidić, similarly, was understandably not in a very talkative mood and the players boarded the coach to get out of town as fast as they could – in disgrace.

In the final match of the qualifying campaign, the Serbs would gain revenge on Kazakhstan, beating them 1-0 in Belgrade in November 2007, but this was of little true consolation. They had failed to make it to Euro 2008.

Once again Vidić was denied acclaim on the international stage. In Germany 2006, this was down to sheer bad luck with his injury, but he would not be at Euro 2008 because he and his team-mates simply had not been good enough over the whole qualifying campaign.

It was disappointing but he would be back, he promised himself that. He made a pledge to his wife Ana that he would finally make his big international stage debut in South Africa in the World Cup finals of 2010. It would be a personal tragedy if a player of his calibre would never feature in a major international final, however gloriously he did at club level.

The draw put Serbia in Group 7 – along with favourites France, Romania, Lithuania, Austria and Faroe Islands. It was by no means a dream group – France would clearly cause problems and even Romania, Lithuania and Austria could pose a threat. Only the Faroe Islands were making up the numbers.

But by the end of June 2009 Serbia were in a fabulous position to qualify. They led the group from France by a massive eight points and a plus nine better goal difference – although the French had played two games less.

Out of seven games played the Serbs had lost just one – a 2-1 defeat in France on September 10, 2008. Goals from Thierry Henry and Nicolas Anelka had sent the French on their way, with Branislav Ivanović pulling one back for the Serbs.

It had been a tough night for Vidić and Co. in the Stade de France in Paris, in what was their second match in the group, but they would gather some of that much-famed Serbian spirit and pull themselves together. They would rally and win their next five games (they had already beaten Faroe Islands, 2-0 in their opening match).

That run would bring excellent results – a 3-0 win over Lithuania, a 3-1 victory away in Austria and a 3-2 win away in Romania. The latter would prove to be a key clash in Serbia's campaign to reach South Africa. Never easy to beat at home, the Romanians were backed by a raucous crowd on 28 March 2009, and no little skill from a team that contained the likes of the talented, if enigmatic Adrian Mutu, who once played for Chelsea and Juventus.

It was truly to their credit that Serbia emerged triumphant and at the same time inflicted on Romania their first defeat in the Black Sea resort of Constanta. Strikes from Milan Jovanović and Branislav Ivanović, plus an own goal from Dorel Stoica saw the Serbs home in a match marred by crowd trouble.

Inspired by Man of the Match Vidić, the Serbs kept their cool and the result meant they now had 12 points from five matches and stood proud at the top of the group. Serbia goalkeeper Vladimir Stojković told Reuters: 'We scored all three goals at the right time and the back four did a superb job after Romania, who are a very good team, launched a spirited fightback.

'If we win our next two games at home to Austria and away to the Faroe Islands, we will have one foot in next year's tournament in South Africa.'

And that was the situation as senior European international football took its summer break. For at the same time as the Serbs were winning, the French were dropping valuable points in the unlikeliest games. They were held to a 2-2 draw in Romania and had begun their campaign with a shock 3-1 loss in Austria.

By the summer of 2009, Nemanja Vidić allowed himself to dream the dream that he had long held: that a year from then, he would play in his first international finals... with his beloved Serbia at the World Cup in South Africa.

And by the time this book went to press at the start of 2010, that dream had become a reality – as long as he did not suffer any injury setbacks before the start of the event in June.

In October 2009, Serbia qualified for the finals as winners of Group 7, beating France to the coveted top spot. It meant the French were consigned to the lottery of the play-offs while Vidić could plan ahead confidently for the extravaganza in South Africa.

'It's brilliant,' he said, once qualification had been assured. 'I am really looking forward to playing in my first Finals, it will be a great experience.' He also said it would silence the dressing room jokers at Old Trafford – such as Wayne Rooney – who had qualified with England and no doubt would have otherwise teased him about not being part of the greatest sporting event in the world.

Vidić had finally made it; now he and Serbia would go all out to win it. That was the nature of the man and his country. And when the Finals were over? The big man had promised his wife Ana that they would go on a well-deserved holiday, maybe taking Luka and Stefan to Disneyland. 'This will be the greatest summer of my life,' he said excitedly. 'I just can't wait for it all to begin...'

Chapter 14
CAPTAIN FANTASTIC

THE SUMMER in South Africa would not be the celebratory one Nemanja hoped for – but he would find major consolation when he returned to Old Trafford in the autumn of 2010, as he was appointed the team's new skipper.

On paper, it appeared Vidić and his Serbian team-mates would at least have an easier time in the World Cup than they had in Germany four years previously. Back then, of course, he failed to play in any of the matches after suffering a knee injury in the build-up. Without him, Serbia crashed out of a veritable 'Group of Death' that also contained Argentina, Holland and the Ivory Coast.

This time around they had been drawn against less worrying opposition – or so it seemed.

In the event, Germany and Ghana would prove classy rivals while the ever-improving Australia would also be no pushover.

As an independent nation (having in 2006 been recognised as Serbia & Montenegro, and previously existing as part of Yugoslavia) this was Serbia's first World Cup appearance – and Vidić was determined that they would not fluff their lines. They were unbeaten in their four build-up games to the tournament but suffered a fright when Nemanja pulled up with a virus before their opener against Ghana.

He had already missed the friendly against Poland with an upset stomach as the build-up to the tournament intensified and was then sidelined in the final friendly against Cameroon with the virus.

As one of the main pillars of the team, he would certainly be needed if they were to avoid another early exit. Coach Raddy Antić moved swiftly to quash speculation that his star man would have to sit out their vital first match in five days' time. Antić said: 'It's true that Vidić has not trained since he had a rash, but he is getting better.'

And as if to prove the point, the big man presented himself at a press conference the same day and took questions on his hopes for the tournament – and how, with hindsight, he viewed the disaster in Germany four years earlier.

'It was not a great experience,' he said of Germany. 'We had a few injuries just before the World Cup started and it got worse the further we went. We have a lot of things to remember and make sure they don't happen again. But I think it will be a bit different. Compared to last time, we have a different team. We have a younger team. The fans are expecting us to do well.'

He admitted he believed entering the tournament as an independent Serbia would be beneficial – that national pride could propel them to great things. Vidi said: 'It will be different. Before we were Yugoslavia, then Serbia and Montenegro, when we knew we were going to split immediately after the World Cup.

'These little things make a difference. It is not that the squad was split but you don't want to be confronted with these things before the World Cup.

'You want to talk about football. Not politics…now we are Serbia and the people are excited because it is the first World Cup for us.'

But Vidić certainly did not subscribe to the view that the group would be any easier than in 2006. He said:

'People don't seem to realise that Ghana and Australia are really good teams and Germany always do well at World Cups. It could be a better draw but it could be worse. We are a better team than the one we had four years ago.

'We have a few young players who are doing well and that's important. They are young and hungry. They want to improve themselves and show how good they are. The World Cup is coming at the right moment in those terms.

'It's a big thing for anyone to play at a World Cup – and I want to play and do well. I want to achieve something I can be proud of. I have reached an age [28] where it could be my last World Cup so I will give everything I can to make it a positive experience.

'We were a little bit inconsistent during qualification but the matches where we played well were very good. There are more goals in this squad too so that should work to our advantage.'

The men of the press were, rather mischievously, also keen to know Nemanja's views on the possibility of coming up against team-mate Wayne Rooney in the next stage. Of course, he knew full well that if Serbia advanced to the last 16 they would have a good chance of meeting England – and Rooney – in the first knockout round.

Vidić played an impressive straight bat, saying: 'If we got to the second round I would like to miss England. England are the strongest team we could play, so I would prefer to avoid them. I play in England. I play against these players and I train with some of them every day.

'But it is best to focus on the first game because success at the World Cup for Serbia would be to reach the second round. If we do that we would be happy. After that everything else is a bonus.'

Five days later and it was finally time for the talk to stop and the action to begin. Vidić lined up in what was Raddy Antić's strongest on Sunday 13 June in Pretoria. Yes, the 13th is unlucky for some...and unfortunately it was for Vidić and Co.

And to rub salt into a cruel wound, the 1-0 loss to the Ghanaians – Africa's first win at the tournament – came at the hands of a Serb, Milovan Rajevac, the coach of the victors. To give him his due, he did make it quickly apparent that he felt sorry for his defeated, demoralised compatriots. He said: 'This is the greatest win of my career but I also feel sorry for Serbia, I saw the anguish on the players' faces after the final whistle.

'I had a job to do and I did it professionally but I hope my countrymen win their next two games against Germany and Australia, I wish them the best of luck.'

Serbia had gone down 1-0 when Asamoah Gyan converted a late penalty, given after Serbia substitute Zdravko Kuzmanović handled the ball in the box.

It had been an uphill struggle for Vidić and his team-mates as they battled to contain the lively Africans with 10-men after Aleksandar Luković was sent off for a second yellow in the 74th minute. Now, as Gyan celebrated the goal that lifted the whole of the African Continent, there would be now way back.

Afterwards Vidić was disappointed but not down. He knew he and the team could not afford to slump – they still had two games to save their tournament. But he had some harsh words for the new Jabulani ball and the constant din of the vuvuzelas.

He said it had been difficult to concentrate with the constant noise they made – and that the bouncy ball had been a contributory factor in the penalty. He felt Kuzmanović had been hit by its unusual flight, rather than having deliberately handled it.

Vidić said: 'Yes, it was hard to blot out the noise and the ball was difficult – it is not easy to control it in the air. It's very quick, more in the air than at the feet. I think if the ball hits the ground you get good control. But all the teams have problems with the ball so it is not an excuse.'

No excuses, no self-pity: it was a good attitude and one that would definitely serve Vidić and the team well as they headed for Port Elizabeth and the absolute make-or-break encounter with the Germans.

This time it would be the opposition who would have to struggle on with 10-men – and who would exit with a 1-0 loss as the Serbs secured the win that blew Group D wide open. Germany, Serbia and Ghana were all now locked on three points – with all to play for.

The two key moments came in the first half as Miroslav Klose was red-carded for two bookings and Milan Jovanović won the game with his fine volley 10 minutes before the interval.

Vidić would play well in the heart of the backline but would also contribute his own moment of madness to proceedings when he flapped at a cross in the box, his hand touching the ball to give away a penalty.

Lukas Podolski stepped up confidently to take the spot kick but his weak effort was easily parried by Vladimir Stojković.

The keeper said: 'After 37 years, to win against Germany at the World Cup is quite something and we deserved it as a group. I thought I would have to be really concentrated during the game and I was. We believe in ourselves and have shown we are a really good team.'

Meanwhile, a relieved Vidić managed to see the lighter side of the incident. He said: 'The goalkeeper owes me a big favour for that handball. It meant I put him in a position to become a great hero for Serbia!

'It's a huge result after the first game. We were disappointed in ourselves. We can be confident and must do the right things in our next game against Australia. They didn't play great in their first game, like us. Anything can happen – we need to be focused and start thinking already about the game.'

He was right about that. Five more days and they would be up against the Aussies in the final match of Group D – but Vidić hoped most fervently it would not be the final match of his World Cup. But it would not be easy; a win for Ghana against the Germans in the other encounter in the group would mean the Aussies would qualify if they beat Serbia (even though they were currently bottom of the group with a single point). So the Socceroos would certainly not be taking it easy in Nelspruit.

Vidić looked uneasy and nervy during the kickabout before the game: of course, he had real reason to...lose and his World Cup dream would be over. Possibly forever...

As it transpired, a 2-2 draw would have kept his dream alive, but it was not to be: the Aussies won 2-1, which meant both they and Serbia exited the tournament at the first stage. Goals from Tim Cahill and Brett Holman wrecked Vida's dream, Marko Pantelić grabbing Serbia's late consolation.

Vidić was an angry man afterwards – and not just because he was out of the World Cup. No, he believed he had been cheated when ref Jorge Larrionda refused his plea for a spot kick when his late header bounced off Cahill's arm.

Nemanja remonstrated with the ref – but to no avail. Afterwards, he was distraught at yet another failure in football's biggest tournament. He said: 'I am disappointed with some decisions. I think my reaction after the "penalty" decision showed what I think and I need to choose my words carefully.

'We had a great first half but I was scared after those chances were missed - that is football, small details can determine the winner. This is the best performance for us in this World Cup but we take nothing from that. We expected to go into the second round and we are going home disappointed.

'We didn't underestimate Australia – we showed in the first half that we are strong and played some good football. But they are a good team, especially in the air. In the second half they had the courage to attack and put more pressure on us – the result was two goals.'

The Aussies were also distraught – even though they had triumphed they were also out. Like Ghana, they had finished on four points, but had an inferior goal difference.

But Australia's disappointment hardly eased the pain Vidić was feeling. 'It is a very sombre atmosphere in the dressing room,' he admitted before getting changed and jumping on the coach back to the team hotel in Johannesburg. Serbia had finished bottom of the group – and Nemanja and his team-mates were now on their way home.

But after a refreshing summer holiday, Vidić would at least find some joy in the new 2010/11 season when he returned to Old Trafford. True, the Red Devils' form was not magnificent as winter drew in at the Theatre of Dreams – but he was so very proud at being made captain by Sir Alex Ferguson in the middle of September.

Fergie confirmed: 'Nemanja Vidić has been given the captain's armband because he has been available all the time.' Many pundits expected Rio Ferdinand to take back the armband when he returned from his latest injury – but the boss decided against that move, adding: 'We want it to be a player who's consistently available for us. Everyone will recognise that if Vidić is fit – and he had been all season – he'll always be there.'

Vidić had skippered the side in the absence of Rio and many people expected the England captain to resume in the leader's role at Old Trafford when he finally shook off his injury jinx. Ferdinand did indeed take the armband in the Champions League 0-0 draw with Rangers at Old Trafford on September 14, but only because Vidić was himself out injured. Five days later Vidić resumed as full-time skipper in the 3-2 home win over bitter rivals Liverpool.

The win was especially sweet for Nemanja given that he was now United's permanent leader and also as nothing gave him more pleasure than beating the team from down the other end of the East Lancs Road – a team he had been red-carded against on numerous occasions!

Vidić admitted he was honoured at being selected for the captain's role – but, in typical humble fashion, tried to play down all the fuss, insisting he was only one of United's leaders. He told the club's website, manutd.com: 'Being captain is a big achievement and honour for me, and I enjoy the responsibility.

But I must say we have a few captains in our team – Gary Neville, [Paul] Scholesy, [Ryan] Giggsy and Rio – they are the real leaders in our team. The other players look to those players.

'For me, as a captain you don't need to do anything special, you just have to be yourself and be an example to the other players.

'I just try to give my best in every game and use the experience I have gained over the years to help the team be successful.'

In fact, by the time he got the job on a permanent basis, he had already won his first silverware in the role. Fergie had tried him out as skipper when United beat Chelsea 3-1 in the Community Shield at Wembley – and the big man did the job asked of him, marshalling his troops and proving a rallying leader.

Vidić was delighted to collect the trophy from United legend Sir Bobby Charlton – the 14th time the Red Devils had won it. Goals from Valencia, Hernandez and Berbatov secured the win, with Kalou scoring for the Blues. And afterwards Nemanja said: 'It's important to win, it's the last game of pre-season, and I think we did well today, especially a lot of players who haven't played much. It was important for Dimitar to score, he's been under a lot of pressure but I think he'll score more this season.'

The new skipper was right about that – as the season unfolded it became clear that Berbatov would be a much different player than in previous campaigns. The nerves and self-doubt that racked so many of his performances seemed a thing of the past as he rammed home the goals and led the United line with distinction.

Berba's renaissance also owed more than a nod of gratitude

to Vidić. The Serb had befriended the Bulgarian when he arrived at Old Trafford and was also keen to support him on and off the field. Vida regularly had Berba round for dinner and 'bigged him up' in press conferences.

None more so than that 3-2 win over Liverpool in his first official match as United skipper. Vidić was much keener to talk about his friend and the wonderful hat-trick he had just scored than his own debut as Reds captain.

The Bulgarian became the first United player since Stan Pearson in 1946 to score a hat-trick against old rivals Liverpool.

And Vidić was effusive about him at the post-match Press conference, saying: 'We are all aware how good Dimitar is. His skills with the ball are incredible.

'The criticism he got last year was because he didn't score many goals. This season he is scoring a lot, and important goals too.

'He has learned what he has to do. He has changed his game compared to last season. He is in the box more and is more of a threat.

'Dimitar has always had a great touch and gave us composure but because he is also going into the box, he is scoring goals. That is why he is getting so much credit.

'If he keeps doing that we have a good chance to win the league and for him to gain some personal reward by becoming player of the year.'

Berba, like captain Vidić, was certainly on a roll at Old Trafford as winter loomed at Old Trafford in 2010. After his hat-trick against the Scousers, he had scored seven times already and was the joint top scorer in the Premier League with Chelsea's Florent Malouda.

But United, even with Vidić in the driving seat, had not been firing on all cylinders. They struggled home against a poor Liverpool outfit and had been chugging along like a car with a blocked exhaust, rather than speeding to glory.

Sure, the 2010/11 season had got off to a fine start with a 3-0 trouncing of newly-promoted Newcastle at Old Trafford and a win by the same scoreline over a poor looking West Ham in the next home match. But in between, the Reds had let Fulham off the hook in the 2-2 draw at Craven Cottage and proceeded to do exactly the same by allowing Everton to grab a 3-3 draw at Goodison after they had led 3-1 as injury time loomed.

Vidić had headed the second United goal at Goodison, his first of the season from a Nani cross, but any joy in that respect was negated by the poor defending from the backline that saw Tim Cahill and Mikel Arteta score the late, late lifesavers for the Toffees.

Then, a week after beating Liverpool, United were once again caught giving free gifts – this time allowing Bolton to snatch a 2-2 draw at the Reebok.

Vidić was fuming after the match and publicly lambasted his team. The 2-2 draw meant United had leaked 11 goals in their eight matches in all competitions.

And Vidić said: 'Yes, we're concerned. Over the last few years we haven't conceded many goals. We always looked strong and we didn't give teams many chances. But in the last few away games we haven't kept clean sheets, which is very disappointing.

'This was a game we wanted to win and before the game we'd have said a draw would be two points dropped.'

Three weeks later – after a couple of promising results including a brilliant 1-0 Champions League win in Valencia and a 0-0 lockout at Sunderland – the Serb was again on the warpath as United leaked two second half goals to lowly West Brom, allowing them to leave Old Trafford with a point after the match ended 2-2.

Vidić was angry that more points had been dropped because of defensive lapses – on this occasion, the finger of blame pointing firmly at veteran keeper Edwin van der Sar who, inexplicably, dropped a cross by Chris Blunt, allowing Somen Tchoyi to equalise.

Typically, Vidić refused to single out Van der Sar, merely pointing out that the keeper had saved both him and his colleagues over the years. But he did demand an improvement – and that it come quickly. 'We've got to start getting results and stop leaking goals,' he admitted. 'We want to win back the league title from Chelsea – and now we've really got to cut out the mistakes...and we can do it.'

It was a strong rallying call from the man who had put his World Cup disappointment behind him to become Manchester United's leader. Nemanja Vidić had played a major part in the glorious past of the club, helping them to that Champions League triumph in 2008, and now he was determined to take them forward to more honours in the future. From humble beginnings in Serbia, Nemanja Vidić had become the future at Old Trafford; the man upon whom the boss now depended and trusted. With total faith.

SOURCES

Hugh McIlvanney
Ian Stafford
John Edwards
Daniel Taylor
Sam Wallace
The Independent
Lee Clayton and the *Daily Mail*
Alex Butler and *The Sunday Times*
Malcolm Vallerius and *The Mail on Sunday*
Nic Petković
Nedeljko Dimitrijević
Zoran Panjković
Dragoljub Vidić
Dave Fowler

The Observer

Ozren Podnar

Dejan Stefanović

PA Sport

The Times

MUTV

Sir Alex Ferguson

Carlos Queiroz

Inside United

Roy Keane

Wayne Rooney

Ruud van Nistelrooy

www.manunited.com

Talking Reds

Edwin van der Sar

Manchester Evening News

Peter Spencer

Paul Hince

www.uefa.com

Tommy Docherty

Radio 5 Live

Bruce Waddell

David Gill

The Daily Telegraph

Sean Connolly

Terry Venables

Martin Phillips

SOURCES

Zoran Djordjević
Lesley Thomas
ITN Sport